Benjamin Thorpe

The Anglo-Saxon Chronicle - According to the Several Original

Authorities

Vol. II

Benjamin Thorpe

The Anglo-Saxon Chronicle - According to the Several Original Authorities
Vol. II

ISBN/EAN: 9783337279646

Printed in Europe, USA, Canada, Australia, Japan

Cover: Foto ©ninafisch / pixelio.de

More available books at **www.hansebooks.com**

THE

ANGLO-SAXON CHRONICLE,

ACCORDING TO THE

SEVERAL ORIGINAL AUTHORITIES.

EDITED, WITH A TRANSLATION,

BY

BENJAMIN THORPE,

MEMBER OF THE ROYAL ACADEMY OF SCIENCE AT MUNICH,
AND OF THE SOCIETY OF NETHERLANDISH LITERATURE AT LEYDEN.

VOL. II.

TRANSLATION.

PUBLISHED BY THE AUTHORITY OF THE LORDS COMMISSIONERS OF HER MAJESTY'S
TREASURY, UNDER THE DIRECTION OF THE MASTER OF THE ROLLS.

LONDON:
LONGMAN, GREEN, LONGMAN, AND ROBERTS.

1861.

ANNALES SAXONICI.

In the year that was past from the birth of Christ cccc.xciv., then Cerdic and Cynric his son landed at 'Cerdices ora' from v. ships. And Cerdic was the son of Elesa, Elesa of Esla, Esla of Giwis, Giwis of Wig, Wig of Freawine, Freawine of Frithugar, Frithugar of Brond, Brond of Bældæg, Bældæg of Woden. And vi. years after they landed they subdued the West Saxons' kingdom ; and they were the first kings who conquered the West Saxons' land from the Welsh ; and he had the kingdom xvi. years, and when he died, then his son Cynric succeeded to the kingdom, and held it xvii. winters. When he died, then Ceol succeeded to the kingdom, and held it vi. years. When he died, then Ceolwulf his brother succeeded, and he reigned xvii. years ; and their kin reaches to Cerdic. ·Then Cynegils,. Ceolwulf's brother's son, succeeded to the kingdom, and reigned xxxi. winters ; and he first received baptism of the West Saxons' kings ; and then Cênwalh succeeded, and held it xxx. winters ; and Cênwalh was the son of Cynegils ; and then Seaxburg his queen held the kingdom one year after him. Then Æscwine succeeded to the kingdom, whose kin reaches to Cerdic, and held it ii. years. Then Centwine, the son of Cynegils, succeeded to the West Saxons' kingdom, and reigned vii. years. Then Ceadwalla succeeded to the kingdom, whose kin reaches to Cerdic, and held it three years. Then Ine succeeded to the [West] Saxons' kingdom, whose kin reaches to Cerdic, and held it xxvii. winters. Then Æthelheard succeeded, whose kin reaches to Cerdic, and held it xiv. winters. Then Cuthred succeeded, whose kin reaches to Cerdic, and held it xvii. years. Then Sigebryht succeeded, whose kin reaches to Cerdic, and held it i. year. Then Cynewulf succeeded to the kingdom, whose

A 2

kin reaches to Cerdic, and held it XXXI. winters. Then
Beorhtric succeeded to the kingdom, whose kin reaches to
Cerdic, and held it XVI. years. Then Ecgbryht succeeded to
the kingdom, and held it XXXVII. winters and VII. months ;
and then Æthelwulf his son succeeded, and held it eighteen
years and a half. Æthelwulf was the son of Ecgbryht, Ecgbryht of Ealhmund, Ealhmund of Eafa, Eafa of Eoppa, Eoppa
of Ingild, Ingild of Cênred ; and Ine of Cênred, and Cuth-
burg [daughter] of Cênred, and Cwenburg [daughter] of
Cênred ; and Cênred [son] of Ceolwald, Ceolwald of Cuthwulf, Cuthwulf of Cuthwine, Cuthwine of Celm, Celm of
Cynric, Cynric of Cerdic. And then Æthelbald his son succeeded to the kingdom, and held it V. years. Then Æthelbryht his brother succeeded, and held it V. years. Then
Æthered their brother succeeded to the kingdom, and held it
V. years. Then Ælfred their brother succeeded to the king-
dom ; and then were past of his age XXIII. winters ; and
CCC.XCVI. winters since his kin first conquered the West
Saxons' land from the Welsh.

THE

ANGLO-SAXON CHRONICLE.

THE island of Britain is eight hundred miles long, and two hundred miles broad : and here are in the island five peoples: English, Brito-Welsh, Scottish, Pictish, and Book-Latin. The first inhabiting this land were Britons : they came from [2]Armenia, and first settled southward in Britain. It then befel, that Picts came from the south from Scythia, with long ships, not many ; and they first landed in north Ireland, and there prayed the Scots that they there might dwell. But they would not allow them ; for they said that they could not all dwell together there. And then said the Scots : " We can, nevertheless, give you counsel. We know another island here to the east, where ye may dwell if ye will ; and if any one withstand you, we will aid you, so that ye may subdue it." Then the Picts went and conquered this land northward ; southward the Britons had it, as we before said. And the Picts obtained them wives from the Scots, on the condition that they should ever choose their royal race on the woman's side, which they have held so long since. And it then befel, after a course of years, that some part of the Scots withdrew from Ireland into Britain, and subdued some part of the land. And their leader was called Reôda, from whom they are named Dalreôdi.

---

[1] N.B.—The numerals in the side margin denote the pages of the Saxon text.

[2] An error for Armorica.—" De " tractu Armoricano advecti," are the words of Beda, H.E. I. 1.

Sixty winters ere Christ was born, Caius Julius, emperor of the Romans, with eighty vessels, sought Britain. There he was at first embarrassed by a fierce fight, and lost a great part of his army. And he then left his army to abide with the Scots, and withdrew south into Gaul, and there gathered six hundred ships, with which he again went to Britain. And when they first rushed together, the emperor's tribune was slain; he was called [1] Labienus. Then the Welsh took great sharp stakes, and drove them into the ford of a river, within the water : the river was called Thames. When the Romans found that, they would not pass over the ford. The Britons then fled to the wood wastes, and the emperor conquered full many a chief burgh, with great labour ; and again withdrew into Gaul.

6, 7.

[2] An. Dom. I. Octavianus reigned LVI. years, and in the XLII. (LII.) year of his reign Christ was born.

An. II. (III.) The three astrologers came from the east part, in order that they might worship Christ ; and the children were slain in Bethlehem, in persecution of Christ, by Herod.

An. III. (IV.) In this year Herod died, stabbed by himself ; and Archelaus his son succeeded to the kingdom. And the child Christ was borne back from Egypt.

An. IV., V. (VI.)

An. VI. (VII.) From the beginning of the world to this year, five thousand and two hundred winters were past.

4.

Before the incarnation of Christ, LX. winters, Caius Julius the emperor, first of the Romans, sought the land of Britain ; and crushed the Britons in fight, and overcame them ; and yet might not there gain power.[a]

---

[1] An error for Laberius.—"Eo "die Q. Laberius Durus, tribunus "militum, interficitur," Cæsar, B.G., v. 15.

[2] The notices which occur between this and the year 449 are derived principally from Jerome's translation of Eusebius' Chronicle and its continuations, and from Bede's Chronicle and Ecclesiastical History, to the latter of which the few incidents relating to Britain during that period are owing.— R.P.

---

[a] MSS. A.B.C.

An. VII. (VIII.)—X.

An. XI. In this year Herod, Antipater's son, received the government in Judea.

An. XII. Philip and Herod divided Lysia and Judea into four governments.

An. XIII. (XIV.)—XV.

An. XVI. (XV.) In this year Tiberius succeeded to the empire.

An. XVII. (XVI.)—XXVI. (XXV.)

An. XXVII. (XXV., XXVI.) In this year Pilate began to rule   8, 9. over the Jews.

An. XXVIII., XXIX. (XXVI.—XXVIII.)

An. XXX. (XXIX.) In this year Christ was baptized, and Peter and Andrew converted; and James and John, and the twelve apostles.

An. XXXL., XXXII.

᷉ An. XXXIII. In this year Christ was crucified; after five thousand two hundred and twenty-six years from the beginning of the world.

᷉ An. XXXIV. In this year St. Paul was converted, and St. Stephen stoned.

An. XXXV. In this year the blessed Peter the apostle filled an episcopal chair in the city of Antioch.

An. XXXVI., XXXVII.

An. XXXVIII. In this year Pilate slew himself with his own hand.

An. XXXIX. In this year Caius (Caligula) succeeded to the empire. ·

An. XL. Matthew in Judea began to write his gospel.

An. XLI.—XLIV. (XLIII.)

An. XLV. (XLIV.) In this year the blessed Peter the apostle filled an episcopal chair in Rome.

An. XLVI. (XLV.) In this year Herod died, who slew James   10, 11. one year before his own death.

An. XII. In this year Judea was divided into four tetrarchates.[a]

---

[a] F.

An. XLVII. (XLVI.) In this year Claudius, second of the Roman kings, sought the land of Britain, and took under his sway the greatest part of the island ; and in like manner subjected the Orkney islands to the kingdom of the Romans. This was in the fourth year of his reign ; and in this same year was the great famine in Syria, which Luke recounts, in the book of the Acts of the Apostles, through Agabus the prophet. Then Nero succeeded to the empire after Claudius, who almost lost Britain through his sloth. Mark the Evangelist begins to write the Gospel in Egypt.

An. XLVIII. (XLVII.) In this year there was a very severe famine.

An. XLIX. In this year Nero began to reign.

An. L. In this year Paul was sent bound to Rome.

An. LI.—LXI.

An. LXII. In this year James, the brother of the Lord, suffered (martyrdom).

An. LXIII. In this year Mark the Evangelist died.

An. LXIV.—LXVIII.

An. LXIX. (LXVIII.) In this year Peter and Paul suffered.

An. LXX. In this year Vespasian succeeded to the empire.

12, 13.   An. LXXI. In this year Titus, son of Vespasian, slew in Jerusalem C.XI. thousand Jews.

An. LXXII.—LXXX.

✔ An. LXXXI. In this year Titus succeeded to the empire after Vespasian, who said that he lost the day on which he did no good.

An. LXXXII., LXXXIII. (LXXXII.)

An. LXXXIV. (LXXXIII.) In this year Domitian, Titus' brother, succeeded to the empire.

✔ An. XLVI. In this year Claudius the emperor came to Britain, and subdued a great part of the island, and also added the island of Orkney to the Roman power.[a]

An. XLVII. In this year Claudius, king of the Romans, went with an army into Britain, and reduced the island, and subjected all the Picts and Welsh to the dominion of the Romans.[b]

An. LXIX. In this year Peter suffered on the cross, and Paul was slain (beheaded).[a]

---

[a] F.   [b] D. E.

An. LXXXV. (LXXXIV.)—LXXXVI. (LXXXIII.) (LXXXIV.)

An. LXXXVII. (LXXXV. LXXXIV.) In this year John the Evangelist, in the island of Patmos, wrote the book Apocalypse.

An. LXXXVIII. (LXXXVI. LXXXV.)—XCVIII. (XCIX.)

An. XCIX. (c.) In this year Simon the apostle, the kinsman of Christ, was crucified; and John the Evangelist rested (died) on that day in Ephesus.

An. C.I. In this year pope Clement died.

An. C.II.—C.IX.

An. C.X. (C.IX.) In this year bishop Ignatius suffered (martyrdom).

An. C.XI.—C.XV.

An. C.XVI. In this year Adrian the emperor began to reign.

An. C.XVII.—C.XXXVI.

An. C.XXXVII. In this year Antoninus began to reign.

An. C.XXXVIII.—C.LIV. (C.LX.)

An. C.LXI. (C.LV.) In this year Marcus Antonius (Antoninus)   14, 15.
and Aurelius his brother succeeded to the empire.

An. C.LXII.—C.LXVI. (C.LVI.—C.LXVI.)

An. C.LXVII. In this year Eleutherius succeeded to the bishopric in Rome, and gloriously (worthily) held it for twelve winters. To him Lucius, king of Britain, sent letters, praying that he might be made a Christian : and he accomplished what he prayed for.

An. C.LXVIII.—C.LXXXVIII.

γ An. C.LXXXIX. (C.LXXXVIII.) In this year Severus succeeded to the empire, and reigned seventeen winters. He begirt Britain with a dike from sea to sea.

An. C.LXVII. In this year Eleutherus succeeded to the popedom, and held it for XV. years ; and in this same year, Lucius, king of the Brito-Welsh, sent and prayed for baptism, and he forthwith sent to him ; and he continued in the true faith till the time of Diocletian.[a]

An. C.LXXXIX. In this year Severus succeeded to the empire, and went with an army to Britain, and by battle subdued a great part of the island ; and then made a wall of turfs, and a broad wall thereupon, from sea to sea, for the protection of the

[a] F.

An. C.XC. (C.LXXXIX.)—C.XCIX.

An. CC. In this year was found the holy rood.

An. CC.I.—CC.LXXXV.

16, 17.   An. CC.LXXXVI. (CC.LXXXIII.) In this year St. Alban the martyr suffered.

An. CC.LXXXVII.—CCC.XLII.

An. CCC.XLIII. In this year St. Nicholas died.

An. CCC.XLIV.—CCC.LXXVIII.

An. CCC.LXXIX. In this year Gratian succeeded to the empire.

An. CCC.LXXX.

An. CCC.LXXXI. In this year Maximus the emperor succeeded to the empire. He was born in Britain, and went thence into Gaul, and he there slew the emperor Gratian, and drove his brother from the country, who was called Valentinian. And Valentinian afterwards gathered an army, and slew Maximus, and succeeded to the empire. At that time the heresy of Pelagius arose throughout the world.

An. CCC.LXXXII.—CCCC.VIII. (CCCC.VII.)

✓ An. CCCC.IX. (CCCC.VIII.) In this year the Goths took Rome by storm ; and never since have the Romans ruled in Britain. That was about XI. hundred and X. winters from the time that it was built. Altogether they ruled in Britain four hundred and seventy winters, from the time that Caius Julius first sought the land.

An. CCCC.X.—CCCC.XVII.

18, 19.   An. CCCC.XVIII. In this year the Romans collected all the treasures that were in Britain, and hid some in the earth, that no man might afterwards find them ; and conveyed some with them into Gaul.

An. CCCC.XIX.—CCCC.XXII.

Brito-Welsh. He reigned seventeen years, and then ended (his days) at York. His son Bassianus succeeded to the empire. His other son was called Geta, who died.[a]

An. C.LXXXVIII. In this year Severus built a wall of turf, after he had won the land by battle ; and a broad wall thereupon from sea to sea. And he reigned seventeen years, and then ended (his days) in York.[b]

---

    [a] B. C.   [b] F.

An. cccc.xxiii. In this year Theodosius the younger succeeded to the empire.

An. cccc.xxiv.—cccc.xxix.

An. cccc.xxx. In this year Palladius the bishop was sent to the Scots by Celestine the pope, that he might confirm their faith.

An. cccc.xxxi.—cccc.xlii.

An. cccc.xliii. In this year the Brito-Welsh sent to Rome, and implored aid against the Picts; but they had none, because they were warring against Attila the king of the Huns. And then they sent to the Angles, and implored the same of the æthelings of the Angle race.

An. cccc.xliv. In this year St. Martin died.

An. cccc.xlv.—cccc.xlviii.

An. cccc.xlix. (cccc.xlviii.) In this year Martian and Valentinian succeeded to the empire, and reigned seven winters.[1] And in their days Hengest and Horsa, invited by⤳ 20, 21.

An. cccc.xxx. This year Palladius (Patricius) was sent by pope Celestine, to preach baptism to the Scots.[a]

An. cccc.xlix. In this year Marcian and Valentinian, &c., and in their days, Wyrtgeorn (Vortigern) invited the Angle race hither, and they then came in three ships hither to Britain, at the place named Heopwines fleot . . . . . . against them. King Wyrtgeorn gave them land in the south-east of this land, on condition that they should fight against the Picts. They then fought against the Picts, and had victory whithersoever they came. They then sent to the Angles; bade them send greater aid, bade them be told of the worthlessness of the Brito-Welsh, and the excellencies of the land. They then forthwith sent hither a larger army, in aid of the others. Then came men from three tribes of Germany : from the Old-Saxons, from the Angles, from the Jutes. From the Jutes came the Kentish people and the people of Wight, that is, the tribe which [2]now dwells in Wight, and the race among the West Saxons

---

[1] Marcian governed the eastern empire from A.D. 450 to 457. | Valentinian III. ruled the western empire from 425 to 455.
[2] That is, in Beda's time.

---

[a] E. F.

Wyrtgeorn (Vortigern) king of the Britons, sought Britain, on the shore which is named Ypwines fleot ; first in support of the Britons, but afterwards they fought against them.

An. CCCC.L. (CCCC.XLIX.)—CCCC.LIV.

An. CCCC.LV. In this year Hengest and Horsa fought against Wyrtgeorn, the king, at the place which is called Ægelsthrep (Aylesford) ; and his brother Horsa was there slain ; and after that Hengest succeeded to the command, and Æsc his son.

An. CCCC.LVI.

An. CCCC.LVII. (CCCC.LVI.) In this year Hengest and Æsc his son fought against the Britons at the place which is called Crecganford (Crayford), and there slew four thousand men ; and the Britons then forsook Kent, and in great terror fled to London.

---

which is yet called the Jute race. From the Old-Saxons came the East Saxons, and South Saxons, and West Saxons. From Angeln—which has ever since stood waste betwixt the Jutes and Saxons—came the East Anglians, the Middle Anglians, the Mercians, and all the Northumbrians. Their leaders were two brothers, Hengest and Horsa. They were sons of Wihtgils ; Wihtgils was son of Witta, Witta of Wecta, Wecta of Woden. From Woden sprang all our royal kin, and the Southumbrians' also.[a]

An. CCCC.XLVIII. In this year John the Baptist discovered his head to two monks, who came from the east, to pray at Jerusalem, in the place that was whilom Herod's dwelling. At the same time Marcian and Valentinian reigned ; and at that time came the Angle race to this land, invited by king Wyrtgeorn (Vortigern), as a help to him in overcoming his foes. They came to this land with three long ships, and their leaders were Hengest and Horsa. First of all they slew and drove away the king's foes, and afterwards they turned against the king, and against the Britons, and destroyed them by fire and by edge of sword.[b]

An. CCCC.LVI. In this year Hengest and Æsc, with edge of sword, slew four hosts of Britons, at the place which is named Creccanford (Crayford).[b]

---

[a] E.　　　　　　　[b] F.

An. CCCC.LVIII.—CCCC.LXIV. (CCCC.LVII.)

An. CCCC.LXV. (CCCC.LXVI.) In this year Hengest and Æsc fought against the Welsh near Wippedes fleot (Ebbsfleet ?), and there slew twelve Welsh aldormen ; and one of their thanes was there slain, whose named was Wipped.

An. CCCC.LXVI.—CCCC.LXXII.

✔ An. CCCC.LXXIII. In this year Hengest and Æsc fought against the Welsh and took countless booty ; and the Welsh fled from the Angles as fire.

An. CCCC.LXXIV.—CCCC.LXXVI.

An. CCCC.LXXVII.—In this year Ælle came to Britain, and his three sons, Cymen, and Wlencing, and Cissa, with three ships, at the place which is named Cymenesora (Shoreham ?), and there slew many Welsh, and drove some in flight into the wood which is named Andredeslea.

An. CCCC.LXXVIII.—CCCC.LXXXI.   24, 25.

An. CCCC.LXXXII. In this year the blessed abbot Benedict, · through the glory of his miracles, shone to this world, as the blessed Gregory relates in the book of Dialogues.

An. CCCC.LXXXIII., CCCC.LXXXIV.

An. CCCC.LXXXV. In this year Ælle fought against the Welsh near the bank of Markredes burne.

An. CCCC.LXXXVI., CCCC.LXXXVII.

An. CCCC.LXXXVIII. In this year Æsc succeeded to the kingdom, and for twenty-four years was king of the Kentish people.

An. CCCC.LXXXIX., CCCC.XC.

An. CCCC.XCI. (CCCC.XC.) In this year Ælle and Cissa besieged Andredesceaster, and slew all that dwelt therein ; not even one Briton was there left.

An. CCCC.XCII. (CCCC.XCI.)—CCCC.XCIV.

An. CCCC.XCV. In this year came two aldormen to Britain, Cerdic, and Cynric his son, with five ships, at the place which is called Cerdices ora (Charford); and on the same day fought against the Welsh.

An. CCCC.XCVI.—D.

An. D.I. In this year came Port to Britain, and his two sons, Bieda and Mægla, with two ships, at the place which is called Portsmouth ; and forthwith landed, and there slew a very noble young British man.

An. D.II.—D.VII.

26, 27.   An. D.VIII. In this year Cerdic and Cynric slew a British king, whose name was Natanleod, and five thousand men with him ; after that the land was named Natanlea as far as Cerdices ford (Charford).

An. D.IX. In this year St. Benedict the abbot, father; of all monks, went to heaven.[1]

An. D.X.—D.XIII.

An. D.XIV. In this year came the West Saxons to Britain, with three ships, at the place which is called Cerdices ora ; and Stuf and Wihtgar fought against the Britons, and put them to flight.

An. D.XV.—D.XVIII.

An. D.XIX. In this year Cerdic and Cynric assumed the kingdom of the West Saxons ; and in the same year they fought against the Britons, where it is now named Cerdic's ford ; and since the royal offspring of the West Saxons has reigned from that day.

An. D.XX.—D.XXVI.

An. D.XXVII. In this year Cerdic and Cynric fought against the Britons at the place which is called Cerdices leag.

An. D.XXVIII., D.XXIX.

An. D.XXX. In this year Cerdic and Cynric took the island of Wight, and slew many men at Wihtgarasburh (Carisbrook).

An. D.XXXI.—D.XXXIII.

An. D.XXXIV. In this year Cerdic, the first king of the West Saxons, died, and Cynric his son succeeded to the
28, 29.   kingdom, and reigned on for twenty-six (twenty-seven) winters ; and they gave all the island of Wight to their two [2] nephews, Stuf and Wihtgar.

An. D.XXXV.—D.XXXVII.

An. D.XXXVIII. In this year the sun was eclipsed fourteen days before the Kalends of March (February 16th), from early morning till nine a.m.

An. D.XXXIX.

---

[1] According to Mabillon, Benedict died in 543.

[2] Here the term nefe (nephew) is used with reference both to father and son.

▼An. D.XL. In this year the sun was eclipsed on the twelfth of the Kalends of July (June 20th), and the stars appeared full nigh half an hour after nine a.m.

An. D.XLI.—D.XLIII.

An. D.XLIV. In this year Wihtgar died, and they buried him at Wihtgarasburh (Carisbrook).

An. D.XLV., D.XLVI.

An. D.XLVII. In this year Ida assumed the kingdom, from whom arose the royal race of the Northumbrians, and reigned twelve years, and he built Bebbanburh (Bamborough), which was at first inclosed by a hedge, and afterwards by a wall. Ida was son of Eoppa, Eoppa of Esa, Esa was son of Ingui, Ingui of Angewit, Angewit of Aloc, Aloc of Benoc, Benoc of Brand, Brand of Bældæg, Bældæg of Woden, Woden of Freothelaf, Freothelaf of Freothewulf, Freothewulf of Finn, Finn of Godulf, Godulf of Geat.

An. D.XLVIII.—D.LI.

An. D.LII. In this year Cynric fought against the Britons at the place which is named Searoburh (Old Sarum), and put the Brito-Welsh to flight. Cerdic was father of Cynric ; Cerdic was son of Elesa, Elesa of Esla, Esla of Giwis, Giwis of Wig, Wig of Freawine, Freawine of Freothogar, Freothogar of Brand, Brand of Bældæg, Bældæg of Woden.

30, 31.

An. D.LIII. —D.LV.

An. D.LVI. In this year Cynric and Ceawlin fought against the Britons at Beranburh (Banbury).

An. D.LVII.—D.LIX.

An. D.LX. (D.LIX.) In this year Ceawlin succeeded to the kingdom of the West Saxons, and Ælle assumed the kingdom of the Northumbrians, Ida being dead ; and each of them reigned thirty winters. Ælle was son of Yffe, Yffe of Uxfrea, Uxfrea of Wilgils, Wilgils of Westerfalena, Westerfalena . of

---

An. D.LII. In this year Cynric fought against the Britons at the place which is called Salisbury; and Æthelberht was born . . . . . . son of Eormenric . . . . year of his reign, he received baptism, first of the kings in Britain.[a]

---

[a] F.

Sǽfugl, Sǽfugl of Sǽbald, Sǽbald of Sigegeat, Sigegeat of
Swebdæg, Swebdæg of Sigegar, Sigegar of Wægdæg, Wægdæg
of Woden, Woden of Frithowulf.

An. D.LXI. (D.LX.)—D.LXIV.

An. [1]D.LXV. In this year Æthelberht succeeded to the
kingdom of the Kentish people, and held it fifty-three winters.
In his days the holy pope Gregory sent us baptism ; that was
in the two and thirtieth year of his reign.   And Columba the
mass-priest came to the Picts and converted them to the faith
of Christ.   They are dwellers by the northern mountains ;
and their king gave him the island which is named Ii (Iona),
where there are five hides, from what men say.   There
32, 33.   Columba built a monastery ; and he was abbot there thirty-
two winters, and there died when he was seventy-seven winters ; his inheritors yet have the place.   The south Picts had
been baptized long before ; to them bishop Nina, who had been
taught at Rome, preached baptism, whose church and his
monastery are at Whiterne, hallowed in the name of St. Martin; there he rests with many holy men.   Now, in Ii (Iona),
there must ever be an abbot, not a bishop ; and to him must
all the Scots' bishops be subjects, because Columba was an
abbot, not a bishop.

An. D.LXVI., D.LXVII.

An. D.LXVIII. In this year Ceawlin and Cutha, Ceawlin's
brother, fought against Æthelberht, and drove him into Kent;
and slew two aldormen at Wibbandûn (Wimbledon), Oslaf
(Oslac) and Cnebba.

An. D.LXIX., D.LXX.

An. D.LXXI. In this year Cuthwulf (Cutha) fought against
the Brito-Welsh at Bedcanforda (Bedford), and took four

V   An. D.LXV. In this year the presbyter (mass-priest) Columba came from the Scots to the Britons, to teach the Picts,
and in the island of Hii (Iona) built a monastery.[a]

---

[1] The correct date, as given by │ he died in 616, after a reign of 56
Wheelocke, would seem to be 560, │ years.
as according to Beda (H.E. II. 5),│

[a] B. C.

towns ; Lygeauburh (Lenbury?), and Æglesburh (Aylesbury), Bænesingtun (Benson), and Egonesham (Ensham) ; and the same year he died. Cutha was Ceawlin's brother.

An. D.LXXII.—D.LXXVI.

An. D.LXXVII. In this year Cuthwine and Ceawlin fought against the Britons, and they slew three kings, Commail, and Condidan, and Farinmail, at the place which is called Deorham (Derham), and took three cities from them, Gloucester, and Cirencester, and Bath.

An. D.LXXVIII.—D.LXXXII.

34, 35.

An. D.LXXXIII. In this year Maurice succeeded to the empire of the Romans.

An. D.LXXXIV. In this year Ceawlin and Cutha fought against the Britons at the place which is named Fethanleng (Frethern ?), and Cutha was there slain ; and Ceawlin took many towns, and countless booty ; and wrathful he thence returned to his own.

An. D.LXXXV.—D.LXXXVII.

An. D.LXXXVIII. In this year *king Ælle died, and Æthel- * of Deira. ric reigned after him for five years.

An. D.LXXXIX., D.XC.

An. D.XCI. In this year *Ceol reigned five years. * of Wessex.

An. D.XCII. In this year there was a great slaughter in Britain at Woddesbeorg (Wansborough), and Ceawlin was driven out. In this year Gregory succeeded to the popedom at Rome.

An. D.XCIII. In this year Ceawlin, and Cwichelm, and *Cryda, perished ; and Æthelfrith succeeded to the king- * k. of Mercia. dom of the Northumbrians : he was son of Æthelric, Æthelric of Ida.

An. D.XCIV., D.XCV.

An. D.XCVI. In this year pope Gregory sent Augustine to Britain with a great many monks, who preached the word of God to the nation of the Angles.

An. D.XCVII. In this year Ceolwulf began to reign over the West Saxons, and he constantly fought and strove against 36, 37. either the Angle race, or against the Welsh, or against the Picts, or against the Scots. He was son of Cutha, Cutha of Cynric, Cynric of Cerdic, Cerdic of Elesa, Elesa of Esla, Esla of Giwis, Giwis of Wig, Wig of Freawine, Freawine of Freothogar, Freothogar of Brand, Brand of Bældæg, Bældæg of Woden. In this year Augustine and his companions came to England.

An. D.XCVIII.—DC.

An. DC.I. In this year pope Gregory sent the pall to archbishop Augustine in Britain, and a great many religious teachers to aid him, and among them was Paulinus the bishop, who afterwards converted Eadwine, king of the Northumbrians, to baptism.

An. DC.II.

An. DC.III. In this year there was a battle at Ægesanstân (Dawston).

An. DC.IV. In this year the East Saxons received the faith and bath of baptism, under king Sǽberht and bishop Mellitus.

An. DC.V.

An. DC.VI. (DC.V.) In this year pope Gregory died, ten years after he had sent us baptism.[1] His father was called Gordian, and his mother Silvia. And in this year Æthelfrith led his army to Chester, and there slew numberless Welsh ; and so was fulfilled the prophecy of Augustine, which

---

An. DC.III. In this year Ægthan king of the Scots fought against the Dalreods, and against Æthelferth, king of the Northumbrians, at Dægsanstân (Dawston), and almost all his army was slain. There was slain Theodbald, Æthelferth's brother, with all his host. Since then no king of Scots has dared to lead an army into this nation. Hering son of Hussa led the army hither.[a]

An. DC.IV. In this year Augustine hallowed two bishops, Mellitus and Justus. Mellitus he sent to preach baptism to the East Saxons, where the king was called Sǽberht, son of Ricole, sister of [*]Æthelberht, whom Æthelberht had there set as king. And Æthelberht gave to Mellitus a bishop's see at London ; and to Justus he gave Rochester, which is twenty-four miles from Canterbury.[b]

[*] k. of Kent.
38, 39.

---

[1] Inserted in A. under DC.VII. According to the Cambrian Annals | and Tigernach, the event took place in 613.

[a] E.   [b] E. F.

he uttered : " If the Welsh refuse peace with us, they shall perish at the hands of the Saxons." There were also slain two hundred priests, who came thither that they might pray for the army of the Welsh. Their chief was named Scromail (Brocmail), who escaped thence with some fifty.

An. DC.VII. (DC.VI., DC.VII.) In this year Ceolwulf fought with the South Saxons.

An. DC.VIII.—DC.X.

An. DC.XI. In this year Cynegils succeeded to the kingdom of the West Saxons, and held it thirty-one winters. Cynegils was son of Ceol, Ceol of Cutha, Cutha of Cynric.

An. DC.XII., DC.XIII.

An. DC.XIV. In this year Cynegils and Cwichelm fought at Beandon (Bampton ?), and slew two thousand and sixty-five Welsh.

An. DC.XV.   40, 41.

An. DC.XVI. In this year Æthelberht king of the Kentish people died ; he reigned LVI. winters ; and Eadbald his son succeeded to the kingdom ; who contemned his baptism, and lived in heathen manner, so that he had his father's relict to wife. Then Laurentius, who was archbishop of Kent, was minded that he would go south over sea, and forsake all. But by night the apostle Peter came to him, and severely scourged him, because he would so forsake God's flock ; and bade him go to the king, and preach to him the true faith ; and he did so, and the king was converted, and was baptized. In this king's days, Laurentius, who was in Kent after Augustine, died,

---

An. DC.XVI. In this year Æthelberht king of the Kentish people died, who first of English kings received baptism ; and he was son of Eormenric ; he reigned fifty-three winters. After him Eadbald his son succeeded to the kingdom, who contemned his Christianity, so that he had his father's relict to wife. At that time Laurentius was archbishop ; and for the affliction that he had on account of the king's unbelief, he was minded to forsake all this land, and go over sea. But one night St. Peter the apostle severely scourged him, because he would so forsake God's flock ; and bade him boldly teach to the king the right faith, and he did so. And the king turned to right. In the days of this same king Eadbald, this same

on the ivth of the Nones of February (Feb. 2nd), and was
buried beside Augustine. After him Mellitus succeeded to
the archbishopric, who had been bishop of London. And
within five years after, Mellitus died. Then after him, Justus
succeeded to the archbishopric, who had been bishop of
Rochester, and hallowed Romanus bishop thereto.

An. DC.XVII. In this year Æthelfrith, king of the Northumbrians, was slain by Rædwald, king of the East Angles ; and
Eadwine son of Ælle succeeded to the kingdom, and ravaged
42, 43.   all Britain, save the Kentish people only ; and drove out the
æthelings, sons of Æthelfrith : that was, first Eanfrith, and
Oswald ; then Oswiu, Oslac, Oswudu, Oslaf, and Offa.

An. DC.XVIII.

An. DC.XIX. In this year archbishop Laurentius died.

An. DC.XX.—DC.XXIII.

An. DC.XXIV. In this year archbishop Mellitus died.

An. DC.XXV. In this year Paulinus was ordained bishop of
the Northumbrians by archbishop Justus, on XII. Kal. of
August (July 21st).

An. DC.XXVI. In this year Eanflæd, king Eadwine's daughter,
was baptized on the holy eve of Pentecost (Jun. 8th). And
Penda had held the kingdom thirty winters ; and he was fifty

Laurentius died. The holy Augustine, while in hale life,
had ordained him bishop, in order that the church of Christ,
which was yet new in England, might not, after his decease,
be at any time without an archbishop. Then after him
Mellitus succeeded to the archiepiscopal see, who had before
been bishop of London. And within five years after the
decease of Laurentius, Eadbald still reigning, Mellitus departed
to Christ.[a]

An. DC.XXV. In this year archbishop Justus hallowed
Paulinus bishop of the Northumbrians, on XII. Kal. of August
(July 21st).[b]

c. XXVII.   An. *DC.XXVI. In this year Eomer came from Cwichelm,
king of the West Saxons, thinking to stab king Eadwine ;
but he stabbed Lilla his thane, and Forthere, and wounded
the king. And on the same night a daughter was born to

---

[a] E. A.   [b] E. F.

winters old when he succeeded to the kingdom. Penda was son of Pybba, Pybba of Cryda, Cryda of Cynewald, Cynewald of Cnebba, Cnebba of Icel, Icel of Eomær, Eomær of Angeltheow, Angeltheow of Offa, Offa of Wærmund, Wærmund of Wihtlæg, Wihtlæg of Woden.

An. DC.XXVII. In this year king Eadwine was baptized with his people at Easter (Apr. 12th) by Paulinus; and this Paulinus also preached baptism in Lindsey, where the first who believed was a powerful man called Blecca, with all his followers. And at this time Honorius, who sent Paulinus the pall hither, succeeded to the popedom after Boniface. And archbishop Justus died on the ivth of the Ides of November (Nov. 10th); and Honorius was consecrated archbishop of Canterbury, by Paulinus, at Lincoln. To Honorius the pope also sent a pall: and he sent a letter to the Scots, that they should turn to the right Easter.

44, 45

An. DC.XXVIII. In this year Cynegils and Cwichelm fought against Penda at Cirencester, and afterwards came to an agreement.

Eadwine, who was called Eanflæd. Then the king promised to Paulinus, that he would give his daughter to God, if by prayer he would obtain from God, that he might slay his foe who had sent the assassin thither. And he then went against the West Saxons with an army, and there slew five kings, and many of the people. And Paulinus baptized his daughter at Pentecost with twelve others. And the king within a twelvemonth was baptized at Easter with all his nobles; Easter was then on iind of the Ides of April (April 12th). This was done at York, where he first commanded a church of wood to be built, which was hallowed in the name of St. Peter. There the king gave to Paulinus a bishop's see; and there he afterwards commanded a larger church to be built of stone. And in this year Penda succeeded to the *kingdom, and reigned thirty winters.[a]   * of Mercia.

An. DC.XXVII. In this year, at Easter (Apr. 12th), Paulinus baptized Eadwine, king of the Northumbrians, with his people; and earlier in the same year, at Pentecost, he had baptized Eanflæd, the same king's daughter, &c.[b]

---

^a E.   ^b F.

An. DC.XXIX.—DC.XXXI.

of E. Anglia. An. DC.XXXII. In this year *Eorpwald was baptized.

An. DC.XXXIII. In this year Eadwine was slain, and Paulinus returned to the Kentish people, and filled the bishop's see at Rochester.

An. DC.XXXIV. In this year bishop Birinus preached baptism to the West Saxons, under king Cynegils. Birinus went thither by command of Honorius the pope, and he there was bishop until his life's end. In this year Osric, whom Paulinus had previously baptized, succeeded to the kingdom of Deira ; he was the son of Ælfric, Eadwine's paternal uncle. And to Bernicia succeeded Eanfrith, the son of Æthelfrith. And in this year also Oswald succeeded to the kingdom of the Northumbrians, and he reigned nine winters : the ninth being reckoned to him, on account of the heathenship which they 46, 47. had practised, who had ruled them for one year, between him and Eadwine.

An. DC.XXXV. In this year Cynegils was baptized by Birinus the bishop at Dorchester, and Oswald king of the Northumbrians received him (for son).

An. DC.XXXVI. In this year king Cwichelm was baptized at Dorchester, and in the same year died. And bishop Felix preached the faith of Christ to the East Angles.

---

45. An. DC.XXXIII. In this year king Eadwine was slain by Cadwalla and Penda at Heathfield (Hatfield chase ?), on the IInd of the Ides of October (Oct. 14th) ; and he reigned seventeen years ; and his son Osfrith was also slain with him. And then afterwards, Cadwalla and Penda went and laid waste all the land of the Northumbrians. When Paulinus saw that, then took he Æthelburh, Eadwine's relict, and withdrew in a ship to Kent. And Eadbald and Honorius received him very honourably, and gave him the bishop's see at Rochester, and he there continued to his end.[a]

An. DC.XXXIII. In this year king Eadwine was slain, and Paulinus returned with Æthelburh, Eadwine's relict, to Canterbury ; and archbishop Honorius received them with great honour, and gave Paulinus the bishop's see at Rochester; and there he continued until his end.[b]

---

[a] E.   [b] F.

An. DC.XXXVII., DC.XXXVIII.

An. DC.XXXIX. In this year Birinus baptized king Cuthred at Dorchester, and received him for son.

An. DC.XL. In this year Eadbald, king of the Kentish people, died, and he reigned twenty-five (twenty-four) winters. He had two sons, Ermenred and Ercenberht; and Ercenberht reigned there after his father. And Ermenred begat two sons, who were afterwards martyred by Thunor. He cast down all the idols in his kingdom, and first of English kings he established the Easter fast. His daughter was called Ercongota, a holy maiden and wondrous person, whose mother was Sexburh, daughter of Anna, king of the East Angles.

An. DC.XLI.

An. DC.XLII. (DC.XLI.) In this year Oswald, king of the Northumbrians, was slain by Penda the Southumbrian at Maserfield (Mirfield ?) on the day of the Nones of August (Aug. 5th), and his corpse was buried at Bardney; whose holiness and miracles were afterwards variously made known throughout this island; and his hands are at Bamborough uncorrupted. And in the same year that Oswald was slain, Oswiu his brother succeeded to the kingdom of the Northumbrians; and he reigned thirty years less two.

48, 49.

An. DC.XLIII. (DC.XLII., DC.XLI.) In this year Kênwealh succeeded to the kingdom of the West Saxons, and held it thirty-one winters. And Kênwealh commanded the old church at Winchester to be built, in the name of St. Peter: and he was son of Kynegils.

An. DC.XLIV. (DC.XLIII.) In this year archbishop Paulinus died at Rochester, on the VIth of the Ides of October (Oct. 10th). He had previously been archbishop of York, and was afterwards at Rochester. He was bishop twenty winters less one, and two months, and twenty-one days. And in this year ¹Oswine son of Osric, Eadwine's uncle's son,' succeeded to the kingdom of Deira, and reigned seven years.

An. DC.XLV. (DC.XLIV.) In this year king Kênwealh was driven out from his kingdom by king Penda.

An. DC.XLVI. (DC.XLV.) In this year king Kênwealh was baptized.

---

¹ Here the original text is evidently corrupt. See An. DC.XXXIV.

An. DC.XLVII.

An. DC.XLVIII. (DC.XLVII.) In this year Kênwealh gave to Cuthred his kinsman three thousand hides of land by Ash-down. Cuthred was son of Cwichelm, Cwichelm of Kynegils. In this year was built the monastery at Winchester, which king Kênwealh had caused to be made and hallowed in the name of St. Peter.

An. DC.XLIX. (DC.XLVIII.)

An. DC.L. (DC.XLIX.) In this year Ægelbyrht of Gaul re-ceived the bishopric of the West Saxons, after Birinus the Romish bishop.

An. DC.LI. (DC.L.) In this year king Oswine was slain ; and *bishop Aidan died.

An. DC.LII. (DC.LI.) In this year Kênwealh fought at Brad-ford by the Avon.

An. DC.LIII. (DC.LII.) In this year the Middle Angles, under the aldorman Peada, received the orthodox faith.

An. DC.LIV. (DC.LIII.) In this year *king Anna was slain ; and Bôtulf began to build a monastery at Ycanho (Boston ?). And this year archbishop Honorius died, on the IInd of the Kal. of October (Sept. 30th).

An. DC.LV. (DC.LIV.) In this year Penda perished ; and the Mercians became Christians. Then had passed, from the beginning of the world, five thousand eight hundred and fifty winters. And Peada, son of Penda, succeeded to the kingdom

---

An. DC.L, In this year Birinus the bishop died, and Ægebert the Frenchman was ordained.[a]

An. DC.L. In this year king Oswiu commanded king Os-wine to be slain, on the XIIIth of the Kalends of September (Aug. 20th) ; and twelve nights after, bishop Aidan died, on the IInd of the Kal. of September (Aug. 31st).[b]

An. DC.LIV. In this year king Oswiu slew king Penda at Winwidfield (Wingfield), and thirty royal persons with him ; and some of them were kings : one of them was Æthelhere, brother of Anna, king of the East Angles, &c.[c]

---

[a] F.   [b] E.   [c] E. F.

of the Mercians.[1] In this year Ithamar, bishop of Rochester, hallowed Deusdedit to Canterbury, on the VIIth of the Kal. of April (Mar. 26th).

An. DC.L.VI. (DC.LV.)

An. DC.LVII. (DC.LVI.) In this year Peada died (was slain),   52, 53. and Wulfhere, son of Peada, succeeded to the kingdom of the Mercians.[2]

---

[1] In his time he and Oswiu, the brother of king Oswald, came together, and said that they would rear a monastery to the glory of Christ and the honour of St. Peter. And they did so, and gave it the name of Medeshamstede ; because there is a well there which is called Mede's well. And they then began the foundation, and thereon wrought, and then committed it to a monk who was called Saxulf. He was greatly the friend of God, and all the nation loved him, and he was very nobly born in the world, and rich ; he is now much richer with Christ. But the king Peada reigned no long while ; for he was betrayed by his own queen at Easter-tide.[a]

[2] In his time the abbacy of Medeshamstede, which his brother had begun, waxed very rich. Now the king loved it much, for love of his brother Peada, and for love of his [3]pledge-brother Oswiu, and for love of Saxulf the abbot. He then said that he would dignify and honour it, by the counsel of his brothers, Æthelred and Merewald ; and by the counsel of his sisters, Kyneburh and Kyneswith ; and by the counsel of the archbishop, who was named Deusdedit ; and by the counsel of all his 'witan,' clerical and lay, who were in his kingdom : and he did so. Then the king sent after the abbot that he should speedily come to him ; and he did so. Then said the king to the abbot, "Lo ! beloved Saxulf, I have sent after thee for my soul's need, and I will plainly tell thee why. My brother Peada and my dear friend Oswiu began a monastery to the glory of Christ and St. Peter. But my brother, as Christ has willed it, is departed from this life, and I will pray to thee, O dear friend ! that they work diligently on the work, and I will find thee thereto gold and silver, lands and

---

[3] *i.e.* baptismal brother.

---

[a] E.

54, 55.   An, DC.LVIII. In this year Kênwealh fought against the Welsh at Peonna (Pen), and put them to flight as far as Pedrida (the Parret). This (battle) was fought after he came

---

possessions, and all that thereto behoveth." Then went the abbot home, and began to work. He so sped as Christ granted him, so that in a few years the monastery was ready. When the king heard that said, he was very glad, bade send through all his people after all his thanes ; after the arch-bisop, and after the bishops, and after his earls, and after all those who loved God, that they should come to him ; and he then set a day when the monastery should be hallowed. At the hallowing of the monastery king Wulfhere was there, and his brother Æthelred, and his sisters, Kyneburh and Kyne-swith ; and Deusdedit, the archbishop of Canterbury, hallowed the monastery ; and the bishop of Rochester, Ithamar ; and the bishop of London, who was named Wine ; and the bishop of the Mercians, who was named Jaruman, and bishop Tuda. And there was Wilfrith the priest, who was afterwards a bishop ; and there were all his thanes that were in his kingdom. When the monastery was hallowed in the name of St. Peter and of St. Paul, and of St. Andrew, then the king stood up before all his thanes, and said with a loud voice, "Thanked be the high almighty God for the worthy deed that is here done ; and I will this day honour Christ and St. Peter, and I will that ye all assent to my words. I, Wulfhere, give to-day to St. Peter, and the abbot Saxulf, and the monks of the monastery, these lands, and these waters, and meres, and fens, and wears, and all the lands that lie thereabout, which are of my kingdom, freely, so that no man, save the abbot and the monks, have any authority there. This is the gift : From Medeshamstede to Northburh (Norborough), and so to the place which is called Folies ; and so all the fen right to Esendic (Asendike), to the place which is called Fethermuth ; and so on the straight way ten miles long to Cuggedic, and so to Raggewilh (Rothwell ?) ; and from Raggewilh five miles to the straight river that goes to Ælm (Elm) and to Wisbec (Wisbech) ; and so about three miles to Throkonholt (Tro-kenholt), and from Throkonholt right through all the fen to Dereword (Dereworth), which is twenty miles long ; and so

from the East Angles. He was there three years in exile : thither had Penda driven him, and had deprived him of his kingdom, because he had forsaken his sister.

An. DC.LIX.

---

to Grætecros (Great Cross) ; and from Grætecros, through a clear water called Brâdan æ ; and thence six miles to Paccelad ; and so on through all the meres and fens which lie towards Huntendun-port (Huntingdon) ; and these meres and lakes, Scœlfremere and Witlesmere, and all the others which lie thereabout, with the land and with the houses which are on the east side of Scœlfremere, and thence all the fens to Medes-hamstede ; and from Medeshamstede to Welmesford (Walmsford); and from Welmesford to Clive (King's Cliff), and thence to Æstûn (Aston); and from Æstûn to Stânford (Stamford), and from Stânford as the water runs to the aforesaid North-burh." These are the lands and the fens which the king gave to St. Peter's monastery. Then said the king, " This gift is little ; but I will that they shall hold it so royally and so freely that there be taken of it neither tax nor gabel, but for the monks alone. Thus will I free this monastery, that it be not subject, save to Rome only; and here I will that we seek St. Peter, all those who cannot go to Rome." Between these words, the abbot desired that he would grant him that which he should desire of him ; and the king granted it to him. "I have here God-fearing monks, who would pass their lives in an anchoretage, if they knew where. But here is an island which is called Ancarig (Thorney Isle ?), and I will crave this, that we may there build a monastery to the glory of St. Mary, that they may there dwell who may desire to lead their lives in peace and in rest." Then the king answered, and thus said, " Lo ! beloved Saxulf, not that alone which thou desirest, but all the things which I know that thou desirest on our Lord's behalf, I will so love and grant. And I pray thee, brother Æthelred, and my sisters, Kyneburh and Kyneswith, for the redemption of your souls, that ye be witnesses, and that ye write it with your fingers. And I pray all those who come after me, be they my sons, be they my brothers, or kings, that come after me, that our gift may stand, as they desire to be partakers in the eternal life, and as they desire to escape

An. DC.LX. In this year bishop Ægelbyrht withdrew from Kênwcalh ; and Wine held the bishopric for three years ; and Ægelbyrht received the bishopric of Paris, in Gaul, by the Seine.

---

from eternal punishment. Whosoever shall lessen our gift, or the gifts of other good men, may the heavenly gateward lessen him in the kingdom of heaven. And whosoever shall amplify it, may the heavenly gateward amplify him in the kingdom of heaven." These are the witnesses who were there, and who wrote it with their fingers on Christ's cross, and agreed to it with their tongues. King Wulfhere was the first that confirmed it, first by his words, and afterwards with his fingers wrote on the cross of Christ, and thus said : "I, king Wulfhere, with the kings, and with earls, and with dukes, and with thanes, the witnesses of my gift, before the archbishop Deusdedit, confirm it with the cross of Christ."✝ "And I, Oswiu, king of the Northumbrians, the friend of this monastery, and of the abbot Saxulf, approve it with the cross of Christ."✝ "And I, king *Sighere, grant it with the cross of Christ."✝ "And I, king *Sebbi, write it with the cross of Christ."✝ "And I, Æthelred, the king's brother, grant the same with the cross of Christ."✝ "And we, the king's sisters, Kyneburh and Kyneswith, we approve it."✝ "And I, Deusdedit, archbishop of Canterbury, grant it."✝ After that, all the others who were there assented to it with the cross of Christ. They were by name: Ithamar, bishop of Rochester ; and Wine, bishop of London, and Jaruman, who was bishop of the Mercians; and Tuda, the *bishop, and Wilfrith the priest, who was afterwards bishop, and Eoppa the priest, whom king Wulfhere sent to preach Christianity in Wight; and Saxulf abbot, and Immine aldorman, and Eadberht aldorman, and Herefrith aldorman, and Wilberht aldorman, and Abon aldorman ; Æthelbold, Brordan, Wilbert, Ealhmund, Frethegist. These and many others who were there, servants of the king, all assented to it.

This writ was written after the birth of our Lord DC.LXIV., the seventh year of king Wulfhere ; the ninth year of archbishop Deusdedit. They then laid the curse of God and the curse of all the saints, and of all Christian people, on him

An. DC.LXI. In this year Kênwealh fought at Easter at Posentesburh (Pontesbury) ; and Wulfhere, son of Penda, committed ravage as far as Æscesdûn (Ashdown). And Cuthred son of Cwichelm and *king Cænbyrht died in one year. *father of Ceadwalla, And Wulfhere, son of Penda, committed ravage on Wight, and gave the people of Wight to Æthelwald, king of the South Saxons, because Wulfhere had received him at baptism. And Eoppa the mass-priest, by order of Wilfrith and king Wulfhere, first brought baptism to the people of Wight.

---

who should undo anything that was there done. "So be it," say all. Amen.[1]

When this thing was done, the king sent to Rome to Vitalian, who was then pope, and desired that he would sanction by his writ and with his blessing all this aforesaid thing. And the pope then sent this writ, thus saying : "I, pope Vitalian, grant to thee, king Wulfhere, and archbishop Deusdedit, and abbot Saxulf, all the things which ye desire. And I forbid that either king or any man have any authority, save only the abbot ; and that he obey any man, save the pope at Rome, and the archbishop of Canterbury. If any one break this in anything, may St. Peter with his sword destroy him ; if any one observe it, may St. Peter with the key of heaven undo for him the kingdom of heaven. Thus was the monastery at Medeshamstede begun, which has since been called Burgh (Peterborough).

After that came another archbishop to Canterbury, who was called Theodorus, a very good and wise man ; and held his synod with his bishops and with the clergy. There was [2]Winfrith bishop *of the Mercians deposed from his bishopric, *of Lichfield. and Saxulf the abbot was there chosen for bishop ; and Cuthbald, a monk of the same monastery, was chosen for abbot. This synod was held six hundred and seventy-three winters after the birth of our Lord.[a]

---

[1] See a late Latin copy of this spurious grant in Cod. Diplom. v. p. 2.

[2] He was deposed for resisting the partition of his see by Theodore.

---

[a] E.

An. DC.LXII., DC.LXIII.

An. DC.LXIV. In this year the sun was eclipsed on the vth of the Nones of May [1](May 3rd); and Earcenbryht, king of the Kentish people, died, and Ecgbryht his son succeeded to the kingdom ; and *Colman with his companions went to his country. In the same year there was a great pestilence in the island of Britain; and of that pestilence died *bishop Tuda, and was buried at Wagel (Wayleigh?). And Ceadda and Wilfrith were ordained ; and the same year archbishop Deusdedit died.

* bp. of Lindisfarne. 56, 57.

* of Lindisfarne.

An. DC.LXV., DC.LXVI.

* k. of Kent.

An. DC.LXVII. In this year Oswiu and *Ecgbriht sent Wigheard the priest to Rome, that he might there be hallowed for archbishop of Canterbury; but he died as soon as he came thither.

An. DC.LXVIII. In this year Theodore was ordained archbishop, and sent to Britain.

An. DC.LXIX. In this year king Ecgbriht gave Reculf (Reculver) to Bass, the mass-priest, to build a monastery thereon.

An. DC.LXX. In this year Oswiu, king of the Northumbrians, died on the xvth of the Kal. of March (Feb. 15th); and Ecgferth his son reigned after him. And Hlothhere, the nephew of bishop Æthelbyrht, succeeded to the bishopric over the West Saxons, and held it seven years ; and bishop Theodore hallowed him. And Oswiu was son of Æthelfrith, Æthelfrith of Æthelric, Æthelric of Ida, Ida of Eoppa.

❤ An. DC.LXXI. In this year was the great destruction of birds.

An. DC.LXXII. In this year king Kênwealh died, and Seaxburh his queen reigned one year after him.

An. DC.LXVII. In this year Wigheard went to Rome, as king Oswiu and Ecgbriht had sent him, &c.[a]

---

[1] This happened on the 1st of May, but the error is Bede's.—R.P.

---

[a] F.

An. DC.LXXIII. In this year Ecgbriht, king of the Kentish people, died ; and in the same year there was a synod   58, 59 at Heorotford (Hertford) ; and St. Ætheldryth began the monastery at Ely.

An. DC.LXXIV. In this year Æscwine succeeded to the kingdom of the West Saxons ; he was son of Cênfûs, Cêufûs of Cênferth, Cênferth of Cuthgils, Cuthgils of Ceolwulf, Ceolwulf of Cynric, Cynric of Cerdic.

An. DC.LXXV. In this year Wulfhere, son of Penda, and Æscwine, son of Cênfûs, fought at Biedanheafod (Bedwin?); and the same year Wulfhere died, and Æthelred succeeded to the kingdom.[1]

-----

[1] In his time he sent bishop Wilfrith to Rome, to the pope that then was, he was called Agatho, and announced to him, by letter and by word, how his brothers, Peada and Wulfhere, and the abbot Saxulf, had built a monastery, which was called Medeshamstede ; and that they had freed it, against king and against bishop, from all service ; and prayed him to sanction it by his writ and with his blessing. And then the pope sent his writ to England, thus saying : [2] "I, Agatho, pope of Rome, greet well the worshipful Æthelred, king of the Mercians, and the archbishop Theodore of Canterbury, and the bishop of the Mercians, Saxulf, who was previously abbot, and all the abbots who are in England, with God's greeting and my blessing. I have heard the yearning of king Æthelred, and of the archbishop Theodore, and of the bishop Saxulf, and of the abbot Cuthbald ; and I will that it be in all wise so as ye have spoken it. And I command, on behalf of God, and of St. Peter, and of all saints, and of all ordained persons, that neither king, nor bishop, nor earl, nor any man have any authority, or gabel, or tax, or military service; nor let any man take service of any kind from the abbacy of Medeshamstede. I command also that the shire-bishop be not so bold that he perform any ordination or consecration in this abbacy, unless the abbot request it of him, or have 'biscop-wite,' or synod, or

-----

[2] See the Latin original in Codex Diplom. v. p. 22, and a Saxon copy at p. 28.

60, 61.

*of the West Saxons.

An. DC.LXXVI. In this year Æscwine died, and Hedde succeeded to the *bishopric ; and Centwine succeeded to the kingdom of the West Saxons. And Centwine was son of Cynegils, Cynegils of Ceolwulf. And Æthered, king of the Mercians, ravaged Kent.

authority there of any kind. And I will that the abbot be holden as legate of Rome over all the island ; and that every abbot who shall be there chosen by the monks, be blessed by the archbishop of Canterbury. I will and grant that every man who had promised to go to Rome, and cannot perform it, either from infirmity, or his lord's need, or from lack of means, or from need of any other kind he cannot go thither, be he of England, or of whatever other island he be, let him go to the monastery at Medeshamstede, and have the same forgiveness of Christ and St. Peter, and of the abbot, and of the monks, that he should have if he went to Rome. I now pray thee, brother Theodore, that thou let be commanded throughout all England, that a synod be gathered, and this writ be read and observed. In like manner I command thee, bishop Saxulf, that so as thou yearnest it that the monastery be free, so I forbid thee and all the bishops who shall come after thee, from Christ and from all his saints, from having any authority over the monastery, save as much as the abbot may allow. I will now say by word, that whoso holds this writ and this announcement, may he be ever dwelling with God Almighty in the kingdom of heaven ; and whoso violates it, be he excommunicated and cast down with Judas and with all the devils into hell, unless he come to repentance. Amen."

This writ pope Agatho and a hundred and twenty-five bishops sent to England by Wilfrith, archbishop of York. This was done after the birth of our Lord DC.LXXX., the sixth year of king Æthelred.

Then the king commanded the archbishop Theodore, that he should appoint a meeting of all the 'witan' at the place which is called Heatfeld (Hatfield). When they were there gathered, he caused the writ to be read which the pope had sent thither, and they all assented to and fully confirmed it. Then said the king: "All the things which my brother

An. DC.LXXVII.

• An. DC.LXXVIII. In this year the star (called) comet appeared in August, and shone for three months every morning like a sun-beam. And bishop Wilfrith was driven from his bishopric by king Ecgferth; and two bishops were hallowed in his stead : Bosa to Deira, and Eata to Bernicia. And Eadhed was hallowed bishop of the people of Lindsey; he was the first of the bishops of Lindsey.

An. DC.LXXIX. In this year *Ælfwine was slain by the ˟ brother of k. Ecgferth. Trent, where Ecgferth and Æthelred fought. And St. Æthelthryth died, and Coldingham was burnt by divine fire.

Peada and my brother Wulfhere, and my sisters, Kyneburh and Kyneswith, gave and granted to St. Peter and the abbot, I will that they stand ; and I will in my day increase it, for their souls and for my soul. I now give to-day to St. Peter, for his monastery of Medeshamstede, these lands and all thereto adjacent : that is, Bredun (Bredon), Hrepingas, Cedenac (Cadney), Swineshæfed (Swineshead), Heanbyrig (Hanbury), Lodeshac (Loddington), Scuffanhalch, Costesford (Cosford), Stretford (Stratford), Wætelleburne (Wellbourne), Lufgeard (Lufwick ?), Æthelhuniglond (Allington ?), Barthanig (Bardney). These lands I give to St. Peter as freely as I myself possessed them, and so that none of my successors take anything therefrom. If any one do it, may he have the curse of the pope of Rome, and the curse of all bishops, and of all those that are here witnesses ; and this I confirm with the sign of Christ." ✚ I, Theodore, archbishop of Canterbury, am witness to this writ of Medeshamstede, and I confirm it with my writing ; and I excommunicate all who shall violate anything thereof, and I bless all who shall hold it. ✚ I, Wilfrith, archbishop of York, I am witness to this writing, and I assent to the same curse. ✚ I, Saxulf, who was first abbot and now am bishop, I give them my curse, and that of all my successors, who shall violate this. I, Osthryth, queen of Æthelred, grant it. I, Adrian, legate, assent to it. I, Putta, bishop of Rochester, subscribe it. I, Waldhere, bishop of London, confirm it. I, Cuthbald, abbot, assent to it, so that whoso shall violate it, have he the cursing of all bishops and of all Christian folk. Amen.

An. DC.LXXX. In this year archbishop Theodore appointed a synod at Hæthfeld (Bishop's Hatfield), because he would set right the faith of Christ. And in the same year Hild, abbess of Whitby, died.

An. DC.LXXXI. In this year Trumbyrht was hallowed bishop of Hexham, and Trumwine of the Picts; because at that time [1] they belonged here.

An. DC.LXXXII. (DC.LXXXIII.) In this year Centwine drove the Brito-Welsh as far as the sea.

An. DC.LXXXIII.

An. DC.LXXXIV. In this year Ecgferth sent an army against the Scots, and Berht, his aldorman, with it; and miserably they afflicted and burned God's churches.

An. DC.LXXXV. In this year king Ecgferth commanded Cuthberht to be hallowed a bishop; and archbishop Theodore hallowed him at York, on the first day of Easter, bishop of Hexham, because Trumbyrht had been [2] deprived of his bishopric. And in this year Ceadwalla began to strive for the kingdom. Ceadwalla was son of Coenbryht, Coenbryht of Cadda (Ceadda), Cadda of Cutha, Cutha of Ceawlin, Ceawlin of Cynric, Cynric of Cerdic. And Mûl was Ceadwalla's brother, and he was afterwards burnt in Kent. And in the same year king Ecgferth was slain by the north sea, and a great army with him, on the XIII. of the Kal. of June (May 20th). He had been king fifteen winters; and Aldfrith, his brother, succeeded to the kingdom after him. Ecgferth was son of Oswiu, Oswiu of Æthelferth, Æthelferth of Æthelric, Æthelric of Ida, Ida of Eoppa. And Hlothhere, king of the Kentish people, died in the same year. And John was hallowed bishop of Hexham, and he was there until Wilfrith came in. John succeeded afterwards to the bishopric of York, for bishop Bosa was dead. Then Wilfrith, his priest, was after that hallowed bishop of Ceaster (York), and John went to his monastery of Derewood (Beverley). In this year there was bloody rain in Britain, and milk and butter were turned to blood.

---

[1] That is, the Picts; they afterwards revolted and threw of the Anglian yoke.

[2] By the revolted Picts, who expelled the Anglian prelate.

An. DC.LXXXVI. In this year Ceadwalla, and Mûl, his brother, ravaged Kent and Wight. This Ceadwalla gave to St. Peter's monastery at Medeshamstede Hoge (Hook), which is in an island called Heabureahg (Egborough). The abbot then of that monastery was called Ecgbald : he was the third abbot after Saxulf. Theodore was then archbishop in Kent.

An. DC.LXXXVII. In this year Mûl was burnt in Kent, and XII. other men with him ; and in that year Ceadwalla again ravaged Kent.

64, 65.

An. DC.LXXXVIII. In this year Ine succeeded to the kingdom of the West Saxons, and held it thirty-seven winters. And he built the monastery at Glastonbury, and afterwards withdrew to Rome, and there dwelt until his dying day. And in the same year Ceadwalla went to Rome, and received baptism from the pope ; and the pope named him Peter ; and after seven nights he died. Now Ine was son of Cênred, Cênred of Ceolwald, Ceolwald was brother of Cynegils ; and they were the sons of Cuthwine, son of Ceawlin, Ceawlin of Cynric, Cynric of Cerdic.

An. DC.LXXXIX.

An. DC.XC. In this year archbishop Theodore died. He was bishop twenty-two winters, and he was buried at Canterbury ; and Beorhtwald succeeded to the bishopric. Previously the bishops had been Roman ; since then they were English.

An. DC.XCI., DC.XCII.

An. DC.LXXXVIII. In this year king Ceadwalla went to Rome, and received baptism of Sergius the pope, and he gave him the name of Peter, and after seven nights he died, on the XIIth of the Kal. of May (Apr. 20th), in his ' baptismal clothes'; and he was buried in St. Peter's church. And Ine succeeded to the kingdom of the West Saxons after him, who reigned twenty-seven winters, and afterwards withdrew, &c.ª

ᴵʼ in albis adhuc positus. Beda, H. E. v. 7. under crisman, Ælfr. Beda.

ª E. F.

66, 67.   An. DC.XCIII. In this year Beorhtwald was hallowed archbishop by Guodun, bishop of the Gauls, on the vth of the
Non. of July (July 3rd). At this time Gefmund, who was
bishop of Rochester, died ; and archbishop Beorhtwald hallowed Tobias in his stead. And Dryhthelm was withdrawn
from life.[1]

An. DC.XCIV. In this year the Kentish people compounded
with Ine, and gave him thirty [2]men (pounds, thousands)
for his friendship, because they had formerly burned Mûl.
And Wihtred succeeded to the kingdom of the Kentish people,[3]
and held it thirty-three winters. Wihtred was son of
Ecgberht, Ecgberht of Erconbryht, Erconbryht of Eadbald,
Eadbald of Æthelbryht.[4]

An. DC.XCII. In this year Brihtwold was chosen archbishop
on the Kal. of July (July 1st) ; he had previously been abbot
of Reculver. There were then two kings in Kent, Wihtred
and Webheard (Swebheard).[5]

[4]And as soon as he was king, he commanded a great
council to be gathered at the place that is called Baccanceld
(Bapchild), in which were sitting Wihtred, king of the
Kentish people, and Beorhtwald, archbishop of Canterbury,·
and Tobias, bishop of Rochester ; and with them abbots and
abbesses, and many wise men were gathered, all to deliberate
concerning the bettering of God's churches that are in Kent.
Now began the king to speak, and said : " I will that all
the monasteries and the churches that were given and
bequeathed in glory to God, in the days of faithful kings,
my predecessors, and in the days of my kinsmen, of king

---

[1] For an account of Dryhthelm
and his vision, see Beda, H.E. v. 12.
[2] The payment, whatever its
amount may have been, was probably the legal compensation for the
death of Mul. (See the vol. of A.S.
Laws). Of the early Latin writers
Ethelweard says it was 30,000 solidi,
'per singulos constanti numero sex-

decim nummis ;' Flor. of Worcester
3,750 pounds ; and Malmesbury
30,000 mancuses, which at 8 to the
pound would agree with Florence.—
R.P.
[3] Probably to the sole government, by the death or expulsion of
Swæbheard. See Beda, H.E. iv.
26.

E. F.

An. DC.XCV., DC.XCVI.

An. DC.XCVII. In this year the Southumbrians slew Osthryth, Æthelred's queen, Ecgferth's sister.

An. DC.XCVIII.

An. DC.XCIX. In this year the Picts slew Beorht the aldorman.

An. DCC., DCC.I.

Æthelberht, and those who followed after him, so remain to the glory of God, and firmly stand to all eternity for evermore. For I, Wihtred, an earthly king, stimulated by the heavenly King, and kindled with the zeal of righteousness, have learned from the institutes of our forefathers, that no layman ought with right to appropriate to himself a church, or any of the things which to a church belong. And therefore strongly and faithfully we appoint and decree, and, in the name of Almighty God and of all saints, we forbid to all kings our successors, and to aldormen, and to all laymen, ever any lordship over churches, and over any of their possessions, which I or my predecessors, in days of old, have given for the glory of Christ, and our lady, St. Mary, and the holy apostles. But be it observed, when it happens, that when a bishop, or an abbot, or an abbess, shall depart from this life, it be announced to the archbishop; and, by his counsel and suggestion, let such be chosen as may be worthy ; and let the archbishop inquire into his life and purity, who shall be chosen to such offices . . . . and in no wise let any one be chosen, nor to such office hallowed, without the archbishop's counsel. Kings are to appoint earls and aldormen, shire-reeves and judges ; and an archbishop is to direct and counsel, and to choose and appoint bishops, and abbots, and abbesses, priests and deacons ; and to hallow and strengthen them by good admonitions and example, lest any of God's herd wander and perish." [a] [1]

---

[1] Besides the mutilated copy of this instrument in MS. F., there is a more perfect one in Cod. Diplom. v. p. 36, from a collation of three MSS.

See also Wilkins, Concil. I. p. 56, and Johnson's Ecclesiastical Laws, I. p. 125, edit. Baron.

---

[a] F.

An. DCC.II. In this year Cênred succeeded to the kingdom of the Southumbrians.

68, 69. An. DCC.III. In this year bishop Hædde died ; and he held the bishopric at Winchester twenty-seven winters.

An. DCC.IV. In this year Æthelred, son of Penda, king of the Mercians, assumed monkhood ; and he had held the kingdom twenty-nine winters ; then Cênred succeeded thereto.

An. DCC.V. In this year Aldferth, king of the Northumbrians, died on the XIXth of the Kal. of January (Dec.
* of Lichfield. 14th) at Driffield, and bishop *Saxwulf. Then Osred, his son, succeeded to the kingdom.

An. DCC.VI.—DCC.VIII.

An. DCC.IX. In this year bishop Aldhelm died : he was
* of Sherborne. *bishop west of Selwood ; and, in the early days of Daniel, the land of the West Saxons was divided into two bishopshires ; and previously it was one : one Daniel held, the other Aldhelm. After Aldhelm, Forthhere succeeded to it. And king Ceolred succeeded to the kingdom of the Mer-
* k. of Essex. cians ; and Cênred went to Rome, and *Offa with him. And Cênred was there till his life's end. And in the
* of Hexham. same year *bishop Wilfrith died at Oundle, and his body was conveyed to Ripon ; he was bishop forty-five winters, whom king Ecgfrith had formerly driven to Rome.

An. DCC.X. (DCC.IX.) In this year Acca, Wilfrith's priest, succeeded to the bishopric which he had before held ; and in the same year the aldorman Beorhtfrith fought against
* 70, 71. the Picts between Hæfe and Cære (Heugh and Caraw); and Ine and Nunna his kinsman fought against Gerent, king of the Welsh ; and in the same year Sigbald (Hygbald) was slain.

An. DCC.XI.—DCC.XIII.

An. DCC.XIV. (DCC.XIII.) In this year St. Guthlac died, and king Pepin.

An. DCC.XV. (DCC.XIV.) In this year Ine and Ceolred fought at Woddesbeorh (Wansborough). In this year king Dagobert died.

An. DCC.XVI. In this year Osred, king of the Northumbrians,
* eleven ? was slain on the southern border ; he had the kingdom *seven (eight) winters after Aldferth ; then Cênred succeeded to the kingdom, and held it two years ; then Osric, and held it eleven years. And also in the same year Ceolred, king of the Mercians,

died, and his body lies in Lichfield, and Æthelred's, the son of Penda, at Bardney. Then Æthelbald succeeded to the kingdom of the Mercians, and held it forty-one winters. Æthelbald was son of Alweo, Alweo of Eawa, Eawa of Pybba, whose kin is before written. And the pious man Ecgberht turned the monks in the island of Iona to right, so that they observed Easter rightly, and the ecclesiastical tonsure.

An. DCC.XVII.

An. DCC.XVIII. (DCC.XVII.) In this year Ingild, the brother of Ine, died, and their sisters were Cwênburh and Cuthburh. And Cuthburh raised the monastery at Wimborne ; and she was given (in marriage) to Ældferth, king of the Northumbrians ; but they separated during his life.　72, 73.

An. DCC.XIX., DCC.XX.

An. DCC.XXI. (DCC.XX.) In this year bishop Daniel went to Rome; and in the same year Ine slew Cynewulf the ætheling. And in this year the holy *bishop John died ; he was bishop * of York. thirty-three years and eight months and thirteen days ; and his body rests at Beverley.

An. DCC.XXII. (DCC.XXI.) In this year queen Æthelburh destroyed Taunton, which Ine had previously built. And Ealdbriht the exile withdrew into Surrey and Sussex ; and Ine fought against the South Saxons.

An. DCC.XXIII., DCC.XXIV.

An. DCC.XXV. In this year Wihtred, king of the Kentish people, died, on the IXth of the Kal. of May (April 23rd); he reigned thirty-four winters ; his kin is *above ; and Ead- * An. DC.XCIV. berht succeeded to the kingdom. And Ine fought against the South Saxons, and there slew Ealdbriht the ætheling, whom he had before driven out.

An. DCC.XXVI.

An. DCC.XXVII. In this year Tobias, bishop of Rochester, died ; and in his stead archbishop Beorhtwald hallowed Aldwulf bishop.

An. DCC.XXVIII. (DCC.XXVI.) In this year Ine went to Rome, and there gave up his life ; and Æthelheard his kinsman succeeded to the kingdom of the West Saxons, and held it fourteen years. And in that same year Æthelheard and Oswald the ætheling fought. And Oswald was son of Æthelbald, Æthelbald of Cynebald, Cynebald of Cuthwine, Cuthwine of Ceawlin.　74, 75.

An. DCC.XXIX. In this year the star comet appeared; and St. Ecgberht died in Iona. And in the same year Osric died; he was king eleven winters; then Ceolwulf succeeded to the kingdom and held it eight years.

An. DCC.XXX. In this year Oswald the ætheling died.

An. DCC.XXXI. In this year Osric, king of the Northumbrians, was slain, and Ceolwulf succeeded to the kingdom, and held it eight years.[1] And Ceolwulf was son of Cutha, Cutha of Cuthwine, Cuthwine of Leodwald, Leodwald of Ecgwald, Ecgwald of Aldhelm, Aldhelm of Ocga, Ocga of Ida, Ida of Eoppa. And archbishop Beorhtwald died on the Ides of January (Jan. 13th); he was bishop thirty-seven winters, and six months and fourteen days. And in the same year Tatwine was hallowed archbishop: he had before been a priest at Breodûn (Bredon) in Mercia: Daniel, bishop of Winchester, and Ingwald, bishop of London, and Aldwine, bishop of Lichfield, and Aldwulf, bishop of Rochester, hallowed him on the 10th of the month of June. He had the archbishopric three years.

76, 77.

An. DCC.XXXII.

An. DCC.XXXIII. In this year Æthelbald captured Somerton; and the sun, was eclipsed and all the sun's disc was like a black shield; and Acca was driven from his *bishopric.

Hexham.

✓ An. DCC.XXXIV. In this year the moon was as if it had been sprinkled with blood; and *archbishop Tatwine and Beda died,[2] and Ecgberht was hallowed bishop.

of Canterbury.
of York.

An. DCC.XXXV. In this year *bishop Ecgberht received the pall at Rome.

of Canterbury.

An. DCC.XXXVI. In this year *archbishop Nothhelm received the pall from the bishop of the Romans.

of Sherborne.
† of Wessex.
‡ of Northumbria.

An. DCC.XXXVII. This year *bishop Forthhere and †queen Frythogith went to Rome; and king ‡Ceolwulf received St. Peter's tonsure, and gave his kingdom to Eadberht, son of his paternal uncle; he reigned twenty-one winters; and *bishop Æthelwold and Acca died, and Cynewulf was hallowed *bishop. And in the same year king Æthelbald ravaged the land of the Northumbrians.

of Lindisfarne.
of Lindisfarne.

---

[1] Erroneously repeated under this date from DCC.XXIX., in which year

Osric's death is placed by Beda, H.E. v. 24.

[2] Beda died in DCC.XXXV.

An. DCC.XXXVIII. In this year Eadberht, son of Eata (Eata   78, 79.
was son of Leodwald), succeeded to the kingdom of the
Northumbrians, and held it twenty-one winters; and his
brother was *archbishop Ecgberht, son of Eata; and they *of York.
both rest at York, in one porch.

An. DCC.XXXIX., DCC.XL.

An. DCC.XLI. (DCC.XL.) In this year king Æthelheard died,
and Cuthred, his kinsman, succeeded to the kingdom of the
West Saxons, and held it sixteen winters; and he warred
boldly against Æthelbald, king of the Mercians. And
*archbishop Nothhelm died, and Cuthbyrht was hallowed *of Canterbury.
archbishop; and bishop Dun to Rochester. This year York
was burnt.

An. DCC.XLII. In this year [1] a great synod was gathered at
Clofeshô (Cliff); and there were Æthelbald, king of the
Mercians, and archbishop Cuthbyrht, and many other wise
men.

An. DCC.XLIII. In this year Æthelbald, king of the
Mercians, and Cuthred, king of the West Saxons, fought
against the Welsh.

An. DCC.XLIV. In this year bishop Daniel resigned the see
of Winchester, and Hunferth succeeded to the bishopric.
And stars went shooting rapidly; and Wilfrith the younger,
who was bishop of York, died, on the IIIrd of the Kal. of May
(April 29th); and he was [2] thirty winters bishop.

An. DCC.XLV. In this year Daniel died: then were forty-   80, 81.
three winters agone since he succeeded to the bishopric.

An. DCC.XLVI. In this year *king Selred was slain.   *of the E. Saxon

An. DCC.XLVII.

An. DCC.XLVIII. In this year Cynric, ætheling of the West
Saxons, was slain; and Eadbryht, king of the Kentish people,

---

[1] The acts of this council are
printed in the Codex Diplomaticus
(I. p. 105) from three MSS. A corrupt copy is also in Wilkins, Con-
cilia, I. p. 86; and a more complete
one in the Latin text of MS. F. See
also Johnson, Eccles. Laws, I. p. 236,
edit. Baron.

[2] Wilfrith succeeded St. John of

Beverley in the see of York in 721,
and was consequently bishop only
twenty-three years. M. Westm.,
Wendover, and other chroniclers
place his death in 743, apparently
confounding him with Wilfrith,
bishop of Worcester, who, according to Florence, died in that year.

died, and Æthelbyrht, son of king Wihtred, succeeded to the kingdom.

An. DCC.XLIX.

An. DCC.L. In this year Cuthred, king of the West Saxons, fought against Æthelhun, the proud aldorman.

An. DCC.LI.

An. DCC.LII. In this year Cuthred, king of the West Saxons, in the twelfth year of his reign, fought at Burford against Æthelbald, king of the Mercians, and put him to flight.

An. DCC.LIII. In this year Cuthred, king of the West Saxons, fought against the Welsh.

An. DCC.LIV. In this year Cuthred, king of the West Saxons, died ; and Cyneheard succeeded to the bishopric of Winchester, after Hunferth ; and in that year Canterbury was

*Cuthred's. burnt ; and Sigebryht, *his kinsman, succeeded to the king-dom of the West Saxons, and held it one year.

82, 83.   An. DCC.LV. In this year Cynewulf and the West Saxon 'witan' deprived Sigebryht, his kinsman, of his kingdom, for his unrighteous deeds, except Hampshire ; and that he held until he slew the aldorman who had longest remained with him. And then Cynewulf drove him into Andred ; and he there abode until a herdsman stabbed him at Pryfetes flôd (Privet) ; and he avenged the aldorman Cumbra. And Cynewulf fought often in great battles against the Brito-Welsh ; [1] and about thirty-one winters after he had the kingdom, he would drive out an ætheling, who was named Cyneheard, and Cyneheard was Sigebryht's brother. And he

---

√ An. DCC.LV. In this year Cynewulf deprived king Sigebryht of his kingdom ; and Sigebryht's brother, named Cyneheard, slew Cynewulf at Merantûn (Merton) ; and he reigned thirty-one years. And in the same year Æthelbald, king of the Mercians, was slain at Repton, and Offa succeeded to the king-dom of the Mercians, Beornred being put to flight.[u]

---

[1] The following narrative is here by anticipation, as the murder of Cynewulf was not perpetrated until 784, under which date it is regularly recorded. It is no doubt an early interpolation.

---

* F.

'then learned that the king, with a small company, was on a
visit to a woman at Merantûn (Merton), and he there beset
him, and surrounded the bower * (bûr), before the men discovered him who were with the king. And when the king
perceived that, he went to the door, and then gallantly
defended himself, until he looked on the ætheling, and then
rushed out on him, and sorely wounded him ; and they were
all fighting against the king, until they had slain him. And
when by the woman's gestures the king's thanes had discovered the tumult, they ran thither, whoever was ready, and
with all speed. And to each of them the ætheling offered
money and life ; and not one of them would accept it ; but
they continued fighting, until they were all slain, save one, a
British hostage, and he was sorely wounded. When in the
morning, the king's thanes, who had remained behind, heard
that the king was slain, they rode thither, and Osric his
aldorman, and Wigferth his thane, and the men whom he had
previously left behind, and found the ætheling in the burgh
where the king lay slain ; and they had ¹locked the gates
against them, and they went thereto. And he then offered
them their own choice of money and land, if they would grant
him the kingdom ; and made known to them that their kinsmen were with him, who would not forsake him. And they
then said, that to them no kinsman was dearer than their lord,
and that they would never follow his murderer. And they
then offered that they should go from him uninjured ; and
they said that the same had been offered to their companions,
who before had been with the king. They then said that they
no more minded it 'than did your companions who were slain
with the king.' And they then were fighting about the gates,
until they followed in and slew the ætheling and the men who
were with him, all save one, who was the aldorman's godson ;
and he saved his life, although he had been repeatedly wounded.
And Cynewulf reigned ²thirty-one winters, and his body lies at

*burh, B.C.

84, 85.

86, 87.

---

¹ 'Fores cunctas seratas invene-
' runt,' Fl. Wigorn. I suspect, nevertheless, that the 'tobelocen' of
the text means that they *unclosed*
the gates, for the purpose of holding
a parley with the king's followers,
a sense which the context seems to
justify.

² According to the dates given in
the chronicles, Cynewulf reigned
only twenty-nine years, viz., from
755 to 784.

Winchester, and the ætheling's at Axminster; and their direct
paternal kin goes to Cerdic. And in the same year Æthelbald, king of the Mercians, was slain at Seckington, and his
body lies at Repton ; and he reigned forty-one winters ; and
Beornræd succeeded to the kingdom, and held it a little while
and unhappily. And in the same year Offa drove out Beornræd and succeeded to the kingdom, and held it thirty-nine
winters ; and his son Ecgferth held it a hundred and forty-one
days. Offa was son of Thincgferth, Thincgferth of Eanwulf,
Eanwulf of Osmôd, Osmôd of Eawa, Eawa of Pybba (Wybba)
Pybba of Creoda, Creoda of Cynewald, Cynewald of Cnebba,
Cnebba of Ikel, Ikel of Eomær, Eomær of Angeltheow,
Angeltheow of Offa, Offa of Wærmund, Wærmund of Wihtlæg,
Wihtlæg of Woden.[1]

An. DCC.LVI.

An. DCC.LVII. In this year Eadberht, king of the Northumbrians, assumed the tonsure, and his son Oswulf succeeded
to the kingdom, and reigned one year, and he was slain by his
household, on the VIIIth of the Kal. of August (July 25th).

88, 89.

An. DCC.LVIII. In this year archbishop Cuthbyrht died ;
and he held the *archbishopric eighteen years.

*of Canterbury.

An. DCC.LIX. In this year Bregowine was ordained *archbishop at St. Michael's tide (Sept. 29th) ; and held the see
four years. And Moll Æthelwald succeeded to the kingdom
of the Northumbrians, and reigned six winters, and then
left it.

*of Canterbury.

An. DCC.LX. In this year Æthelbryht, king of the Kentish
people, died; he was son of king Wihtred. [2]And Ceolwulf
also died.

✔ An. DCC.LXI. In this year was the great winter ; and
Moll, king of the Northumbrians, slew Oswine at Eadwine's
cliff (Edwinstow ?) on the VIIIth of the Ides of August
(Aug. 6th).[3]

*of Canterbury.

An. DCC.LXII. In this year *archbishop Bregowine died.

90, 91.

An. DCC.LXIII. (DCC.LXII.) In this year Ianbryht was ordained *archbishop on the fortieth day after Midwinter (Feb.

*of Canterbury.

---

[1] See Flor.Wigorn. I. p. 251, edit.
Engl. Histor. Society.

[2] See An. DCC.XXXVII.
[3] See Sim. Dunelm. col. 105.

3rd), and held the sec twenty-six years; and Frithuwald, bishop of Whiterne, died on the Nones of May (May 7th); he was hallowed at York on the XVIIIth of the Kal. of September (Aug. 15th), the sixth winter of the reign of Ceolwulf, and he was bishop twenty-nine winters. Then Pehtwine was hallowed bishop of Whiterne at Ælfet-ee (Adlingflet ?) on the XVIth of the Kal. of August (July 17th).

An. DCC.LXIV. In this year archbishop Ianbryht received the pall.

An. DCC.LXV. In this year Alchred succeeded to the kingdom of Northumbria, and reigned nine (eight) winters.

An. DCC.LXVI. In this year archbishop Ecgberht died at York on the XIIIth of the Kal. of December (Nov. 19th); he was bishop [1] thirty-seven (thirty-six) winters; and Fritheberht at Hexham; he was bishop thirty-three winters (thirty-four); and Æthelberht was hallowed to York, and Alchmund to Hexham.

An. DCC.LXVII.

An. DCC.LXVIII. In this year died king [2] Eadberht, son of Eata, on the XIIIth of the Kal. of September (Aug. 20th).

An. DCC.LXIX.—DCC.LXXI.

An. DCC.LXXII. In this year *bishop Milred died.   * of Worcester.

✔ An. DCC.LXXIII. (DCC.LXXIV.) In this year a red cross appeared in the heavens after sunset; and in this year the Mercians and Kentish men fought at Otford ; and wondrous   92, 93. serpents were seen in the South Saxons' land.

An. DCC.LXXIV. In this year, at Easter-tide (April 3rd), the Northumbrians drove their king Alchred from York, and took Æthelred, son of Moll, for their lord, who reigned four winters.

An. DCC.LXXV.

An. DCC.LXXVI. In this year *bishop Pehtwine died, on * of Whiterne. the XIIIth of the Kal. of October (Sept. 19th); he was bishop fourteen winters.

An. DCC.LXXVII. In this year Cynewulf and Offa fought at Benson, and Offa took the town. And in the same year

---

[1] This is incorrect; he was consecrated in 734.   [2] Formerly king of the Northumbrians. See An. DCC.LVII.

Æthelberht was hallowed bishop of Whiterne, at York, on the xviith of the Kal. of July (June 15th).[1]

An. DCC.LXXVIII. In this year Æthelbald and Heardberht slew three high reeves, Ealdulf son of Bosa, at King's cliff, and Cynewulf and Ecga at Helathyrn (Ellerton ?), on the xith of the Kal. of April (March 22nd); and then Alfwold *of North- umbria. succeeded to the *kingdom, and drove Æthelred from the land ; and he reigned ten winters.[3]

An. DCC.LXXIX. (DCC.LXXX.) In this year the Old-Saxons and the Franks fought ; and the high reeves of the Northumbrians burned the aldorman Beorn at Seletûn (Silton), on

---

[1] In the days of king Offa there was an abbot of Medeshamstede called Beonna. The same Beonna, by the advice of all the monks of the monastery, let to the aldorman Cuthbriht ten [2] "bonde-lands" at Swineshead, with leasow and with meadow, and with all thereto adjacent, and so that Cuthbriht should give to the abbot fifty pounds for it, and every year one night's entertainment, or thirty shillings in pennies ; and also that after his day the land should revert to the monastery. At this was witness the king Offa and king *of Lichfield. Ecgferth and *archbishop Hygeberht, and †bishop Ceolwulf, †of Lindsey. *of Leicester. and *bishop Inwona, and abbot Beonna, and many other bishops and abbots, and many other great men.[3] In the days of this same Offa there was an aldorman who was called Brordan. He desired of the king that, for his love, he would free[4] his one monastery called Woking, because he would give it to Medeshamstede and to St. Peter, and to the abbot that then was, who was called Pusa. Pusa was after Beonna, and the king loved him greatly. And the king then freed the monastery of Woking against king, and against bishop, and against earl, and against all men, so that no one should have there any authority, save St. Peter and the abbot. This was done in the king's vill called Freoricburne.

---

[2] 'terram x. manentium.' Cod. Diplom. i. p. 201.

[3] See the Latin documents in Cod. Diplom. i. pp. 201, 204, from a MS.

belonging to the Society of Antiquaries.

[4] From all secular services.

[5] See Sim. Dunelm., H. Hunt. a. 778.

the VIII. of the Kal. of January (Dec. 25th); and archbishop Æthelberht died at York, in whose stead Eanbald was hallowed; and bishop Cynewulf resigned the bishopric of Lindisfarne. 94, 95.

An. DCC.LXXX. In this year Alchmund, bishop of Hexham, died on the VII. of the Ides of September (Sept. 7th), and Tilberht was hallowed in his stead, on the VIth of the Nones of October (Oct. 2nd); and Higbald was, at Soccaburh (Sockburn), hallowed bishop of Lindisfarne. And king Alfwold sent to Rome for a pall, and made Eanbald *archbishop. * of York.

An. DCC.LXXXI.

An. DCC.LXXXII. In this year died Werburh, *Ceolred's queen; and Cynewulf bishop of Lindisfarne; and there was a synod at Aclea (Ockley). * k. of Mercia.

An. DCC.LXXXIII.

An. DCC.LXXXIV. In this year Cyneheard slew king Cynewulf, and he was there slain, and eighty-four men with him; and then Beorhtric succeeded to the kingdom of the West-Saxons, and he reigned sixteen years, and his body lies at Wareham; and his direct paternal kin goes to Cerdic. At this time king Ealhmund reigned in Kent. This king Ealhmund was father of *Ecgberht, and Ecgberht was father of Athulf (Æthelwulf) * of Wessex.

An. DCC.LXXXV. In this year there was a contentious synod at Cealchyth (Chalk ?), and archbishop Ianbryht resigned [1] a part of his bishopric, and Higebryht was chosen by king Offa; and Ecgferth was hallowed *king. In this year abbot Bôtwine died at Ripon. And at this time messengers were sent from Rome to England by pope Adrian, to renew the faith and the peace which St. Gregory had sent us by the bishop Augustine; and they were received with honour and sent back in peace. 96, 97. * of Mercia.

An. DCC.LXXXVI.

✔ An. DCC.LXXXVII. In this year king Beorhtric took Eadburh, king Offa's daughter, to wife. And in his days first came three ships of Northmen from [2] Hæretha land. And then the reeve rode thereto, and would drive them to the king's

---

[1] Of which Offa created the temporary archiepiscopal see of Lichfield.

[2] Probably Haurðaland, a district on the west coast of Norway.

vill, for he knew not what they were, and they there slew him. Those were the first ships of Danish men that sought the land of the English race.

An. DCC.LXXXVIII. In this year a synod was gathered in the land of the Northumbrians at Pincanheal (Finchale), on the IVth of the Nones of September (Sept. 2nd); and abbot Aldberht died at Ripon.

98, 99.   An. DCC.LXXXIX. In this year Alfwold, king of the Northumbrians, was slain by Sicga, on the VIIIth of the Kal. of October (Sept. 24th); and a heavenly light was frequently seen there, where he was slain ; and he was buried at Hexham, within the church ; and Osred son of Alchred succeeded to the kingdom after him ; he was his nephew. And a great synod was gathered at Aclea (Ockley).

* of Canterbury.   An. DCC.XC. In this year *archbishop Ianbryht died; and in the same year, abbot Æthelheard was chosen archbishop. And Osred, king of the Northumbrians, was betrayed, and driven from the kingdom ; and Æthelred, son of Æthelwold, afterwards succeeded to the kingdom.

An. DCC.XCI. In this year Baldwulf was hallowed bishop of Whiterne, on the XVIth of the Kal. of August (July 17th), by

* of York.
† of Hexham.   *archbishop Eanbald, and by †bishop Æthelberht.

An. DCC.XCII. In this year Offa, king of the Mercians, com-

* of the E. Angles. manded the head of *king Æthelbryht to be struck off; and Osred, who had been king of the Northumbrians, having come home after exile, was seized and slain, on the XVIIIth of the Kal. of October (Sept. 14th) ; and his body rests at Tynemouth ; and king Æthelred took a new wife, who was called Ælfled, on the IIId of the Kal. of October (Sept. 29th).

100, 101.   An. DCC.XCIII. In this year dire forewarnings came over the land of the Northumbrians, and miserably terrified the people : these were excessive whirlwinds and lightnings, and fiery dragons were seen flying in the air. A great famine soon followed these tokens ; and a little after that, in the same year, on the VIth of the Ides of January (Jan. 8th), the havoc of heathen men miserably destroyed God's church at Lindisfarne, through rapine and slaughter. And ¹Sicga died on the VIIIth of the Kal. of March (Feb. 22nd).

---

¹ See DCC.LXXXIX.

An. DCC.XCIV. In this year ¹pope Adrian and king Offa
died ; and Æthelred, king of the Northumbrians, was slain by
his own people, on the XIIIth of the Kal. of May (Apr. 19th) ;
and *bishop Ceolwulf and bishop Eadbald departed from the *of Lindsey.
land ; and Ecgferth succeeded to the kingdom of the Mercians,
and died the same year. And Eadberht succeeded to the
kingdom in Kent, whose other name was Præn. And the
aldorman Æthelheard died on the Kal. of August (Aug. 1st).
And the heathens ravaged among the Northumbrians, and
plundered Ecgferth's monastery at Donemuth (Wearmouth) ;
and there one of their leaders was slain, and also some of their
ships were wrecked by a tempest, and many of them were
there drowned, and some came to shore alive, and they were   102, 103.
forthwith slain at the mouth of the river.

An. DCC.XCV. In this year the moon was eclipsed between
cock-crowing and dawn, on the Vth of the Kal. of April
(Mar. 28th) ; and Eardwulf succeeded to the kingdom of the
Northumbrians, on the IInd of the Ides of May (May 14th) ;
and he was afterwards blessed for king, and raised to his
throne on the VIIth of the Kal. of June (May 26th), at York,
by archbishop Eanbald, and bishop *Æthelberht, and bishops *of Hexham.
*Higbald and †Badwulf.   *of Lindisfarne.
                                                              †of Whiterne.

An. DCC.XCVI. In this year Cynulf (Ceolwulf), king of the
Mercians, ravaged Kent as far as the marsh, and took Præn
their king, and led him bound into Mercia, [and caused his
eyes to be put out, and his hands cut off]. And Æthelheard,
archbishop of Canterbury, appointed a synod, and confirmed
and ratified, by command of pope Leo, all the things concerning God's monasteries, that were established in Wihtgar's day,

---

¹ Charlemagne, in his letter to
Offa, (W. Malmesb. p. 129), men-
tions the death of Adrian, which
happened on the 25th Dec. 795, or,
according to the reckoning then in
use, on the first day of 796. Offa's
death could not therefore have taken
place in 794, but must, no doubt, be
assigned to 796, under which date it
is again given in MSS. D. and E.

Offa began to reign in 756, and
reigned 39 years, or, according to
MSS. D. and E., 40 years. A charter of Offa, in Cod. Diplom. (I. p.
204), is dated 796, though it does
not appear on what authority it is
assigned to that year ; it is the basis
of the document here given under
DCC.LXXVII.

_and in the day of other kings.[1] In this year died Offa, king of the Mercians, on the IVth of the Kal. of August (July 29th); he reigned forty winters; and archbishop Eanbald, on the IVth of the Ides of August (Aug. 10th) of the same year, and his

* of Lindsey.

body lies at York; and in the same year died *bishop Ceolwulf; and a second Eanbald was hallowed in the other's stead, on the XIXth of the Kal. of September (Aug. 14th).

104, 105.

An. DCC.XCVII. In this year the Romans cut out the tongue of pope Leo, and put out his eyes, and drove him from his see; and then soon after, with the aid of God, he could see and speak, and was pope again as he had been before.[2] And Eanbald received the pall on the VIth of the Ides of September

* of Hexham.

(Sept. 8th); and *bishop Æthelberht died on the XVIIth of the Kal. of November (Oct. 16th), and Heardred was hallowed bishop in his stead, on the IIIrd of the Kal. of November

* of Dunwich.

(Oct. 30th). And *bishop Alfhun died at Sudbury, and he was buried at Dunwich; and Tidfrith was chosen after him;

---

[1] And thus said: "I Æthelheard, humble archbishop of Canterbury, with the unanimous counsel of the whole synod, and with . . . . of all . . . . to the congregation of all the monasteries, to which in old days immunity was given by faithful men, in the name of God, and by his awful doom, I enjoin, as I have command from pope Leo, that henceforth none dare to choose themselves lords over God's heritage from laymen. But

* privilegia, Cod. Diplom.

as it is in the *writ which the pope has given, or as those holy men have established, who are our fathers and teachers, concerning holy monasteries, thus let them continue inviolate without any gainsaying. If there is any man who will not hold this command of God, and of our pope, and of us, but contemns and holds it for naught, let them know that they shall give account before the judgment-seat of God. And I, archbishop Æthelheard, with twelve bishops, and with three and twenty abbots, confirm and ratify this same with the sign of Christ's rood.[3]

---

[2] See the story in Gibbon, Decl. and Fall, c. xlix., and the authorities there cited.

[3] F., *inserted in the text.* See Cod. Diplom. v. p. 56, date 798.

and Sigeric, king of the East Saxons, went to Rome. In this same year the body of [1]Wihtburh was found at Dereham, all whole and uncorrupted, five and fifty years after she had departed from this life.

An. DCC.XCVIII. In this year there was a great fight in the land of the Northumbrians, in Lent, on the IVth of the Nones of April (Apr. 2nd), at Whalley ; and there Alric, the son of Heardberht, was slain, and many others with him.

An. DCC.XCIX. In this year *archbishop Æthelheard and [*]of Canterbury. Cynebryht, *bishop of the West Saxons, went to Rome. [*]of Winchester.

An. DCCC. In this year king Beorhtric and the aldorman Worr died ; and Ecgbryht succeeded to the kingdom of the West Saxons ; and on the same day, the aldorman Æthelmund   106, 107. rode over from the Hwiccas (Worcestershire) at Cynemæresford (Kempsford), when the aldorman Weohstân met him with the Wiltshire men ; and there was a great fight, and both the aldormen were slain ; and the Wiltshire men got the victory. In this year the moon was eclipsed at the second hour of night, on the XVIIth of the Kal. of February (Jan. 16th).

An. DCCC.I. [2]In this year Beornmôd was ordained bishop of Rochester.

An. DCCC.II. (DCCC.I.) In this year. the moon was eclipsed at dawn, on the XIIIth of the Kal. of January (Dec. 20th) ; and Beornmôd was hallowed bishop of Rochester in the same year.

An. DCCC.III. (DCCC.II.) In this year archbishop Æthelheard died in Kent ; and Wulfred was ordained archbishop ; and abbot Forthred died. In this year Higbald, bishop of Lindisfarne, died, on the VIIIth of the Kal. of July (June 24th) ; and Ecgberht was hallowed in his stead, on the IIIrd of the Ides of June (June 11th).

An. DCCC.IV. (DCCC.III.) In this year archbishop Wulfred received the pall.

An. DCCC.V. (DCCC.IV.) In this year king Cuthred died among the Kentish people ; and the *abbess Ceolburh, and [*]of Berkeley. Heabryht (Heardbryht) aldorman.

---

[1] A daughter of Anna, king of the East Angles; she was a nun at Ely.

[2] Repeated with the variation of gehalgod (hallowed) for gehádod (ordained), in the following year.

An. DCCC.VI. In this year the moon was eclipsed on the Kal. of September (Sept. 1st); and Eardwulf, king of the Northumbrians, was driven from his kingdom; and Eanberht, bishop of Hexham died. Also in this same year, on the IInd of the Nones of June (June 4th), a sign of the cross appeared in the moon, one Wednesday at dawn. And again, on the IIIrd of the Kal. of September (Aug. 30th), a wonderful circle appeared about the sun.

103, 109.

An. DCCC.VII., DCCC.VIII.

An. DCCC.IX. In this year the sun was eclipsed in the beginning of the fifth hour of the day, on the XVIIth of the Kal. of August (July 16th), on the 2nd day of the week, the 29th of the moon.

An. DCCC.X., DCCC.XI.

*the emperor Charlemagne.

An. DCCC.XII. (DCCC.XI. DCCC.XIV.) In this year king Charles died, and he reigned five and forty winters; and archbishop Wulfred and Wigbryht, bishop of the West Saxons, went both to Rome.

An. DCCC.XIII. (DCCC.XII. DCCC.XV.) In this year archbishop Wulfred, with the blessing of pope Leo, returned to his own bishopric; and in this year king Ecgbryht harried in West Wales from eastward to westward.

An. DCCC.XIV. (DCCC.XIII. DCCC.XVI.) In this year the noble and holy pope Leo died, and after him Stephen succeeded to the popedom.

An. DCCC.XV.

An. DCCC.XVI. (DCCC.XIV. DCCC.XVII.) In this year pope Stephen died, and after him Paschal was ordained (hallowed) pope; and in the same year the [1] Angle race's school was burnt.

An. DCCC.XVII., DCCC.XVIII.

110, 111.

An. DCCC.XIX. (DCCC.XXII.) In this year Cênwulf, king of the Mercians, died, and [2] Ceolwulf succeeded to the kingdom; and the aldorman Eadbryht died.

An. DCCC.XX.

---

[1] At Rome; founded, according to Matthew of Westminster, (a. 727), by king Ine.

[2] Ceolwulf succeeded Cênhelm, a child, son of Cênwulf, who was basely murdered at the instigation of his sister Cwênthryth.

An. DCCC.XXI. In this year Ceolwulf was deprived of his kingdom.

An. DCCC.XXII. In this year two aldormen, Burhhelm and Muca, were slain; and there was a synod at Clovesho (Cliff).

An. DCCC.XXIII. In this year there was a fight of the Welsh and Devonians at Gafulford (Camelford ?); and in the same year, king Ecgbryht, of the West Saxons, and king Beornwulf, of the Mercians, fought at Ellendun (Allington ?); and Ecgbryht gained the victory, and a great slaughter was there made. He then sent Æthelwulf his son, from the army, and Ealhstân his bishop, and Wulfheard his aldorman, to Kent, with a large force, and they drove Baldred the king north, over the Thames; and the Kentish people, and those of Surrey, and the South Saxons, and the East Saxons, turned to him, because they had formerly been unjustly forced from his kinsmen. And in the same year the king of the East Angles, and the nation, sought Ecgbryht for peace and as protector, 12, from dread of the Mercians; and in this same year the East Angles slew Beornwulf, king of the Mercians.

An. DCCC.XXIV.

An. DCCC.XXV. In this year Ludecan, king of the Mercians, was slain, and his five aldormen with him, and Wiglâf succeeded to the kingdom.

An. DCCC.XXVI.

An. DCCC.XXVII. In this year the moon was eclipsed on Midwinter's mass-night; and the same year king Ecgbryht subdued the kingdom of the Mercians, and all that was south of the Humber, and he was the eighth king who was BRYTENWALDA (Bretwalda, Bretenanwealda). The first was Ælle, king of the South Saxons, who had thus much sway; the second was Ceawlin, king of the West Saxons; the third was Æthelbryht, king of the Kentish people; the fourth was Rædwald, king of the East Angles; the fifth was Eadwine, king of the Northumbrians; the sixth was Oswald, who reigned after him; the seventh was Oswiu, Oswald's brother; the eighth was Ecgbryht, king of the West Saxons. And Ecgbryht led an army to Dore against the Northumbrians, 114, and they there offered him obedience and concord; and thereupon they separated.

An. DCCC.XXVIII. In this year Wiglâf again obtained the

* of Lichfield.   kingdom of the Mercians ; and * bishop Æthelwald died ; and
in the same year king Ecgbryht led an army against the
North Welsh, and he reduced them to humble obedience.

* of Canterbury.   An. DCCC.XXIX. In this year * archbishop Wulfred died,
and after him abbot Felogild was chosen to the archiepiscopal
see, on the VIIth of the Kal. of May (April 25th) ; and he
was hallowed on the vth of the Ides of June (Jun. 9th), one
Sunday ; and he was dead on the IIIrd of the Kal. of September (Aug. 30th).

An. DCCC.XXX. In this year Ceolnoth was chosen bishop,
and ordained ; and abbot Felogild died.

of Canterbury.   An. DCCC.XXXI. (DCCC.XXXII.) In this year * archbishop
Ceolnoth received the pall.

An. DCCC.XXXII. In this year heathen men ravaged Shepey.

116, 117.   An. DCCC.XXXIII. (DCCC.XXXIV.) In this year king Ecg-
bryht fought against the crews of thirty-five ships at Carrum
(Charmouth), and there was great slaughter made, and the
Danes held possession of the battle place. And * Hereferth

* of Winchester. and * Wigthen, two bishops, died ; and Dudda and Osmôd,
two aldormen, died.

An. DCCC.XXXIV. (DCCC.XXXV.)

An. DCCC.XXXV. In this year a great naval force came to
the West Welsh, and they combined together, and warred
against Ecgbryht, king of the West Saxons. When he heard
that, he went thither with an army, and fought against them
at Hengestesdûn (Hengston), and there put to flight both the
Welsh and the Danes.

An. DCCC.XXXVI. In this year [1] king Ecgbryht died ; and
before he was king, Offa, king of the Mercians, and Beorhtric,
king of the West Saxons, had driven him from the Angle
race's land into France, for three years ; and Beorhtric assisted Offa, because he had his daughter for his queen. And

118, 119.   Ecgbryht reigned thirty-seven winters and seven months ;
and Æthelwulf, son of Ecgbryht, succeeded to the kingdom of

---

[1] Ecgberht's accession is invari-
ably placed in the year 800. If,
therefore, the length of his reign be
rightly stated, his death could not
have happened before 837.—R.P.

If Ecgberht's expulsion took place
on the marriage, in 787, of Beorhtric
with Eadburh, we ought apparently
to read *thirteen* years instead of *three*,
for its duration.

the West Saxons; ' and he gave his son Æthelstân the kingdom of the Kentish people, and of the East Saxons, and of Surrey, and of the South Saxons.'

An. DCCC.XXXVII. In this year the aldorman Wulfheard fought at Southampton against the crews of thirty-three (thirty-four) ships, and there made great slaughter, and gained the victory. And in the same year Wulfheard died. And in the same year the aldorman Æthelhelm fought against a Danish ² army at Port (Portland) with the Dorset men, and for a good while put the army to flight; but the Danes held possession of the battle place, and slew the aldorman,

An. DCCC.XXXVIII. In this year the aldorman Herebryht was slain by heathen men, and many with him among the marsh-dwellers; and again, in the same year, in Lindsey, and in East Anglia, and among the Kentish people, many men were slain by the army.

An. DCCC.XXXIX. In this year there was a great slaughter at London, and at ³ Cwantawic, and at Rochester.

An. DCCC.XL. In this year king Æthelwulf fought at Carrum (Charmouth) against the crews of thirty-five ships, and the Danes held possession of the battle place. And ⁴ Lewis the emperor died.

120, 121.

An. DCCC.XLI.—DCCC.XLIV.

An. DCCC.XLV. In this year the aldorman Eanulf, with the men of Somerset, and bishop Ealhstân, and the aldorman Osric, with the men of Dorset, fought at the mouth of the

---

¹' and Æthelstân, his second son, succeeded to the kingdom of the Kentish people, and to Surrey, and to the kingdom of the South Saxons.a

---

² By the word ' here,' the army of the Danes, or Northmen, is usually understood in the Chronicle, while the English force is denominated the ' fyrd.'

³ Quantovic or Quêntawich was the ancient name of S. Josse-sur-Mer, or Estaples; it was sacked in 842. *Ann. Bertin. Bouquet*, vii. 61. According to MS. C. it is Canterbury.—R.P.

⁴ The *Debonnaire*, or, as the Germans style him, the *Pious*.

ᵃ D. E. F.

Parret against the Danish army, and there made great slaughter, and gained the victory.

An. DCCC.XLVI.—DCCC.L. (DCCC.LII.)

An. DCCC.LI. (DCCC.LIII.) In this year the aldorman Ceorl, with the men of Devonshire, fought against the heathen men at Wieganbeorh (Wembury ?), and there made great slaughter, and gained the victory. And in the same year king Æthelstân and the aldorman Ealchere, fought in ships, and slew a great force at Sandwich in Kent, and took nine ships, and put the others to flight. [And the heathen men, for the first time, took up their quarters over winter in Thanet. And in the same year came three hundred and fifty ships to the mouth of the Thames, and landed, and took Canterbury and London by storm, and put to flight Beorhtwulf, king of the Mercians, with his army, and then went south, over the Thames into Surrey, and there king Æthelwulf and his son Æthelbald, with the army of the West Saxons, fought against them at Aclea (Ockley), and there made the greatest slaughter among the heathen army that we have heard tell of until this present day, and there gained the victory.[1]]

122, 123.

[1] An. DCCC.LII. At this time Ceolred, abbot of Medeshamstede, and the monks let to Wulfred the land at Sempringham, on the condition, that after his day the land should revert to the monastery ; and that Wulfred should give the land at Sleaford to Medeshamstede, and that he should give every year to the monastery sixty fothers of wood, and twelve fothers of pit coal, and six fothers of faggots, and two tuns full of bright ale, and two neats for the slaughter, and six hundred loaves, and ten measures (mittan) of Welsh ale ; and every year a horse, and thirty shillings ; and for one night give entertainment. Here, were present, the king Burhred, and Ceolred *(r. Ceolnoth) archbishop, and †Tûnbirht bishop, and *Cênred bishop, and †Alhhun bishop, and *Berhtred bishop, and Wihtred abbot, and Werhtherd abbot, Æthelheard aldorman, Hunberht aldorman, and many others.*[2]

* of Canterbury.
† Lichfield.
* of Selsey.
† of Worcester.
* of Lindsey.

[2] See a more complete copy in Cod. Diplom. II. p. 46.

E.

An. DCCC.LII.

An. DCCC.LIII. (DCCC.LIV.) In this year Burhred, king of
the Mercians, and his ' witan,' prayed king Æthelwulf that he
would aid him, that he might reduce the North Welsh to
obedience. He then did so, and went with an army over
Mercia against the North Welsh, and made them all obedient
to him. And in the same year king Æthelwulf sent his son
Ælfred to Rome. Then at that time, the lord Leo was pope   124, 125.
of Rome ; and he hallowed him king, and took him for his
episcopal son. Then, in the same year, Ealhhere with the
Kentish men, and Huda with those of Surrey, fought in Thanet
against a heathen army, and at first gained the victory, and
there was many a man slain and drowned on each side ; and
both aldormen fell. And the Easter after this, king Æthelwulf gave his daughter to king Burhred, from the West
Saxons to the Mercians.

An. DCCC.LIV. (DCCC.LV.)

An. DCCC.LV. (DCCC.LVI.) In this year heathen men first   ²
took up their quarters over winter in Shepey. ² And in the
same year king Æthelwulf chartered the tenth part of his land
over all his kingdom, for the glory of God and his own eternal
salvation : and in the same year went to Rome with great
pomp, and dwelt there twelve months, and then returned
home ;¹ and *Charles, king of the Franks, then gave him his ∗ the Bald.
daughter for queen ; and after that he came to his people, and
they were rejoiced thereat ; and two years after he came from   126, 127.
France, he died, and his body lies at Winchester, and he
reigned eighteen years and a half. And Æthelwulf was son
of Ecgbryht, Ecgbryht of Ealhmund, Ealhmund of Eafa, Eafa

---

¹ An. DCCC.LV. —and when he was homewards, he obtained
the daughter of Charles, king of the Franks; she was called
Judith, and he came home safe ; and then after two years
he died, and his body lies at Winchester; and he reigned
eighteen years and a half ; and he was son of Ecgbryht.
And then his two sons succeeded to the kingdom, Æthelbald

---

² For this grant of Æthelwulf's, | sion, see Asser, A. 855, and Cod.
which has caused so much discus- | Diplom. II. pp. 50, 56, 57.

of Eoppa, Eoppa of Ingild ; Ingild was brother of Ine, king
of the West Saxons, who held the kingdom thirty-seven
winters, and afterwards went to St. Peter's, and there gave
up his life. And they were sons of Cênred, Cênred of Ceol-
wald, Ceolwald of Cutha, Cutha of Cuthwine, Cuthwine of
Ceawlin, Ceawlin of Cynric, Cynric of Cerdic, Cerdic of Elesa,
Elesa of Esla, Esla of Giwis, Giwis of Wig, Wig of Freawine,
Freawine of Frithogar, Frithogar of Brond, Brond of Bældæg,
Bældæg of Woden, Woden of Frithowald, Frithowald of Frealâf,
Frealâf of Frithuwulf, Frithuwulf of Finn, Finn of Godwulf,

128, 129.   Godwulf of Geat, Geat of Tætwa, Tætwa of Beaw, Beaw of
Sceldwa, Sceldwa of Heremôd, Heremôd of Itermon, Itermon
[of Hathra, Hathra of Hwala, Hwala of Bedwig, Bedwig of
Sceaf, that is, the son of Noah] ; he was born in Noah's ark ;
Lamech, Mathusalem, Enoch, Jared, Malalahel, Cainan, Enos,
Seth, Adam, the first man and our father, that is, Christ.
Amen. And then Æthelwulf's two sons succeeded to the
kingdom ; Æthelbald to the kingdom of the West Saxons, and
Æthelbryht to the kingdom of the Kentish people, and to the
kingdom of the East Saxons, and to Surrey, and to the king-
dom of the South Saxons. And then Æthelbald reigned five

* r. fourth.   years. Ælfred, his ʼthird son, he had sent to Rome; and when
pope Leo heard say that he (Æthelwulf) was dead, he blessed
Ælfred as king, andʼ held him to episcopal hands, as his father
Æthelwulf, in sending him thither, had requested.

An. DCCC.LVI.—DCCC.LIX.

An. DCCC.LX. (DCCC.LXI.) In this year king Æthelbald died,
and his body lies at Sherborne ; and Æthelbryht succeeded to
all the kingdom of his brother ; and he held it in good har-
mony, and in great tranquillity. And in his day there came
a great naval force to land, and took Winchester by storm.

130, 131.   And the aldorman Osric with the Hampshire men, and the
aldorman Æthelwulf with those of Berkshire, fought against

---

to the kingdom of the West Saxons, and Æthelbyrht to
the kingdom of the Kentish people, and of the East Saxons,
and of Surrey, and of the South Saxons, and he reigned five
years. [a]

---

[a] D. E. F.

the army, and put them to flight, and held possession of the battle place. And Æthelbryht reigned five years, and his body lies at Sherborne.

An. DCCC.LXI. In this year died St. Swithin *bishop.   * of Winton.

An. DCCC.LXII.—DCCC.LXIV.

An. DCCC.LXV. (DCCC.LXVI.) In this year a heathen army took up their quarters in Thanet, and made peace with the people of Kent, and the people of Kent promised them money for the peace ; and during the peace and the promise of money, the army stole itself away by night, and ravaged all Kent eastward.

An. DCCCLXVI. (DCCC.LXVII.) In this year Æthered (Æthelred), Æthelbryht's brother, succeeded to the kingdom of the West Saxons. And in the same year came a great heathen army to the land of the Anglo race, and took winter-quarters among the East Angles, and were there horsed ; and they (the East Angles) made peace with them.

An. DCCC.LXVII. (DCCC.LXVIII.) In this year the army went from the East Angles, over the mouth of the Humber, to York in Northumbria : and there was great dissension of the people   132, 133. betwixt themselves ; and they had cast out their king, Osbryht, and received a king, Ælla, not of royal blood ; and late in the year, they came to the resolution that they would   ⅄. fight against the army ; and yet they gathered a large force, and sought the army at York, and stormed the city, and some got within, and there was an immense slaughter made of the Northumbrians, some within, some without ; and both kings were slain ; and the remainder made peace with the army.] And in the same year bishop Ealhstân died ; and he had the bishopric of Sherborne fifty winters ; and his body lies there in the town.

An. DCCC.LXVIII. (DCCC.LXIX.) In this year the same army went into Mercia to Nottingham, and there took up winter-quarters. And Burhred, king of the Mercians, and his ' witan ' prayed Æthered, king of the West Saxons, and Ælfred his brother, that they would aid them, that they might fight   134, 135. against the army. And they then went, with a force of West Saxons, into Mercia as far as Nottingham, and there found the army in the works, and there besieged them. But there was no hard battle there ; and the Mercians made peace with the army.

An. DCCC.LXIX. (DCCC.LXX.) In this year the army went
again to York, and sat there one year.

An. DCCC.LXX. (DCCC.LXXI.) In this year the army rode over
Mercia into East Anglia, and took winter-quarters at Thetford ; and in that winter king Eadmund fought against them,
and the Danes gained the victory, and slew the king, and
subdued all that land, and destroyed all the monasteries which
they came to. The names of the chiefs who slew the king
were [1] Ingvar and Ubba. At that same time they came to
Medeshamstede, burned and broke, slew the abbot and the
monks, and all that they found there ; then made that which
was ere full rich, that it was reduced to nothing. And in
the same year died [*] archbishop Ceolnoth at Rome.[2] And
[3] Æthered, bishop of Wiltshire, was chosen archbishop of
Canterbury.

137.

* of Canterbury.

[2] Then went king Æthered and Ælfred his brother, and took
[3] Æthelred, bishop of Wiltshire, and appointed him archbishop
of Canterbury, because he had formerly been a monk of the
same monastery at Canterbury. As soon as he came to Canterbury, and he was firmly settled in his archiepiscopal chair,
he thought how he might drive out the clerks who were
therein, whom the archbishop Ceolnoth had before placed
there, for such need . . . . as we shall relate. The first
year that he was appointed archbishop there was so great a
mortality, that of all the monks that he found there within,
no more than five monks remained. Then for the . . . .
. . he commanded his private priests, and also some of his
vill-priests, that they should help the few monks who remained to do Christ's service, because he could not so readily
find monks who might by themselves do the service ; and for
this he commanded that the priests the while, until God
should give peace in the land, should help the monks. At
the same time this land was greatly harassed by frequent
conflicts, and on that account the archbishop could not attend

[1] They were the sons of Ragnar
Lodbrök, by a concubine. By the
Danish writers Ingvar is usually
called Ivar.

[2] Or Ethered. Of the Wiltshire
see nothing occurs elsewhere before
the beginning of the following century.—R.P.

An. DCCC.LXXI. (DCCC.LXXII.) In this year the army came ✗136.
to Reading in Wessex, and three nights after, two jarls rode
up, when the aldorman Æthelwulf met them at Inglefield, and
there fought against them, and gained the victory, and one of
them was there slain, whose name was Sidroc. Four nights
after this king Æthered and Ælfred his brother led a large force
to Reading, and fought against the army, and there was great
slaughter made on each side ; and the aldorman Æthelwulf
was slain, and the Danes held possession of the battle place.
And four nights after, king Æthered and Ælfred his brother
fought with all the army at ¹Ashdown ; and they were in two   138, 139.
divisions ; in one were Bagsecg (Bagsecg) and Hálfdán, the
heathen kings, and in the other were the jarls ; and then king
Æthered fought with the kings' division, and there was the
king Bagsecg slain ; and Ælfred his brother fought against
the jarls' division, and there were the elder jarl Sidroc slain,

to this object ; for all that time there was strife and sorrow
over England ; and therefore the clerks remained with the
monks. Nor was there ever a time that monks were not
there within, and they ever had lordship over the priests.
Again the archbishop Ceolnoth thought, and also said to those
who were with him : " As soon as God shall give peace in
this land, either these priests shall be monks, or . . . . '.
elsewhere I will place within the monastery as many monks
as may do the service ² by themselves ; for God knows that
I . . . ." ³

An. DCCC.LXXI. '—and the Danes were overcome ; and they
had two heathen kings, Bagsecg and Hálfdán, and many jarls ;
and there was the king Bagsecg slain, and these jarls, Sidroc
the old, and also Sidroc the young, Asbiörn, Fræna, and
Harald, and the army put to flight, &c.ᵃ

---

² The original has ' ðe,' apparently | ³ F., inserted in the text. For the
an error for ' be :' see above. | Latin, see vol. I. p. 136.

ᵃ F.

and the younger jarl Sidroc, and Asbiörn jarl, and Frœna jarl, and Harald jarl, and both divisions put to flight, and many thousands slain ; and they were fighting until night. And fourteen nights after, king Æthered and Ælfred his brother fought against the army at Basing, and there the Danes gained the victory. And two months after, king Æthered and Ælfred his brother fought against the army at Merton ; and they were in two divisions, and they put both to flight, and far in the day were victorious ; and there was great slaughter on each side, but the Danes held possession of the battle-place ; and there were *bishop Heahmund slain, and many good men. And after this fight there came a great ¹summer-force to Reading. And the Easter after, king Æthered died ; and he reigned five years, and his body lies in *Wimborne monastery.

Then Ælfred, son of Æthelwulf, his brother, succeeded to the kingdom of the West Saxons ; and one month after, king Ælfred, with a small force, fought against all the army at Wilton, and far in the day put them to flight ; but the Danes held possession of the battle-place. And this year nine great battles were fought against the army in the kingdom south of the Thames ; besides which, Ælfred, the king's brother, and individual aldormen, and king's thanes, often rode raids on them, which were not reckoned. And within the year nine jarls and one king were slain ; and that year the West Saxons made peace with the army.

An. DCCC.LXXII. (DCCC.LXXIII.) In this year the army went from Reading to London, and there took winter-quarters ; and then the Mercians made peace with the army.

An. DCCC.LXXIII. (DCCC.LXXIV.) In this year the army went into Northumbria, and took winter-quarters at Torksey in Lindsey ; ²and then the Mercians made peace with the army.'

An. DCCC.LXXIV. (DCCC.LXXV.) In this year the army went from Lindsey to Repton, and there took winter-quarters, and drove the king Burhred over sea, two and twenty winters after

Margin notes: 140, 141. — *of Sherborne. — *Sherborne, C. — 142, 143.

---

¹ This compound word has undergone divers interpretations. Æthelweard (p. 514) has, I think, given the true sense of the passage : " ad-

" venit sine numero æstivus exercitus in loco Readingon."

² Omitted in D. and E., perhaps rightly, being apparently a repetition from the preceding year.

he had obtained the kingdom, and they subdued all the land ; and he went to Rome, and there settled, and his body lies in St. Mary's church, in the school of the Angle race. And in the same year they gave the kingdom of Mercia to the custody of Ceolwulf, an unwise king's thane ; and he swore oaths to them, and gave hostages, that it should be ready for them, on whatever day they would have it ; and that he would be ready in his own person, and with all who would follow him, for the behoof of the army.

An. DCCC.LXXV. (DCCC.LXXVI.) In this year the army went from Repton ; and Hâlfdân went with a part of the army into Northumbria, and took winter-quarters by the river Tyne ; and the army subdued the land, and often harried on the Picts and on the Strathclyde Welsh ; and the three kings, Guthorm, and Oskytel, and Amund, went from Repton to Cambridge with a large army, and sat there one year. And in the summer, king Ælfred went out to sea with a naval force, and fought against the crews of seven ships, and took one of them, and put to flight the others.   144, 145.

An. DCCC.LXXVI. (DCCC.LXXVII.) In this year the army stole away to Wareham, a fortress of the West Saxons ; and after that the king made peace with the army ; and they gave to the king as hostages those who were most honourable in the army, and they then swore oaths to him on the [1] holy ring, which they before would not do to any nation, that they

---

[1] The 'beag' or bracelet appears to have been of a somewhat oval form, and open on one side; but it also signifies a ring. The ceremony here noticed may perhaps be elucidated by the following passage from Arngrim Jonas : " In ara præterea " annulus asservabatur argenteus, " vel ex orichalco, unciarum xx., " quem forensi aliquo munere fun- " gentes, jusjurandum jam præstituri, " victimarum illinitum cruore, re- " ligiose inter jurandum contrecta- " bant." Rer. Islandic. I. 7 ; and see Bartholinus de Armillis, p. 101. Compare Asser, A. 876.—R.P.

Of the solemn oath on the arm-let or bracelet, we find mention in Sæmund's Edda, (see edit. Arnæ Magn. III. p. 116, and II. p. 395):—

Baug-eið Óðinn hygg ek at unnit hafi.
Annulare juramentum Othinum opinor præstitisse.
Hâvamâl, Str. 111.

Ok at hringi Ullar.
Et per Ulleri annulum.

Atlaquiða in Grænl. Str. 31. On which the editor remarks: " Gentiles nostri proavi præstitere " juramenta ad sacrum quendam an- " nulum, in templo servatum, ac " interdum, quasi armillam, a sacer- " dote gestatum."

would speedily depart from his kingdom; and notwithstanding this, the mounted body stole away from the army by night to Exeter. And in that year Hâlfdân divided the Northumbrians' lands, [1] and from that time were ploughing and tilling them. In this year Rolf (Rollo) overran Normandy with his army, and he reigned fifty winters.

An. DCCC.LXXVII. (DCCC.LXXVIII). In this year the army came to Exeter from Wareham; and the naval force sailed west about; and then a great storm met them at sea, and there perished a hundred and twenty ships at Swanwick. And king Ælfred with his force rode after the mounted army as far as Exeter, but could not overtake them before they were in the fastness, where they could not be come at. And they there gave him as many hostages as he would have, and swore great oaths, and then held good peace. And then, in the autumn, the army went into the Mercians' land, and divided some of it, and gave some to Ceolwulf.

An. DCCC.LXXVIII. (DCCC.LXXIX.) In this year, at Midwinter, after Twelfth night, the army stole itself away to Chippenham, and harried the West Saxons' land, and settled there, and drove many of the people over sea, and of the remainder the greater portion they harried, and the people submitted to them, save the king Ælfred, and he, with a little band, withdrew to the woods and moor-fastnesses.[*] And in the same winter the brother of Ingvar and Hâlfdân was in Wessex, in Devonshire, with twenty-three ships, and he was there slain, and with him eight hundred and forty men of his force. (And there was the standard taken which they call the Raven.) And the Easter after, Ælfred, with a little band, wrought a fortress at Æthelney, and from that work warred on the army,

---

[1] An. DCCC.LXXVI. And in this same year the army of the Danes in England swore oaths to king Ælfred upon the holy ring, which before they would not do to any nation, and also gave to the king as hostages those who were most honourable in the army, that they would speedily depart from his kingdom; and that by night they brake.[a]

---

with that portion of the men of Somerset that was nearest. Then in the seventh week after Easter he rode to Ecgbryht's stone, on the east of Selwood, and there came to meet him all the Somersetshire men, and the Wiltshire men, and that part of Hampshire [1] which remained of it on this side of the sea ; and they were rejoiced on seeing him; and one night after, he went from the camp to Iley, and one night after that to Ethandûn (Heddington ?), and there fought against all the army, and put it to flight, and rode after it, as far as the works, and there sat fourteen nights. And then the army gave him hostages with great oaths, that they would depart from his kingdom ; and also promised him that their king would receive baptism ; and that they so fulfilled ; and three weeks after, king Guthorm came to him, with thirty of the men who were most honourable in the army, at Aller, which is opposite to Athelney; and the king received him there at baptism ; and his [2] chrism-loosing was at Wedmore ; and he was twelve nights with the king ; and he largely gifted him and his companions with money.

148, 149.

An. DCCC.LXXIX. (DCCC.LXXX.) In this year the army went to Cirencester from Chippenham, and sat there one year. And in that year a body of [3]vikings assembled, and sat down at Fulham on the Thames. And that same year the [4] sun was eclipsed one hour of the day.

150, 151.

An. DCCC.LXXX. (DCCC.LXXXI.) In this year the army went from Cirencester to East Anglia, and occupied and divided the land. And in the same year the army, which had before sat down at Fulham, went over sea to Ghent in France, and sat there one year.

An. DCCC.LXXXI. (DCCC.LXXXII.) In this year the army went up into France, and the French fought against them ; and there was the army horsed, after the fight.

---

[1] Those that had not emigrated beyond sea, see above : "qui non ultra "mare pro metu navigaverant pa- "ganorum." Flor. Wigorn.

[2] Apparently the removal of the fillet which, covering the chrism on the forehead, was bound round the head at confirmation.—R.P.

[3] So called from their custom of lurking in creeks, O. Nor. vik.

[4] The eclipse happened on the 14th of March 880.—R.P. "Eodem "anno eclipsis solis inter nonam et "vesperam, sed propius ad nonam, "facta est." Flor. Wigorn. a. 879.

An. DCCC.LXXXII. (DCCC.LXXXIII.) In this year the army went up along the Maese far into France, and there sat one year. And that same year king Ælfred went out to sea with ships, and fought against four ship-crews of Danish men, and took two of the ships, and the men were slain that were therein; and two ship-crews surrendered to him; and they were sorely fatigued and wounded before they surrendered.

An. DCCC.LXXXIII. (DCCC.LXXXIV.) In this year the army went up the Scheldt to Condé, and there sat one year. And Marinus the pope then sent 'lignum Domini' (of Christ's cross) to king Ælfred. And in the same year Sighelm and Æthelstân conveyed to Rome the alms which the king had vowed (to send) thither, and also to India to St. Thomas, and to St. Bartholomew, when they sat down against the army at London; and there, God be thanked, their prayer was very successful, after that vow.

An. DCCC.LXXXIV. (DCCC.LXXXV.) In this year the army went up the Somme to Amiens, and there sat one year. [1] In this year died the benevolent *bishop Æthelwold.

An. DCCC.LXXXV. (DCCC.LXXXVI.) In this year the fore-mentioned army separated into two; one part (went) east, the other part to Rochester, and besieged the city, and wrought another fastness about themselves; but they, nevertheless, defended the city until king Ælfred came without with his force. Then the army went to their ships, and abandoned the fastness; and they were there [2]deprived of their horses, and forthwith, in the same summer, withdrew over sea. And the same year king Ælfred sent a naval force from Kent to East Anglia. As soon as they came to the mouth of the Stour, then met them sixteen ships of vikings, and they fought against them, and captured all the ships, and slew the men. When they were returning homeward with the booty, a great naval force of vikings met them, and then fought against them on the same day, and the Danish gained the victory. In the same year, before midwinter, Carloman, king of the Franks, died, and a wild boar killed him; and one year before his brother died: he also had

152, 153.

* of Winton.

154, 155.

---

[1] A clerical error; Æthelwold died in 984. See that year.

[2] "Omnibus equis, quos de Fran-

"cia adduxerant, derelictis." Flor. Wigorn.

the western kingdom ; and they were both sons of Lewis, who also had the western kingdom, and died in the year when the sun was eclipsed, who was son of *Charles, whose daughter *tɪe Bald. Æthelwulf, king of the West Saxons, had for his queen. And in the same year a large naval force assembled among the Old-Saxons ; and there was a great fight twice in that year, and the Saxons had the victory ; and there were Frisians with them. In the same year *Charles succeeded to the western *the Fat. kingdom, and to all the kingdom on this side of the Mediterranean sea, and beyond this sea, as his great-grandfather had it, excepting the ¹Lidwiccas. Charles was son of Lewis, Lewis was brother of Charles, who was father of Judith, whom king Æthelwulf had ; and they were sons of Lewis ; Lewis was son of the old Charles, Charles was son of Pepin. And in the same year the good pope Marinus died, who freed the Angle race's school, at the prayer of Ælfred, king of the West   156, 157. Saxons : and he sent him great gifts, and part of the rood on which Christ suffered. And in the same year the army in East Anglia brake peace with king Ælfred.

  An. DCCC.LXXXVI. (DCCC.LXXXVII.) In this year ²the army   886 again went west, which had before landed in the east, and then up the Seine, and there took winter-quarters at the city of Paris. In the same year king Ælfred ³ restored London ; and all the Angle-race turned to him that were not in the bondage of the Danish men; and he then committed the burgh to the keeping of the aldorman Æthered.

  An. DCCC.LXXXVII. (DCCC.LXXXVIII.) In this year the army went up through the bridge at Paris; and then up along the Seine as far as the Marne, and then up on the Marne as far as

---

¹ Of this word various etymons have been suggested. The words butan Lidwiccum are rendered by Florence "absque Armoricano "regno ;" and suðan of Lidwiccum (a. 918), " de provincia quæ Lid-"wiccum dicitur." I am inclined to derive it from Llydaw, the British name of Brittany ; though it may, after all, be Norse, and composed of lid, a ship, and vik, a creek, firth,

(see a. 879, note); in which case Lidwic would signify the habitation, and Lidwicing (as in MSS. C. and D.), the inhabitant.

² " Orientali Francia derelicta, " iterum in Occidentalium Franco- " rum regionem venit." Flor. Wigorn. ex Assero.

³ Sax. gesette, " honorifice restau- " ravit et habitabilem fecit." Ibid.

Chezy, and then sat there, and in the [1] Yonne, two winters in
the two places. And in the same year *Charles, king of the
Franks died; and six weeks before he died Arnulf, his brother's
son, bereft him of the kingdom. And then was the realm
divided into five; and five kings thereto hallowed ; that was
however, with the consent of Arnulf ; and they said that they
would hold it from his hand, because none of them on the
paternal side was born thereto, save him alone. Arnulf then
dwelt in the land east of the Rhine, and Rodolf then obtained
the middle kingdom, and Eudes the western portion, and
Berenger and Wido the Lombards' land and the lands on that
side of the mountain ; and they held that in great hostility,
and fought two great battles, and oft and frequently ravaged
the land, and repeatedly drove out each other. And the same
year that the army went forth up over the bridge at Paris the
aldorman Æthelhelm conveyed the alms of the West Saxons
and of king Ælfred to Rome.

An. DCCC.LXXXVIII. (DCCC.LXXXIX.) In this year the aldorman Becca conveyed the alms of the West Saxons and of king
Ælfred to Rome. And queen Æthelswith, who was king
Ælfred's sister, died on the way to Rome, and her body lies
at Pavia. And in the same year archbishop Æthelred of Canterbury and the aldorman Æthelwold died in one month.

An. DCCC.LXXXIX. (DCCC.XC.) In this year there was no
journey to Rome, except that king Ælfred sent two couriers
with letters.

An. DCCC.XC. (DCCC.XCI.) In this year the abbot Beornhelm
conveyed the alms of the West Saxons and of king Ælfred to
Rome. And Guthorm, the Northern king, died, whose baptismal name was Æthelstân ; he was king Ælfred's godson, and
he abode in East Anglia, and *first occupied that land. And
in the same year the army went from the Seine to St. Lô,
which is between the Bretons and the Franks ; and the Bretons fought against them, and had the victory, and drove
them out into a river, and drowned many of them. In this
year Plegemund was chosen of God and of all the people to
the archbishopric of Canterbury.

*the Fat.

158, 159.

160, 161.

---

[1] " In ostium fluminis quod dicitur | " tyrium sancti regis Eadmundi,
" Iona." Flor. Wigorn. | " primitus incoluit et possedit."
    " Provinciam illam, post mar- | Ibid.

An. DCCC.XCI. (DCCC.XCII.) In this year the army went east, and king Arnulf, with the East Franks, and Saxons, and Bavarians, fought against the mounted force before the ships came, and put it to flight.[1] And three Scots came to king Ælfred in a boat without any oars, from Ireland, whence they had stolen away, because they desired, for love of God, to be in a state of pilgrimage, they recked not where. The boat in which they came was wrought of two hides and a half, and they took with them food sufficient for seven nights ; and on the seventh night they came to land in Cornwall, and then went straightways to king Ælfred. Thus they were named : Dubslane, and Macebethu, and Maclinmum. And Swifneh, the best teacher that was among the Scots, died.

162, 163.

An. DCCC.XCII. And in the same year after Easter, about the Rogations (May 29th) or earlier, appeared the star which in Book-Latin is called *cometa*. Some men say in English, that it is a long-haired (feaxed) star, because there stands a long ray from it, sometimes on one side, sometimes on each side.

An. DCCC.XCIII. (DCCC.XCII.) In this year the great army, of which we 'long before spoke, came again from the east kingdom westward to Boulogne; and was there shipped, so that they in one voyage made the transit, with horses and all; and they came up to the mouth of the Limen with two hundred and fifty ships. The mouth is in the east of Kent, at the east end of the great wood which we call Andred. The wood is in length, from east to west, one hundred and twenty miles long, or longer, and thirty miles broad. The river, of which we before spoke, flows out from the weald. On the river they towed up their ships as far as the weald, four miles from the outward mouth, and there stormed a work : within the fastness a few countrymen were stationed, and it was only half constructed. Then soon after that, came Hæsten with eighty ships into the Thames' mouth, and wrought him a work at Middleton (Milton), and the other army one at Appledore.

164, 165.

An. DCCC.XCIV. In this year, that was a twelvemonth after they had wrought a work in the 'east kingdom, Northumbria

* An. DCCC.XCI.

(which was made at St. Lô)

* An. DCCC.XCI.

* at Middleton.

---

[1] This celebrated battle was fought on the 1st Sept. on the banks of the Dyle near Louvain ; it freed the interior of Germany for ever from the invasions of the Northmen. See Depping, "Expéditions Maritimes des Normands," II. p. 35, and the authorities there cited.

and East Anglia had given oaths to king Ælfred, and East
Anglia six hostages ; and yet against the compact, as often as
the other armies with all their force went out, then they went
out, either with them or on their side.   And then king Ælfred
gathered his force, and went until he encamped between the
two armies, the nearest where he had room, for wood-fastness
and for water-fastness, so that he might reach either, [1] if they
would seek any field.   Then after that, they went through the
weald in bands and troops, on whichever side was then without a force.   And they also were sought by other bands,
almost every day, or by night, both from the (king's) force
and also from the burghs.   The king had divided his force into
two, so that they were constantly half at home, half abroad,
besides those men that held the burghs.   The whole army did
not come out of their quarters oftener than twice, one time,
when they first came to land, before the (king's) force was
assembled ; the other time, when they would go from their
quarters. They had then taken a great booty, and would con-
vey it northwards over the Thames into Essex towards the
ships.   The (king's) force then rode before them, and fought
against them at Farnham, and put the army to flight, and
rescued the booty ; and they fled over the Thames without
any ford ; then up by the Colne to an *island.   The (royal)
army then beset them there from without, for the longest time
that they had provisions ; but they had then stayed their
appointed time and consumed their provisions; and the king
was then on his march thitherwards with the division which
was advancing with himself.   Then he was thitherward, and
the other force was homeward, and the Danish remained there
behind, because their king had been wounded in the fight, so
that he could not be conveyed. Then those who dwell with
the Northumbrians and with the East Angles gathered some
hundred ships, and went south about, and besieged a work
in Devonshire by the north sea ; and those who went south
about besieged Exeter.   When the king heard that, he turned
west towards Exeter with all the force, save a very
body of the people eastwards. These went on until they
came to London, and then, with the townsmen and with the

Margin notes:
166, 167.
* Thorney.
  Ethelw.

---

[1] " Si aliquem campum prædæ vel prælii causa peterent." Flor. Wigorn.

aid which came to them from the west, marched east to Benfleet. Hæsten was then come there with his army, which had
previously sat at Middleton (Milton); and the great army
also was come thereto, which had before sat at the mouth of
the Limen, at Appledore. Hæsten had before wrought the
work at Benfleet, and was then gone out harrying, and the 168.
great army was at home. They then marched up and put
the army to flight, and stormed the work, and took all that
there was within, as well *money, as women and children, *or property.
and brought all to London; and all the ships they either
broke in pieces, or burned, or brought to London, or to Ro- 169.
chester; and Hæsten's wife and his two sons were brought
to the king, and he restored them to him, because one of them
was his godson, the other the aldorman Æthered's. They
had been their sponsors before Hæsten came to Benfleet, and
he had given him oaths and hostages; and the king had also
given him much money, and so likewise, when he gave up
the boy and the woman. But as soon as they came to Benfleet, and had wrought the work, he harried on that end of
his realm which Æthered his had to defend; and
again, a second time, he had arrived on a plundering expedition on that same kingdom, when his work was taken by
storm. When the king turned west with his force towards
Exeter, as I before said, and the army had beset the burgh,
when he had arrived there, they went to their ships. While
he was busied in the west against the army there, and both
the armies had formed a junction at Shoebury in Essex, and
there wrought a work, they then went both together up along
the Thames, and a great increase came to them, both from
the East Angles and the Northumbrians. They then went
up along the Thames, until they reached the Severn, then up
along the Severn. Then the aldorman Æthered, and the
aldorman Æthelm, and the aldorman Æthelnoth, and the
king's thanes, who were then at home in the works, gathered
together, from every town east of the Parret, as well west as
east of Selwood, as also north of the Thames and west of the 170.
Severn, and also some part of the North Welsh race. When
they were all gathered together, they followed after the army
to Buttington on the bank of the Severn, and there beset
them on every side in a fastness. When they had sat there
many weeks on the two sides of the river, and the king was 171.

west in Devon ag.   the naval force, they were distressed
for want of food, and had eaten a great part of their horses,
and the others had died of hunger ; they then went out to
the men who were encamped on the east side of the river,
and fought against them, and the Christians had the victory.
And there was Ordheh, a king's thane, slain, and also many
other king's thanes were slain ; (and of the Danish there was
a very great slaughter made); and the part that came away
thence was saved by flight. When they came into Essex to
their work and to their ships, the remnant gathered again a
great army from the East Angles and from the Northumbrians,
before winter, and committed their wives and their ships and
their chattels to the East Angles, and went at one stretch, by
day and by night, until they arrived at a [1]desolated city in
Wirrall, which is called Legaceaster (Chester).   Then could
the force not overtake them before they were within the
work ; they however beset the work from without for two
days, and took all the cattle which was there without, and
slew the men that they might intercept outside of the work,
and burned all the corn, and with their horses consumed it on
every [2]plain.   And that was a twelvemonth after they had
come over sea hither.

An. DCCC.XCV. And then soon after that, in this year, the
army went from Wirrall, because they could not abide there,
into North Wales ; that was because they had been deprived
both of the cattle and of the corn which they had obtained by
plunder.   When they had again wended out of North Wales
with the booty which they had there taken, then they went
over Northumberland and East Anglia, so that the (king's)
force could not reach them, until they came into the eastward
part of the East Saxons' land, to an island that is out in the
sea, which is called Mersey. And when the army which had
beset Exeter again turned homewards, they harried on the
South Saxons near Chichester, and the townsfolk put them
to flight, and slew many hundreds of them, and took some
of their ships.   Then, in the same year, before winter, the

---

[1] " Civitatem Legionum, tunc
" temporis *desertam*, quæ Saxonice
" Legeceaster dicitur . . . . intrant."
Flor. Wigorn.

[2] The original word is efennehð,
or efenchð, the Old high Ger.
ebanôd, *Ger.* ebene, *planities.*

Danish who sat in Mersey, towed their ships up the Thames, and then up the Lea. This was two years after they had come over sea hither.]

An. DCCC.XCVI. [In the same year the fore-mentioned army had wrought a work on the Lea, twenty miles above London. Then, in the summer after, a great number of the townspeople, and also of other folk went until they came to the Danish work, and were there put to flight, and some four king's thanes slain. Then afterwards, during harvest, the king encamped in the neighbourhood of the town, while the people reaped their corn, so that the Danish might not deprive them of the crop. Then one day the king rode up by the river, and observed where the river might be obstructed, so that they might not bring out their ships. And they then did so: they wrought two works on the two sides of the river. When they had actually begun the work, and had encamped thereby, then the army perceived that they could not bring out their ships. They then abandoned them, and went over land, until they arrived at Quatbridge (Bridge) on the Severn, and there wrought a work. Then rode the (king's) force west after the army, and the men of London brought away the ships, and all those which they could not bring off they broke up, and those that were *stalworth* they brought into London. And the Danish had intrusted their wives to the East Angles before they went out from their work. They then sat that winter at Quatbridge (Bridge). That was three years after they had come hither over sea to the mouth of the Limen.]

An. DCCC.XCVII. [Then the summer after, in this year, the army went, some to East Anglia, some to Northumbria; and they who were moneyless got themselves ships, and went south over sea to the Seine. Thanks be to God, the army had not utterly broken up the Angle race; but they were much more broken, in those three years, by a mortality of cattle and of men; most of all thereby, that many of the king's most excellent thanes that were in the land died in those three years: of these one was Swithulf, bishop of Rochester, and Ceolmund, alderman of Kent, and Beorhtulf, alderman of the East Saxons, and Wulfred, alderman of Hampshire, and Ealhheard, bishop of Dorchester, and Eadulf, a king's thane in Sussex, and Beornulf, wick-reeve at Win-

174, 175.

chester, and Ecgulf, the king's horse-thane, and many, also besides these, although I have named the most eminent. In the same year the armies from the East Angles and Northumbrians harassed the West Saxons' land, very much on the south coast, by predatory bands ; (though) most of all by the long ships (æscas), which they had built many years before. Then king Ælfred commanded long ships to be built against them, which were full nigh twice as long as the others ; some

177.   had sixty oars, some more ; they were both swifter and steadier, and also higher than the others ; they were shapen neither as the Frisian nor as the Danish, but as it seemed to himself that they might be most useful. Then on a certain time in the same year, there came six ships to Wight, and did there much evil, both in Devon and elsewhere on the seashore. Then the king commanded (his men) to go thither with nine of the new ships, and they blockaded against them the mouth into the outer sea. They then went with three ships out against them, and three lay high up in the mouth, in the dry : the men were gone off on shore. They then took two of the three ships at the outward mouth, and slew the men, and the one escaped, in which also the men were killed, save five, who came away because the ships of the others were aground. They were also aground very inconveniently ; three were aground on the side of the deep on which the Danish ships were aground, and all the others on the other side, so that not one of them could get to the others. But when the water had ebbed many furlongs from the ships, then the Danish went from the three ships to the other three which had been left by the ebb on their side, and they then fought there. There were slain Lucumon the king's reeve, and Wulfhard the Frisian, and Æbbe the Frisian, and Æthelhere the Frisian, and Æthelferth the king's companion, and of all the men, Frisian and English, sixty-two, and of the Danish a hundred and twenty. But then the flood came to the Danish ships before the Christians could shove theirs out ; and they therefore rowed away out ; they were then so damaged that they could not row round the South Saxons' land, for there the sea cast two of them on land, and the men

179.   were led to the king at Winchester, and he commanded them to be there hanged ; and the men who were in the one ship came to East Anglia sorely wounded. In the same summer

no less than twenty ships, with men and everything, perished on the south coast. In the same year died Wulfric the king's horse-thane, who was also Welsh-reeve.

An. DCCC.XCVIII. In this year died Æthelm, aldorman of Wiltshire, nine nights before Midsummer ; and in this year died Heahstân, who was bishop of London.

An. DCCC.XCIX., D.CCCC.

✔ An. DCCCC.I. In this year died Ælfred son of Athulf (Æthelwulf), six nights before All-hallowmass (Oct. 26th). He was king over all the Angle race, except the part that was under the dominion of the Danes ; and he held the kingdom one year and a half less than thirty winters. And then Eadweard his son succeeded to the kingdom. Then Æthelwald ætheling, [1] son of his paternal uncle, forcibly entered the vill at Wimborne and that at Tweoxneam (Twynham, Christchurch) against the will of the king and his ' witan.' Then the king rode with a force, until he encamped at Badbury, near Wimborne; and Æthelwald sat within the vill with the men who submitted to him ; and had obstructed all the entrances to him, and had said that he would one or other, either there live or there lie. Then, in the meanwhile, he stole away by night, and sought the army in Northumbria, and they received him for their king and submitted to him. And the king commanded that he should be ridden after, but it was impossible to overtake him. They then beset the woman whom he had before taken without the king's leave, and against the bishops' ordinance ; because she had previously been hallowed a nun. And in this same year died Æthered, who was aldorman of Devon, four weeks before king Ælfred.

An. DCCCC.II. In this year [2] Ealhswyth died ; and in the same year was the fight at the Holme between the Kentish men and the Danish.

An. DCCCC.III. In this year died the aldorman Athulf, brother of Ealhswyth, mother of king Eadweard ; and Virgilius, abbot of the Scots, and Grimbald, the mass-priest, on the VIIIth of the Ides of July (July 8th). And in the same

---

[1] Æthelwald was son of Æthered, Ælfred's brother and predecessor.

[2] Her death is again recorded under An. DCCCC.V.

year the new monastery was hallowed at Winchester ; and the [1] coming of St. Ludoc.

An. DCCCC.IV. In this year Æthelwald came hither over sea with the fleet that he was able to get, and he was submitted to in Essex. In this year the moon was eclipsed.

An. DCCCC.V. In this year Æthelwald allured the army in East Anglia to a violation of the peace, so that they harried over all the Mercians' land, until they came to Cricklade, and there they went over the Thames, and took, both in [2] Bredon and thereabont, all that they could carry off, and then again went homewards. Then king Eadweard went after them as speedily as he conld gather his force, and harried [3] all their land between the dikes and the Ouse, all as far north as the fens. When he again would withdraw thence, he commanded it to be proclaimed over all the force, that they should all withdraw together : then the Kentish men remained there behind against his command, although he had sent seven messengers to them. Then the army there surrounded them, and they there fought, and there were the aldorman Sigulf slain, and the aldormen Sigelm, and Eadwold, the king's thane, and the abbot Cênwulf, and Sigebriht, son of Sigulf, and Eadwald, son of Acca, and with them many others, though I have named the most distinguished. And on the side of the Danish were slain Eric their king, and Æthelwald ætheling, who had allured him to the infraction of the peace, and Byrhtsige, son of Byrhtnoth ætheling, and Ysopa [4] hold, and Oskytel hold, and likewise very many others with

182, 183.

---

[1] The relics of St. Judoc (Ludoc) were brought from Ponthieu by certain monks, and placed in the New Minster.—R.P.

[2] " Silva quæ Saxonice Bradene " vocatur." Fl. Wigorn. Bredon forest, near Malmesbury.

[3] " Terras illorum quæ inter terræ " limitem sancti regis Eadmundi et " flumen Usam sitæ sunt, devastat." Ibid. See Lappenberg, Engl. under the A. S. Kings, I. p. 242.

[4] A title of honour introduced by the Danes into E. Anglia. Biörn Haldorsen defines höldr as *dominus*

fundi aviti vel *allodialis*, and in the Index to the Grágás a höldr is described as *colonus odulicus* vel *fundum avitum tenens.* From his 'wergild,' (or legal valuation),which is double that of a priest or thane it is evident that he was of very high rank in the state ; though the disparity may, perhaps, be justly ascribed to the assumed superiority of the victors over the vanquished ; the thanes and priests being of the latter class. See Ancient Laws and Institutes of England, tit. Wergilds, 4.

them, whom we are unable now to name. And there was a great slaughter made on either hand; and of the Danish there were more slain, though they held possession of the place of carnage. And Ealhswyth died in the same year. This year a comet appeared on the xiiith of the Kal. of November (Oct. 20th).

An. DCCCC.VI. In this year died Ælfred, who was reeve at Bath. And in the same year peace was concluded at Yttinga-ford (Hitchen?), as king Eadweard dictated, both with the East Angles and with the Northumbrians.

An. DCCCC.VII. [1] In this year Chester was renovated.

An. DCCCC.VIII.

An. DCCCC.IX. In this year died Denulf, who was bishop of Winchester.

In this year St. Oswald's body was conveyed form Bardney into Mercia.

An. DCCCC.X. In this year Frithestân succeeded to the bishopric of Winchester; and after that died Asser, who was bishop of Sherborne. And in the same year king Eadweard sent a force both from the West-Saxons and from the Mercians; and they made very great ravage on the north army, both in men and in every kind of cattle, and slew many of the Danish men; and were five weeks therein. In this year the Angles and Danes fought at Tettenhall, on the viiith of the Ides of August (Aug. 6th), and the Angles gained the victory. And in the same year [2]Æthelflæd built the burgh at Bramsbury.

184, 1

ᐁ An. DCCCC.XI. In this year the army in Northumbria broke the peace, and disdained every right (peace) which king

---

.An. DCCCC.VI. In this year king Eadweard, of necessity, concluded a peace both with the East Angles' army and with the Northumbrians'. [a]

An. DCCCC.X. In this year the army of the Angles and of the Danes fought at Tettenhall.[a]

---

[1] See An. DCCC.XCIV.　　|　　[2] Sister of king Eadweard.

---

[a] F.

Eadweard and his 'witan' offered them, and harried over the Mercians' land. And the king had gathered some hundred ships, and was then in Kent, and the ships went south-east along the sea towards him. Then weened the army that the greatest part of his support was in the ships, and that they might go unassailed wheresoever they would. When the king learned that they were gone out to ravage, he sent his force, both from the West Saxons and from the Mercians, and overtook the army when it was returning homewards, and fought against them and put the army to flight, and slew many thousands of them; and there was king Eowils slain, and king Hâlfdân, and Ottar jarl, and Skurfa jarl, and Othulf hold, and Benesing hold, and Olaf the Black, and Thurferth ¹hold, and Osferth Hlytte, and Guthferth hold, and Agmund hold, and Guthferth.

Then in the year next after, died Æthered, aldorman of the Mercians.

186, 187.   ✔ An. DCCCC.XII. In this year died Æthered, aldorman of the Mercians; and king Eadweard took possession of London, and Oxford, and all the lands which thereto belonged.

In this year Æthelflæd, the lady of the Mercians, came to Scergeat (Sarrat ?), on the holy eve of the Inventio Sanctæ Crucis (May 3rd), and there built the burgh; and in the same year that at Bridgenorth.

An. DCCCC.XIII. In this year, about ²Martinmas (April 14th), king Eadward commanded the north burgh to be built at Hertford, between the Memera (Maran), and the Beneficca (Bean), and the Lygea (Lea). And then, the summer after that, betwixt the Rogation days (May 3rd) and Midsummer, king Eadweard went with some of his force to Maldon in Essex, and there encamped, while the burgh at Witham was being wrought and built; and a good deal of the folk submitted to him, who were before under the power of the Danish men. And some of his force the while wrought the burgh at Hertford, on the south side of the Lea.

In this year, God granting, Æthelflæd, lady of the Mer-

---

¹ See An. DCCCC.V. *note*⁴.
² From the following dates, this would appear to be the anniversary, not of St. Martin of Tours, but of 'Martin pope and martyr,' which was celebrated on the 14th of April.

cians, went with all the Mercians to Tamworth, and built
the burgh there, in the early summer ; and before the following Lammas (Aug. 1), that at Stafford.

Then in the year after this, that at Eddesbury, in the
early summer ; and afterwards, in the same year, towards the
end of autumn, that at Warwick.

Then in the next year, after Midwinter, that at Chirbury,
and that at Wardbury ; and that same year, before Midwinter,
that at Runcorn.

188, 189.

An. °DCCCC.XIV. In this year the army rode out after * DCCCC.XVII. A
Easter from Northampton and from Leicester, and broke the
peace, and slew many men at Hocneratûn (Hockerton?) and
thereabouts. And then, very soon after that, when the one
came home, then they raised another troop, which rode out
against Lygtûn (Leighton) ; and then were the country
people aware of them, and fought against them and put them
to full flight, and rescued all that they had taken, and also a
great portion of their horses and their weapons.

✓ An. °DCCCC.XV. ¹In this year there came a great naval * DCCCC.XVIII. A
force over hither from the south, from the ²Lidwiccas, and
with it two jarls, Ottar and ³Hraold, and went west about
until they arrived in the mouth of the Severn ; and they
harried on the North Welsh everywhere by the sea, where it
pleased them ; and took bishop Cameleac in Irkenfield, and
led him with them to the ships ; and then king Eadweard
afterwards ransomed him with forty pounds. Then after that,
all the army landed, and would still go to harry towards
Irkenfield. Then met them the men of Hereford and of
Gloucester, and of the nearest burghs, and fought against
them, and put them to flight, and slew the jarl Hraold, and

---

¹ An. DCCCC.XV. In this year Warwick was built.＊

---

² See An. DCCC.LXXXV. *note*. | by transposition, as hros and hors,
³ Apparently the same as *Harold* | *horse*.

＊ D.

the brother of Ottar the other jarl, and many of the army,
and drove them into an ¹ inclosure, and there beset them from
without, until they gave them hostages, that they would
190, 191.   depart from king Eadweard's dominion.   And the king had
contrived so that his force sat opposite to them on the south
side of the mouth of the Severn, west from the Welsh (shore),
as far as the mouth of the Avon east, so that they durst not
anywhere seek the land on that side.   Then, nevertheless,
they stole away by night, on some two occasions, on one
occasion, up to the east of Watchet, and on another occasion,
to Porlock.   Then they were beaten on both occasions, so
that few of them came away, save those only who there swam
out to the ships ; and these seated themselves out on the
island of Flatholme (Steepholm), until the time that they
were greatly destitute of food ; and many men perished from
hunger, because they could not obtain any food.]   They then
went to South Wales, and then out to Ireland ; and this was
in autumn.   And then after that, in the same year, before
Martinmas (Nov. 11th), king Eadweard went with his force
to Buckingham, and sat there four weeks, and wrought
both the burghs on each side of the river, before he went
thence.   And Thurkytel jarl sought him for his lord, and
all the ²holds, and almost all the chief men belonging to
Bedford, and also many of those belonging to Northampton.

An. DCCCC.XVI.   In this year abbot Ecgbriht was guiltless
slain, before Midsummer, on the XVIth of the Kal. of July
(June 16th).   On the same day was the feast of St. Ciricus
the martyr and his companions.   And three nights after,
Æthelflæd sent a force into Wales, and took Brecknock by
storm, and there captured the king's wife with four and
thirty persons.

An. DCCCC.XVII.   In this year Æthelflæd, lady of the Mercians, God aiding her, before Lammas (Aug. 1), acquired the
192, 193.   burgh which is called Derby, with all that belonged thereto ;
and there also were slain four of her thanes, within the gates,
whose loss was a great sorrow to her.

---

¹ Sax. pearruc, hence our *park* ; | ² See An. DCCCC.V. *note⁴*.
the word is Keltic.

An. DCCCC.XVIII. In this year, with the aid of God, in the early part of the year, she got into her power peacefully the burgh at Leicester ; and the greatest part of the army which belonged thereto became subjected to her. And the people of York had also promised her, and some given a pledge, and some confirmed by oaths, that they would be at her disposal. But very soon after they had agreed thereon, [1] she died at Tamworth twelve nights before Midsummer (June 12th), in the eighth year from the time she rightfully held the lordship over the Mercians ; and her body lies in Gloucester, in the east porch of St. Peter's church.

An. DCCCC.XIX. In this year king Eadweard went with an army to Bedford, before Martinmas (Nov. 11th), and gained the burgh ; and almost all the townsmen who had previously dwelt there turned to him, and he remained there four weeks, and commanded the burgh on the south side of the river to be built, before he went thence. In this year also the daughter of Æthered, lord of the Mercians, was deprived of all power, and conveyed into Wessex, three weeks before Midwinter. She was called Ælfwyn.

An. DCCCC.XX. In this year, before Midsummer, king Eadweard went to Maldon, and built and established the burgh, ere he went thence. And in the same year Thurkytel jarl went over sea to France, with the men who would follow him, with the peace and support of king Eadweard.

An. DCCCC.XXI. In this year, before Easter (April 1st), king Eadweard gave orders to proceed to Towcester, and build the burgh. And then again, after that, in the same year, in the Rogation days (May 7th), he commanded the burgh at Wigmore to be built. In the same summer, betwixt Lammas (Aug. 1st) and Midsummer, the army broke the peace from Northampton

194.

An. DCCCC.XVIII. In this year died Æthelflæd, lady of the Mercians.[a]

---

[1] See p. 83, where her death is again recorded under DCCCC.XXII.

---

[a] E.

and from Leicester, and north from thence, and went to Towcester, and fought against the burgh a whole day, and thought
that they should take it by storm; but, nevertheless, the
people who were within defended it, until a greater force
arrived ; and they then abandoned the burgh, and went away.
And then again, very soon after that, they again went out
with a predatory band by night, and came upon men unpre-
pared, and took no little, both in men and in cattle, betwixt
Bernwood and Aylesbury. At the same time, the army from
Huntingdon, and from the East Angles, went and wrought
the work at Tempsford, and inhabited it, and built, and forsook
the other at Huntingdon ; and thought that from thence they
could, by warfare and hostility, again obtain more of the land.
And they went until they arrived at Bedford; and then the
men who were there within went out against them, and fought
with them, and put them to flight, and slew a good part of
them.   Then again, after that, a great army was gathered
from the East Angles and from the Mercians' land, and went
to the burgh at Wigingamere (Wigmore ?), and beset it round
about, and fought against it far in the day, and took the cattle
about it ; and, nevertheless, the men defended the burgh who
were therein ;. and then they abandoned the burgh and went
away.   Then, after that, in the same summer, a great body of
people assembled in king Eadweard's dominion, from the
nearest burghs, who could then go, and went to Tempsford,
and beset the burgh, and fought against it until they took it
by storm, and slew the king, and Toglos jarl, and Manna jarl
his son, and his brother, and all those who were there within
and would defend themselves, and took the others, and all that
was therein.   Then, very shortly after that, a great body of
people assembled in autumn, as well from Kent as from Surrey
and from Essex, and everywhere from the nearest burghs, and
went to Colchester, and beset the burgh, and fought against it
until they reduced it, and slew all the people, and took all that
was there within, except the men who fled away over the
wall.   Then, after that, yet in the same autumn, a great army
assembled from the East Angles, both of the land-army and
of the vikings whom they had allured to their aid, and thought
that they might avenge their injuries. And they went to
Maldon, and beset the burgh, and fought against it, until there
came greater aid to the townspeople from without ; and the

army then abandoned the burgh and departed. And then the men from the burgh went out after them, and also those who had come to their aid from without, and put the army to flight, and slew many hundreds of them, both of the [1] seamen and of the others. Then, very soon after this, in the same autumn, king Eadweard, with a force of West Saxons, went to Passenham, and sat there while they surrounded the burgh at Towcester with a stone wall. And Thurferth jarl, and the [2] holds, and all the army which belonged to Northampton, north as far as the Welland, submitted to him, and sought him for their lord and protector. [3]And when that army corps went home, then went another out, and reduced the burgh at Huntingdon, and repaired and renovated it, where it was before in a state of ruin, by order of king Eadweard; and all the folk that were left there of the peasantry submitted to king Eadweard, and sought his peace and his protection. Then again, after that, in the same year, before Martinmas (Nov. 11th), king Eadweard, with an army of West Saxons, went to Colchester, and repaired and renovated the burgh, where it had previously been ruined; and a great number of people submitted to him, both in East Anglia and in Essex, who had before been under the power of the Danes. And all the army in East Anglia swore unity with him, that they all that would that he would, and would protect all that the king would protect, both by sea and by land. And the army which belonged to Cambridge chose him specially for their lord and protector, and confirmed it by oaths, as he it then dictated. In this year king Eadweard built the burgh at Cledemutha. In this year king Sihtric slew Niel his brother. ⌄An. DCCCC.XXII. In this year, between the Rogations (May 27th) and Midsummer, king Eadweard went with a force to Stamford, and commanded the burgh to be wrought on the south side of the river; and all the people who belonged to the northern burgh submitted to him, and sought him for their lord. And then, while he was there sitting, Æthelflæd his sister died at Tamworth, twelve nights before Midsummer. And then he

195.

---

[1] The shipmen; from sæc, a ship, a pirate vessel, so called apparently from being made of ash.

[2] See An. DCCCC.V., note, p. 76.
[3] See An. DCCC.XCIV., p. 70.

took possession of the burgh at Tamworth ; and all the people in the Mercians' land, who had/before been subject to Æthelflæd, submitted to him ; and the kings of the North Welsh, Howel, and Cledauc, and Jeothwel, and all the North Welsh race, sought him for lord. He then went thence to Nottingham, and reduced the burgh, and ordered it to be repaired, and peopled, both with Englishmen and with Danish. And all the people who were settled in the Mercians' land submitted to him, both Danish and English.

196.

197.

An. DCCCC.XXIII. In this year king Eadweard went, after autumn, with a force to Thelwall, and commanded the burgh to be built, and inhabited, and manned ; and commanded another force also of the Mercian nation, while he there sat, to reduce Manchester in Northumbria, and repair and man it. In this year died archbishop Plegemund : (and) in this year king Ragnald won York.

An. DCCCC.XXIV. In this year, before Midsummer, king Eadweard went with a force to Nottingham, and commanded the burgh to be built on the south side of the river, opposite to the other ; and the bridge over the Trent, betwixt the two burghs ; and then went thence into Peakland, to Bakewell, and commanded a burgh to be built and manned there in the immediate neighbourhood. [And then the king of the Scots and all the nation of Scots, and Ragnald, and the sons of Eadulf,] and all those who·dwell in Northumbria, as well English as Danish and Northmen, and others, and also the king of the Strathclyde Welsh, and all the Strathclyde Welsh, chose him for father and for lord.

An. DCCCC.XXIV. In this year king Eadweard was chosen for father and for lord by the king of the Scots, and by the Scots, and by king Ragnald, and by all the Northumbrians, and also by the king of the Strathclyde Welsh, and by all the Strathclyde Welsh.[a]

199.

An. DCCCC.XXIV. In this year king Eadweard died in Mercia at Farndon ; and very shortly, in sixteen days after, his son Ælfweard died at Oxford ; and their bodies lie at Winchester.

---

[a] F.

✓ An. DCCCC.XXV. In this year king Eadweard died, and
Æthelstân his son succeeded to the kingdom. And St.
Dûnstân was born, and Wulfhelm succeeded to the arch-
bishopric of Canterbury. In this year king Æthelstân and
Sihtric, king of the Northumbrians, came together at Tam-
worth on the IIIrd of the Kal. of February (Jan. 30th); and
Æthelstân gave him his sister.

198.

An. DCCCC.XXVI. In this year fiery beams of light appeared
in the north part of the sky. And Sihtric died; and king
Æthelstân assumed the kingdom of the Northumbrians; and
he subjugated all the kings who were in this island: first,
Howel king of the West Welsh, and Constantine king of the
Scots, and Owen king of Gwent, and Ealdred son of Ealdulf
of Bamborough: and with pledge and with oaths they confirmed peace, in the place which is named Eâmôt (Emmet?),
on the IVth of the Ides of July (July 12th), and renounced
every kind of idolatry; and after that departed in peace.

An. DCCCC.XXVII. In this year king Æthelstân expelled
king Guthfrith; and in this year archbishop Wulfhelm went
to Rome.

An. DCCCC.XXVIII. In this year William succeeded to Normandy, and held it fifteen years.

201.

An. DCCCC.XXIX., DCCCC.XXX.

An. DCCCC.XXXI. In this year Byrnstân was ordained bishop
of Winchester, on the IVth of the Kal. of June (May 29th);
and he held the bishopric two years and a half.

200.

An. DCCCC.XXXII. In this year died *bishop Frythestân.

* of Winton.

An. DCCCC.XXXIII. In this year Eadwine ætheling was
drowned in the sea. In this year king Æthelstân went into
Scotland, with both a land-force and a ship-force, and ravaged

---

And Æthelstân was chosen king by the Mercians, and hallowed at Kingston. And he gave his sister to Otho, son of
the king of the Old-Saxons.[a]

An. DCCCC.XXV. In this year bishop Wulfhelm was hallowed; And in the same year king Eadweard died.[b]

An. DCCCC.XXXI. In this year died Frithestân, bishop of
Winchester, and Byrnstân was blessed in his stead.[c]

ᵃ B. C. D.   ᵇ E., partly repeated.   ᶜ F.

a great part of it. And bishop Byrnstân died at Winchester at All-Hallows tide.

An. DCCCC.XXXIV. In this year bishop Ælfheah succeeded to the bishopric of Winchester.

An. DCCCC.XXXV., DCCCC.XXXVI.

An. [1] DCCCC.XXXVII.

This year king Æthelstân, | Eadward's offspring,
lord of earls, | as was to them congenial
[2] ring-giver of warriors, | from their ancestors,   202, 203.
and his brother eke, | that they in conflict oft,
Eadmund ætheling, | 'gainst every foe,
life-long glory | should the land defend,
in battle won, | treasure and homes.
with edges of swords, | The foes lay low,
at Brunanburh. | the Scots' people,
The board-wall clave, | and the shipmen
hew'd the [3] war linden, | death-doom'd fell.
with [4] hammers' leavings, | The field [5] stream'd

An. DCCCC.XXXVII. In this year king Æthelstân and Eadmund his brother led a force to Brunanburh, and there fought against Olaf, and, Christ aiding, had victory: and they there slew five kings and seven jarls.[a]

---

[1] DCCCC.XXXVIII.—W.

[2] Rings were worn about the head, round the neck, the arms, the wrists, on the fingers, the ankle, and probably even round the waist. See ' Guide to Northern Archæ-'ology,' edited by the Earl of Ellesmere, 8vo. 1848, p. 54; also Weinhold, Altnordisches Leben, 8vo. Berlin, 1856, p. 185. See also An. DCCC.LXXVI. and note, p. 63.

[3] shields, being made of the lime or linden tree.

[4] gomel láf, eald láf, yrfe láf, hamora (homera) láf, are all poetic expressions for a sword ; a sword being the leaving, or produce, of the operation of forging (hammering).

[5] This translation of dæniede (dennade) is countenanced by the O. Norse dundi, from dynia, resonare, irruere : Blôdid dundi, og târin tîdt, creberrima erat stillatio tum sanguinis tum lacrymarum. Biörn Haldorsen, voce dyn. The reading of MS. A. seems to be the error of an illiterate scribe, writing, as was customary, from dictation, and deceived by similarity of sound.

---

[a] F.

with warriors' [1] blood,
what time the sun up,
at morning tide,
the glorious star,
glided o'er grounds,
God's candle bright,
the eternal Lord's,
until the noble creature
sank to its setting.
There many a warrior lay,
by javelins scatter'd,
northern men,
o'er the shield shot,
so the Scots eke,
weary, war-sated.
The West Saxons forth,
the live-long day,
– in martial bands,
follow'd the footsteps
of the hostile nations.
They hew'd the fugitives
from behind amain,
with falchions [2] mill-sharp.
The Mercians refus'd not
the hard hand-play
to any of the warriors,
who with [3] Olaf,
o'er the waves' mingling,
in the ship's bosom,
the land had sought,
death-doom'd in fight.
205. Five lay
on that battle-stead,

young kings,
by swords laid to sleep :
so seven eke
of Olaf's jarls,
of the army countless,
shipmen and Scots.
There was put to flight
the Northmen's prince,
by need constrain'd,
to the vessel's prow,
with a little band.
The bark drove afloat,
the king departed
on the fallow flood,
his life preserved.
So there eke the aged
came by flight
to his country north,
Constantine,
hoary warrior ;
he needed not exult
in the falchions' intercourse ;
he of his kinsmen was bereft,
of his friends depriv'd,
on the trysting place,
in conflict slain ;
and his son he left
on the slaughter place,
mangled with wounds,
young in warfare.
Needed not boast
the grizzly lock'd warrior
of the bill-clashing,

---

[1] swát here, as often in poetry, signifies *blood*. In German, the blood of game is called schweiss, *sweat*.

[2] From the grindstone, on which they were sharpened. The reading of MS. D. (mycel scearpum) requires no comment.

[3] The form of Anlaf for Olaf in A.S. (O. Nor. Ólafr) seems quite unaccountable. Besides Anlaf, we find Onlaf and Unlaf. It has been supposed to have arisen from a clerical error of *n* for *u*, and that we should read Aulaf ; but this supposition will hardly apply to the reading Unlaf ; and even on his coins the name stands Anlaf.

tho old deceiver,
nor Olaf tho more,
with their armies' relics ;
they needed not to laugh
that they in works of war
the better were
206, 207. on tho battle-stead,
at tho rush of banners,
the meeting of javelins,
the tryst of men,
the clash of weapons,   [they
that on the field of slaughter
with Eadweard's
offspring play'd.
Departed then the Northmen
in their nail'd barks,
the darts' gory leaving,
on tho [1] roaring sea,
o'er the deep water,
Dublin to seek,
Ireland once more,
in mind abash'd.
Likewise tho brothers,
both together,
king and ætheling,
their country sought,
tho West Saxons' land,
in war exulting.

They left behind them,
the carcases to share,
with [2] pallid coat,
tho swart raven,
with horned neb,
and him of goodly coat,
[3] the eagle white behind,
the carrion to devour,
tho greedy war-hawk,
and that grey beast,
the wolf in the weald.
No slaughter has been greater
in this island
over yet
of folk laid low,
before this,
by the sword's edges,
from what books tolls us,
old chroniclers,   **208, 209.**
since hither from tho east
Angles and Saxons
came to land,
o'er the broad seas
Britain sought,
proud war-smiths,
tho Welsh o'ercame,
men for glory eager,
tho country gain'd.

---

[1] This rendering of "on dynges" "(dyniges) mere" is quite conjectural.

[2] The word 'pade' of the original is here taken as synonymous with the Goth. paida, Ohg. pheit, O. Sax. pêda. *coat, indusium.* ' Salowig 'pádan' is, I have no doubt, an apposition to hrá, as both salowig and sweart cannot well be said of tho raven, though 'salowig,' *pale,* well applies to a corpse. The following is offered as a freer version of the

lines :—*They left behind them the swart raven with horned neb, to share the pale-hued carcases ; and the white-tailed eagle with goodly plumage, the greedy war-hawk, and that grey beast, the wolf in the wood, the carrion to devour.*

[3] Grimm (Andr. and El. p. xvi.) proposes to read, earn æftan hwæt. cæses brúcan, *aquilam pone se escæ aliquid edere (siverunt).* The emendation seems hardly needed, or, indeed, admissible.

An. DCCCC.XXXVIII., DCCCC.XXXIX.

An. DCCCC.XL. In this year king Æthelstân died, at Gloucester, on the vith of the Kal. of November (Oct. 27th), forty-one winters, save one night, after king Ælfred died; and Eadmund ætheling, his brother, succeeded to the kingdom; and he was then eighteen winters old. And king Æthelstân reigned fourteen years and ten weeks. Wulfhelm was then archbishop in Kent.

An. DCCCC.XLI. In this year the Northumbrians belied their fealty oaths, and chose Olaf of Ireland for their king.

Here Eadmund king,	so Stamford eke,
of Angles lord,	and Derby,
of his kin (tribes) protector,	were erewhile Danish,
Mercia subdued,	under the Northmen,
dear deed-performer,	by need constrain'd,
as the ¹ Dore it bounds,	in heathens'
and Whitwell's gate,	captive bonds,
and Humber's river,	for a long space,
² broad ocean-stream.	until again releas'd them,
Five towns,	through his worthiness,
Leicester,	the warrior's refuge,
211. and Lincoln,	Eadward's offspring,
and Nottingham,	Eadmund king.

An. DCCCC.XLII. In this year ³ king Olaf died.

An. DCCCC.XLIII. In this year Olaf took Tamworth by storm, and great slaughter was made on either side; and the Danes had the victory, and led away great booty with them: there, during the pillage, was Wulfrûn taken. In this year king Eadmund beset king Olaf and archbishop Wulfstân

---

¹ The Dore would seem to be intended for the western boundary of Mercia, while Whitwell's gate and the mouth of the Humber are its southern and northern limits on the east coast.

² This line seems merely an apposition to the one immediately preceding it.

³ See H. Huntingdon and Sim. of Durham, a. 941. There were several chiefs of that name at this period: Anlaf the son of Guthferth, Anlaf the son of Sihtric, and Anlaf Cwiran, mentioned a. 949. --R.P. Ólaf Kvaran was king of Dublin. See Saga Ólafs Konúngs Tryggvasonar. I. p. 149, edit. 1825; also his Saga in Snorra Heimskr. cap. 33. Mention occurs of him also in the Annals of Ulster, aa. 944, 946.

in Leicester; and would have captured them, had it not been that they escaped out of the town by night. And after that, king Olaf gained king Eadmund's friendship; and king Eadmund then received king Olaf at baptism, and he royally gifted him. And in the same year, after a good long interval, he received king Ragnald at the bishop's hand. In this year king Eadmund delivered Glastonbury to St. Dûnstân, where he afterwards first became abbot.

212, 213.   An. DCCCCXLIV. In this year king Eadmund subdued all Northumberland into his power, and expelled two kings, Olaf son of Sihtric, and Ragnald son of Guthferth.

An. DCCCCXLV. In this year king Eadmund harried over all Cumberland, and gave it all up to Malcolm king of the Scots, on the condition, that he should be his co-operator both on sea and on land.

An. DCCCCXLVI. In this year king Eadmund died, on St. Augustine's mass-day (May 26th). It was widely known how he ended his days, that Liofa stabbed him at Pucklechurch. And Æthelfled at Domerham, daughter of the aldorman Ælfgar, was then his queen. And he had the kingdom six years and a half; and then after him, Eadred ætheling, his brother, succeeded to the kingdom, and reduced all Northumberland under his power: and the Scots gave him oaths, that they would all that he would.

An. DCCCCXLVII. In this year king Eadred came to Taddenes Seylf (Shelf), and there Wulfstân the archbishop and all the Northumbrian 'witan,' swore fealty to the king; and within a little space belied it all, both pledges and also oaths.

An. DCCCCXLVIII. In this year king Eadred harried over all Northumberland, because they had taken Eric for their king: and then in that harrying was the famous monastery at Ripon burnt, which St. Wilferth built. And when the king was homeward, the army within York overtook him: (the rear of the king's force was at Chesterford), and there made great slaughter. Then was the king so indignant, that he would again march in, and totally destroy the country. When the Northumbrian 'witan' understood that, they forsook Eric, and made compensation for the deed to king Eadred.

215.   An. DCCCCXLIX. In this year came Olaf Cwiran to Northumberland.

An. DCCCC.L.

An. DCCCC.LI. In this year died Ælfheah, bishop of Win-   214.
chester, on St. Gregory's mass-day (Mar. 12th).

An. DCCCC.LII. In this year king Eadred commanded archbishop Wulfstân to be brought into the fastness at Jedburgh,
because he had been often accused to the king. And in
this year also, the king commanded a great slaughter to be
made in the town of Thetford, in revenge for the abbot
Eadelm, whom they had before slain. In this year the Northumbrians expelled king Olaf, and received Eric, Harald's
son.

An. DCCCC.LIII.

An. DCCCC.LIV. In this year the Northumbrians expelled
Eric, and Eadred assumed the kingdom of the Northumbrians. In this year archbishop Wulfstân again received a
bishopric, at Dorchester.

An. DCCCC.LV. In this year died king Eadred, on St.
Clement's mass-day (Nov. 23rd) at Frome, and he rests in
the *Old monastery; and he reigned nine years and a half; * at Winchester.
¹ and then Eadwig ₔsucceeded to the kingdom, the son of
king Eadmund and St. Ælfgifu. And he drove St. Dûnstân
out of the land.

An. DCCCC.LVI.

An. DCCCC.LVII. In this year died archbishop Wulfstân of
York, on the XVIIth of the Kal. of January (Dec. 16th), and
he was buried at Oundle. And in the same year abbot Dûn-   217.
stân was driven away over sea. In this year Eadgar ætheling
succeeded to the kingdom of the Mercians.

An. DCCCC.LVIII. In this year archbishop * Oda separated * of Canterbury.
king Eadwig and Ælfgyfu, because they were too near akin.
In this year king Eadwig died, on the Kal. of October   216.
(Oct. 1st.); and Eadgar his brother succeeded to the king-

---

¹—and Eadwig succeeded to the kingdom of the West
Saxons, and Eadgar his brother succeeded to the kingdom of
the Mercians; and they were the sons of king Eadmund and
St. Ælfgifu.ᵃ

ᵃ D.F.

dom, as well of the West Saxons as of the Mercians, and of
the Northumbrians ; and he was then sixteen winters old.

In his days   and on God's law meditated
it prosper'd well,   oft and frequently,
and God him granted   and God's praise exalted   219.
that he dwelt in peace,   wide and far ;
the while that he lived ;   and wisely rul'd
and he did as him behoved,   oftenest ever constantly,
diligently earn'd it.   'fore God
He up-rear'd   and 'fore the world,
the praise of God widely,   all his people.
and God's law lov'd,   One misdeed he did
and the folk's peace better'd however too frequently,
the most of the kings   that he foreign
that were before him   vices lov'd,
in memory of men.   and heathen manners
And God him eke aided,   within this land
so that kings and earls   brought too fast,
willingly to him submitted,   and outlandish men
and became subject   hither enticed,
to that which he will'd ;   and pernicious people
and without contest,   allur'd to this country.
he govern'd all   But may God grant him,
that he himself will'd.   that his good deeds
He was widely among nations,   be more prevailing
greatly, honour'd,   than his misdeeds,
because he honour'd   for his soul's protection,
God's name zealously,   on the longsome journey.

218.   An. DCCCC.LIX. In this year Eadgar sent after St. Dûnstân,
and gave him the bishopric of Worcester ; and afterwards the
bishopric of London.

An. DCCCC.LX.

An. DCCCC.LXI. In this year died Oda, the good archbishop ;
and St. Dûnstân succeeded to the archbishopric.

An. DCCCC.LXII. In this year died Ælfgar, the king's kinsman, in Devon ; and his body rests at Wilton. And king
Sigferth killed himself, and his body lies at Wimborne. And
then within the year there was a great mortality, and the
220.   great fever was in London, and Paul's monastery was burnt,
and in the same year was again founded. In the same year

Athelmôd the mass-priest went to Rome, and there died, on the xviiith of the Kal. of September (Aug. 15th).

An. DCCCC.LXIII. In this year Wulfstân the deacon died on Childermas day (Dec. 28th) ; and after that died Gyric the mass-priest. In this same year, abbot Athelwold succeeded to the bishopric of Winchester, and he was hallowed on the vigil of St. Andrew (Nov. 29) : it was Sunday on that day.

An. DCCCC.LXIII. In this year Athelwold was chosen to the bishopric of Winchester by king Eadgar ; and the archbishop of Canterbury, St. Dûnstân, hallowed him on the first Sunday of Advent, that was on the IIIrd of the Kal. of December (Nov. 29th).[1] *

221.

[1] In the year after he was hallowed he made many monasteries, and drove the clerks out of the bishopric; because that they would not hold any rule, and set monks there. He made there two abbacies, one of monks, one of nuns ; all that was within Winchester. Then afterwards he came to king Eadgar, and besought him that he would give him all the monasteries which heathen men had before ruined ; because that he would restore them ; and the king blithely granted it. And the bishop then came first to Ely, where St. Ætheldrith lies, and caused the monastery to be made ; then gave it to one of his monks who was named Brihtnoth : then hallowed him abbot, and there set monks to serve God where whilom there were nuns. Then bought he many villages (cotlîf) of the king, and made it very rich. After that, bishop Athelwold came to the monastery that was called * Medeshâmstede, which whilom * Peterborough. was destroyed by heathen folk : there found he nothing but old walls and wild woods. Then found he, hidden in the old walls, writings that abbot Headda had erewhile written, how king Wulfhere and Æthelred his brother had built it, and how they had freed it against king, and against bishop, and against all secular service ; and how the pope Agatho had confirmed it by his writ, and the archbishop Deusdedit. He then caused the monastery to be wrought, and set there an abbot who was

* E.

222, 223.
* Winchester.

An. DCCCC.LXIV. In this year king Eadgar drove out the priests in the *city, from the Old monastery and from the New monastery, and from Chertsey, and from Milton (Middle-

---

called Aldulf; and placed monks there where before there was nothing. He then came to the king, and caused him to look at the writings which had before been found : and the king then answered and said : "I, Eadgar, grant and give to-day, before God and before the archbishop Dûnstân, freedom to St. Peter's monastery, Medeshamstede, from king and from bishop ; and all the villages which are thereto adjacent, viz., Eastfield, and Dosthrop, and Eye, and Paston. And so I free it, that no bishop have any command there, besides the abbot of the monastery. And I give the ¹ town which is called Oundle, with all that is thereto adjacent, that is, that which is called the Eight Hundreds, and market, and toll, so freely, that neither king, nor bishop, nor earl, nor shire-reeve have any command there, nor any one save the abbot only, and him whom he shall appoint thereto. And I give to Christ and St. Peter, and through the prayer of bishop Athelwold, those lands : that is, Barrow, Warmington, Ashton, Kettering, Castor, Eylesworth, Walton, Witrington, Eye, Thorp ; and one moneyer in Stamford. These lands and all the others that are adjacent to the monastery, these I declare ² clear, that is, (with) 'saca' and 'socn,' 'toll' and 'team,' and 'infangenthef.' These rights and all others I declare clear to Christ and St. Peter. And I give the two parts of Witlesmere, with waters, and with weirs, and fens, and so, through Merelade, direct to the water that is called Nen, and so eastward to King's delf (Knut's dike). And I will that there be a market in the same town, and that there be none other betwixt Stamford and Huntingdon. And I will that the toll be given thus : first from Witlesmere all to the king's toll of Norman's Cross hundred, and then back again from Witlesmere, through Merelade, at once to the Nen; and so as the water runs to Crowland, and from Crowland to Muston, and from Muston to

---

¹ It would seem that when this document was made, the word tún had assumed its present signification of *town*.
² i.e. without restriction or burthen.

ton), and planted them with monks ; and he set abbot Æthelgar for abbot to the New monastery, and Ordbriht to Chertsey, and Cyneward to Milton.

An. DCCCC.LXV. In this year king Eadgar took [1]Ælfthryth for his queen ; she was the daughter of the aldorman Ordgar.

King's delf, and to Witlesmere. And I will that all the immunities, and all the remissions that my predecessors have given, stand. And (this) I write and confirm with the sign of Christ's rood." ✚

Then answered Dûnstân, the archbishop of Canterbury, and said : "I consent to all the things which are here given and said ; and all the things which thy predecessors and mine have conceded, those will I that they stand : and whosoever shall violate this, then give I him the curse of God, and of all saints, and of all ordained heads, and of myself, unless he come to repentance. And I give, in acknowledgment to St. Peter, my mass-mantle, and my stole, and my robe, for the service of Christ." "I, Oswald, archbishop of York, assent to all these words, by the holy rood on which Christ suffered." ✚ "I, Athelwold bishop, bless all who hold this, and I excommunicate all who violate this, unless he come to repentance." Here were Ælfstân bishop, Athulf bishop, and Escwi abbot, and Osgar abbot, and Æthelgar abbot, and Ælfere aldorman, Æthelwine aldorman, Brihtnoth, Oslac aldorman, and many other great men : and all assented to it, and all signed it with Christ's cross. ✚ This was done after the birth of our Lord DCCCC.LXXII., the king's sixteenth year.

Then the abbot Aldulf bought much and many lands, and then largely endowed the monastery with all : and he was there so long as until the archbishop Oswald of York was dead, and then he was chosen for archbishop. And then forthwith another abbot was chosen of the same monastery, who was called Kênulf, who was afterwards bishop of Winchester. And he first made the walls about the monastery; then gave it for name 'Burch' (Borough), that was before called Medeshamstede. He was there so long as until he was appointed bishop of Winchester. Then another abbot was chosen of the

---

[1] The Elfrida of the Latin chroniclers.

An. DCCCC.LXVI. In this year Thored Gunnar's son harried Westmoreland. And in the same year Oslac obtained an aldordom.

An. DCCCC.LXVII.

An. DCCCC.LXVIII. In this year king Eadgar commanded all Thanet-land to be ravaged.

An. DCCCC.LXIX., DCCCC.LXX.

An. DCCCC.LXXI. In this year died archbishop Oskytel : he was first hallowed suffragan bishop of Dorchester, and afterwards, by favour of king Eadred and all his ' witan,' he was hallowed archbishop of York ; and he was twenty-two winters bishop, and he died on All-Hallows mass-night (Nov. 1st), ten nights before Martinmas, at Thame ; and abbot Thurkytel, his kinsman, conveyed the bishop's body to Bedford ; because he was then at that time abbot there.

224.

225.

An. DCCCC.LXXII. (DCCCC.LXX.) In this year died Eadmund ætheling, and his body lies at Rumsey.

An. DCCCC.LXXIII.

This year was Eadgar,	hallow'd king,
of Angles ruler,	in the old town
in a great assembly,	Akemansceaster ;

same monastery, who was called Ælfsi. Ælfsi was then abbot fifty winters from that time. He took up St. Kyneburh and St. Kyneswith, who lay at Castor, and St. Tibba, who lay at Ryhall, and brought them to Burch, and offered them all to St. Peter in one day, and held it the while that he was there.[a]

An. DCCCC.LXXII. In this year Eadgar ætheling was hallowed king, on the mass-day of Pentecost, on the vth of the Ides of May (May 11th) in the thirteenth year that he succeeded to the kingdom, at the Hot-baths, (that is, at Bath) ; and he was then thirty years old, wanting one. And forthwith after that, the king led all his naval force to Chester ; and there came to meet him [1] six kings, and all swore fealty to him, that they would be his co-operators by sea and by land.[b]

---

[1] Eight, according to Florence, (A. 973), who gives their names; so also Malmesbury, Wendover, &c.

---

[a] E., and a Latin copy in Cod. Diplom. III. p. 92. | [b] D. E. F.

also it the islanders,
by another word,
men, name Bath.
There was great bliss,
on that happy day,
fall'n upon all,
which children of men
name and call
Pentecost's day.
There was of priests a throng,
a great band of monks,
as I have heard,
of sages, gather'd ;
and was then agone
ten hundred winters,
in number counted,
from the birth-tide

An. DCCCC.LXXIV.

An. DCCCC.LXXV.

Here ended
the joys of earth
Eadgar of Angles king,
chose him another light,
beauteous and winsome,
and left this frail,
this perishable, life.
Children of people name,
men on earth,
the month everywhere
in this land,
those who erewhile were
in the art of numbers
rightly instructed,
July month,
when departed,
on the eighth day,

of the glorious King,
light's Guardian,
save that there yet remaining
was of winter-number,   226.
from what writings say,
seven and twenty ;
so nigh of the victor Lord was
a thousand run out,
when this befel ;
and himself, Eadmund's
offspring, had
nine and twenty
(stern against works of evil)
years in the world,
when this took place, .
and then, in the thirtieth, was
sovereign hallow'd.

the young Eadgar from life,
¹ ring-giver of men ;
and then his child succeeded
to the kingdom,
a babe ungrown,
prince of earls,
whose name was Eadweard.
And a glorious man,
ten nights before,   228.
from Britain departed,
the * bishop good   * of Wells.
through natural virtue,
whose name was Cyneweard.
Then was in Mercia,
as I have heard,
widely and everywhere,
the Supreme Ruler's praise

¹ See page 86, *note* ².

laid low on earth;
many were driven away
of God's sage servants:
that was a great affliction,
to him who in his breast bare
a burning love
of the Creator in his mind.
Then the Source of marvels
too greatly was despis'd,
the Lord of victories,
Ruler of the skies,
when his right was violated;
and then was eke driven away
the beloved hero
Oslac from the land,
over the billows' roll,
over the gannet's bath,
hoary-lock'd hero,
wise and eloquent,
over the waters' throng,

o'er the whale's country,
of home bereft.
And then appear'd,
up in the skies,
a star in its station,
which strong-soul'd
men, sage-minded,
widely call
comet by name,
men skill'd in arts,
wise interpreters.
Throughout mankind was
the Ruler's vengeance
widely proclaim'd,
famine o'er the earth :
that again heaven's guardian,
Lord of angels, better'd,
gave again bliss,
to each isle-dweller
through the fruits of earth.

230.

227.   An. DCCCC.LXXV. The VIIIth of the Ides of July (July 8th).

This year died Eadgar,
of Angles ruler,
West Saxons' friend,
and Mercians' protector.
Widely was it known,
through many nations,
that Eadmund's offspring,
over the gannet's bath,
kings remote

greatly honoured,
to the king submitted,
as to him was fitting.
Was no fleet so insolent,
no host so strong,
that in the Angle race
took from him aught,
the while the noble king
rul'd on the royal seat.[a]

An. DCCCC.LXXV. In this year king Eadgar died, and Eadward his son succeeded to the kingdom. And in this same year, in autumn, the star cometa appeared ; and in the

[a] D. E.

An. DCCCC.LXXVI. Here in this year was the great famine in England.

An. DCCCC.LXXVII. Here was the great mote at Kyrtlington, after Easter (April 8th) ; and there died bishop Sideman, by sudden death, on the IInd of the Kal. of May (April 30th). He was bishop of Devonshire, and he desired that his body's resting-place might be at Crediton, at his episcopal see. Then commanded king Eadweard and archbishop Dûnstân that he should be conveyed to St. Mary's monastery that is at Abingdon, and so it was also done ; and he is also honourably buried on the north side, in St. Paul's porch.[1]

An. DCCCC.LXXVIII. In this year all the chief 'witan' of the Angle race fell at Calne from an [2]upper floor, except the holy archbishop Dûnstân, who alone was stayed upon a beam ; and some there were sorely maimed, and some did not escape with life.   231.

---

following year came a very great famine, and very many   229.
troubles over the Angle race.[a] And Ælfhere commanded the monasteries to be demolished, which king Eadgar had before commanded the holy bishop Æthelwold to found. And at that time also was Oslac the great earl expelled from England.[b]

In his days,	whom Eadgar king ere order'd
for his youth,	the holy bishop
God's adversaries	Æthelwold to establish.
God's law brake ;	And widows plunder'd,
Ælfhere aldorman,	oft and frequently,
and others many,	and many wrongs,
and monkish rule obstructed,	and evil, lawless deeds,
and monasteries destroy'd,	afterwards arose :
and monks expel'd,	and ever afterwards
and God's servants persecuted,	it greatly grew in evil.[a]

---

[1] Here ends MS. Cott. Tiber. A. VI.   [2] " de solario corruerunt." Flor. Wigorn.

---

[a] D. E.   [b] D. E. F.

G 2

232, 233.   An. DCCCC.LXXVIII. (DCCCC.LXXIX.) In this year king Eadweard was slain [martyred], and Æthelred ætheling, his brother, succeeded to the kingdom ; and in the same year he was hallowed king. In that year died bishop Alfwold, who

* Sherborne.   was bishop of *Dorset, and his body lies in the monastery at Sherborne.

An. DCCCC.LXXIX. In this year king Eadweard was slain at eventide, at Corfe-gate, on the xvth of the Kal. of April (Mar. 18th), and then was buried at Wareham, without any kingly honour. To the Angle race was no worse deed done than this was, since they first sought Britain. Men murdered him, but God him glorified. He was in life an earthly king ; he is now, after death, a heavenly saint. Him his earthly kinsmen would not avenge, but his heavenly Father has amply avenged him. The earthly murderers would his memory blot out on earth ; but the Avenger above has spread abroad his memory in the heavens and on earth. They who before

234, 235.   would not to his living body bow, now humbly bend on their knees to his dead bones. Now may we understand, that men's wisdom, and their machinations, and their counsels, are like naught against God's decree. Then Æthelred succeeded to the kingdom ; and he was after that, very quickly, with great joy of the 'witan' of the Angle race, hallowed king at Kingston.[a]

Then were past from the birth of Christ four hundred and ninety-four winters, when Cerdic and Cynric his son arrived at Cerdices ora with five ships ; and Cerdic was son of Elesa, Elesa of Esla, Esla of Giwis, Giwis of Wig, Wig of Freawine, Freawine of Freothogar, Freothogar of Brand, Brand of Bældæg, Bældæg of Woden. And six years after their arrival, they subdued the West Saxons' land ; and they were the first kings that took the West Saxons' land from the Welsh ; and he had the kingdom sixteen winters. Then he departed, and his son Cynric succeeded to the kingdom, and held it twenty-six winters. When he departed, Ceawlin his son succeeded, and held it seventeen years. When he departed, Ceol succeeded to the kingdom, and held it five years. When he

---

* D. E. F.

An. DCCCC.LXXIX. In this year Æthelred was hallowed king at Kingston, on the Sunday, fourteen nights after Easter (Mar. 28th); and there were at his hallowing two archbishops, and ten suffragan bishops. In the same year was seen oftentimes a bloody cloud, in likeness of fire ; and that was most apparent at midnight ; and was coloured in various rays. Then when it was about to dawn, it glided away.

---

departed, Ceolwulf his brother succeeded, and reigned seventeen years ; and their kin goes to Cerdic. Then Cynegils, Ceolwulf's brother's son, succeeded to the kingdom, and reigned twenty winters ; and he first of the West Saxons' kings received baptism. And then Cênwalh succeeded, and held it thirty-one winters. Cênwalh was son of Cynegils. And then queen Sexburh held the kingdom one year after him. Then Æscwine succeeded to the kingdom, whose kin goes to Cerdic, and held it two years. Then Centwine son of Cynegils succeeded to the West Saxons' kingdom, and reigned nine years. Then Ceadwalla succeeded to the kingdom, whose kin goes to Cerdic, and held it three years. Then Ine succeeded to the West Saxons' kingdom, whose kin goes to Cerdic, and held it thirty-seven winters. Then Æthelheard succeeded, whose kin goes to Cerdic, and held it sixteen years. Then Cuthred succeeded, whose kin goes to Cerdic, and held it seventeen winters. Then Sigebriht succeeded, whose kin goes to Cerdic, and held it one year. Then Cynewulf succeeded, whose kin goes to Cerdic, and held it thirty-one winters. Then Brihtric succeeded to the kingdom, whose kin goes to Cerdic, and held it sixteen years. Then Ecgbriht succeeded to the kingdom, and held it thirty-seven winters and seven months. Then Æthelwulf his son succeeded, and held it eighteen years and a half. Æthelwulf was son of Ecgbriht, Ecgbriht of Ealhmund, Ealhmund of Eafa, Eafa of Eoppa, Eoppa of Ingild, Ingild of Cênred. And Ine [was] son of Cenred, and Cuthburh and Cwenburh [were] daughters of Cênred. Cênred [was] son of Ceolwald, Ceolwald of Cuthwulf, Cuthwulf of Cuthwine, Cuthwine of Celm, Celm of Cynric, Cynric of Creoda, Creoda of Cerdic. And then Æthelbald his son succeeded, and held it five years. Then Æthelbriht his brother succeeded, and held it five years,

* of the New Monastery.

An. DCCCC.LXXX. In this year *abbot Æthelgar was hallowed bishop, on the VIth of the Nones of May (May 2nd), of the episcopal see of Selsey. And in the same year Southampton was ravaged by a naval force, and most of the townsfolk slain or captured. And in the same year Thanet-land was ravaged. And in the same year Cheshire was ravaged by a North naval force. In this year St. Dûnstân and the alderman Alf'here fetched the body of the holy king St. Eadweard from Wareham, and conveyed it with great honour to Shaftesbury.

An. DCCCC.LXXXI. In this year was Padstow ravaged; and in the same year great harm was done everywhere by the sea-coast, both in Devonshire and in Wales. And in the same year died [1]Ælfstân, bishop of Wiltshire, and his body lies in the monastery at Abingdon; and Wulfgar then succeeded to the bishopric. And in the same year died *abbot Womær at Ghent.

* of St. Peter's.

[Then Æthered his brother succeeded to the kingdom and held it five years.] Then Ælfred their brother succeeded to [the kingdom; and then had passed three-and-twenty winters of his age, and three hundred and ninety-six winters from the time that his kin first subdued the West Saxons' land in Britain;] and held it a year and a half less than thirty winters. Then succeeded Eadweard son of Ælfred, and held it thirty-four years. When he departed, Æthelstân his son succeeded, and held it fourteen years, and seven weeks, and three days. Then Eadmund his brother succeeded, and held it six years and a half, less two nights. Then Eadred his brother succeeded, and held it nine years and six weeks. Then Eadwig, son of king Eadmund, succeeded, and held it three years and thirty-six weeks, less two days. When he departed, his brother Eadgar succeeded, and held it sixteen years, and eight weeks, and two nights. When he departed, Eadweard, Eadgar's son, succeeded, and held   *   *   *   *ᵃ

---

[1] See Flor. Wigorn. I. p. 147, *note.*

ᵃ MS. Cott. Tiber. A. III.

An. DCCCC.LXXXII. In this year arrived in Dorsetshire three ships of vikings, and ravaged in Portland. In the same year London was burnt ; and in the same year died two aldormen, Æthelmær in Hampshire, and Eadwine in Sussex ; and Æthelmær's body lies in the New Monastery at Winchester, and Eadwine's in the monastery at Abingdon. In the same year died two abbesses in Dorsetshire, Herclufu at Shaftesbury, and Wulfwin at Wareham. And in the same year Otho, emperor of the Romans, went to Greece ; and then met he a great army of the Saracens coming up from the sea, and would go on a plundering expedition upon the Christian folk. And then the emperor fought against them, and there was a great slaughter made on each side, and the emperor had possession of the place of carnage ; and nevertheless he was greatly exhausted before he departed thence ; and as he homeward went, his brother's son died, who was called Otho ; and he was son of Liudolf the ætheling ; and Liudolf was son of the old Otho and of the daughter of king * Eadweard.

236, 237.

* the Elder.

An. DCCCC.LXXXIII. In this year died Ælfhere aldorman, and Ælfric succeeded to the same * aldormanship. And pope Benedict died.

* of Mercia.

An. DCCCC.LXXXIV. In this year died Æthelwold, the benevolent bishop of Winchester, father of monks, on the Kal. of August (Aug. 1st) ; and the hallowing of the following bishop, Ælfheah, who by another name was called Godwine, was on the XIIIIth of the Kal. of November (Oct. 19th) ; and he took possession of the episcopal chair at Winchester, on the mass-day of the two apostles Simon and Jude.

An. DCCCC.LXXXV. In this year Ælfric aldorman was driven from the country. And in the same year Eadwine was hallowed abbot of the monastery at Abingdon.

238, 239.

An. DCCCC.LXXXVI. In this year the king laid waste the bishopric of Rochester. In this year first came the great murrain among the cattle into England.

An. DCCCC.LXXXVII.

An. DCCCC.LXXXVIII. In this year Watchet was ravaged, and Goda, the Devonshire thane, slain, and with him great slaughter made. And in this year died the holy archbishop Dûnstân, and passed to the heavenly life ; and after him * bishop Æthelgar succeeded to the archiepiscopal chair ; and a little while afterwards lived, only one year and three months.

* of Selsey.

An. DCCCC.LXXXIX.

An. DCCCC.XC. In this year Sigeric was hallowed *archbishop, and afterwards went to Rome after his pall. And *abbot Eadwine died, and abbot Wulfgar succeeded to the dignity.

An. DCCCC.XCI. In this year Ipswich was sacked ; and very speedily after that, the aldorman Brihtnoth was slain at Maldon. And in that year it was first decreed that tribute should be paid to the Danish men, on account of the great terror which they caused by the sea-coast : that was at first ten thousand pounds. That counsel first advised archbishop Sigeric.

An. DCCCC.XCII. In this year the holy *archbishop Oswald left this, and passed to the heavenly, life ; and the aldorman Æthelwine died in the same year. Then the king and all his ' witan' decreed, that all the ships that were of any worth should be gathered at London. And the king then committed the leading of the force to the aldorman Ælfric and to the
earl Thored, to *bishop Ælfstân, and to † bishop Æscwig ; and they were to try whether they might anywhere abroad entrap the army. Then sent the aldorman Ælfric, and bade the army take warning ; and then in the night when they should have encountered in the day, he departed by night from the force, to his great disgrace ; and the army then escaped, except one ship, the crew of which was there slain. And then the army met the ships from East Anglia, and from London, and they there made a great slaughter, and took the ship, all armed and equipped, in which the aldorman had been.

An. DCCCC.XCII. In this year died the blessed archbishop
Oswald, and *abbot Eadulf succeeded to York and to Worcester. And in this year the king and all his ' witan' decreed that all the ships which were of any worth should be gathered at London, in order that it might be tried whether they might anywhere without entrap the army. But the aldorman Ælfric, one of those in whom the king had the greatest trust, bade the army take warning, and in the night, when on the morrow they should have engaged, the self-same Ælfric fled from the force, and the army then escaped.ª

---

* F.

And then, after the death of archbishop Oswald, abbot Ealdulf of Peterborough succeeded to the see of York, and to that of Worcester ; and Kênulf to the abbacy at Peterborough.

An. DCCCC.XCIII. In this year Bamborough was stormed, and a great booty there taken. And after that the army came to the mouth of the Humber, and there wrought great evil, both in Lindsey and in Northumbria. Then a very great force was gathered ; and when they should have engaged, then the leaders the first took to flight : they were Frœna, and God-wine, and Frythegyst. In this year the king commanded Ælfgar, son of the alderman Ælfric, to be blinded.

An. DCCCC.XCIV. In this year came [1]Olaf (Anlaf) and [2]Svein to London, on the Nativity of St. Mary (Sept. 8th), with ninety-four ships, and then they were obstinately fighting against the town, and would also have set it on fire. But they there sustained more harm and evil than they ever weened that any townsmen could do to them. For the holy mother of God, on that day, manifested her mercy to the townsmen, and delivered them from their foes. And they then went thence, and wrought the greatest evil that ever any army could do, in burning, and harrying, and in man-slayings, as well by the sea-coast, as in Essex, and in Kent,

242, 243.

An. DCCCC.XCIII. [3]In this year came [1]Olaf with ninety-three ships to Staines, and harried without it ; and then went thence to Sandwich, and so thence to Ipswich, and ravaged all over it ; and so to Maldon ; and the alderman Brihtnoth came against him with his force, and fought against him ; and they there slew the alderman, and had possession of the place of carnage. And after that, peace was made with him ; and the king afterwards received him at the bishop's hand, through the instruction of Sigeric, bishop of the Kentish people, and Ælfheah of Winchester.[a]

---

[1] Olaf Tryggvason, king of Norway.
[2] King of Denmark, and father of Cnut.

[3] The events here noticed belong to the years 991 and 994 of the text.—R.P.

---

[a] A.

and in Sussex, and in Hampshire. And at last they took them horses, and rode as far as they would, and were doing unspeakable evil. Then the king and his 'witan' resolved that they should be sent to, and promised tribute and food, provided that they would cease from ravaging; and they then accepted that. And all the army then came to Southampton, and there took winter-quarters; and there they were fed from all the realm of the West Saxons, and they were paid sixteen thousand pounds of money. Then the king sent bishop Ælfheah and the aldorman Æthelweard after king Olaf; and the while hostages were given to the ships; and they then led Olaf with great worship to the king at Andover. And king Æthelred received him at the bishop's hand, and royally gifted him. And Olaf then promised him, as he also fulfilled, that he would never again come with hostility to England.

An. DCCCC.XCV. In this year appeared cometa the star; and
* of Canterbury. * archbishop Sigeric died; and Ælfric, bishop of Wiltshire, was chosen on Easter day (Apr. 21st) by king Æthelred and by all his 'witan.' This Ælfric was a very wise man, so that there was no more sagacious man in England. Then went Ælfric to his archiepiscopal see, and when he came thither, he was received by those men in orders, who of all were most distasteful to him, that was, by clerks.[1]

---

[1] And forthwith he sent for all the wisest men that he anywhere knew of, and in like manner, the old men, who were able to say the truest how everything was in this land in the days of their forefathers, besides what he himself had learned in books and from wise men. Very old men then told him, both ecclesiastical and lay, that their parents had told them how it had been by law established, soon after St. Augustine came to this land. "When Augustine had obtained the episco-
* Canterbury.
* Beda, 1. 26. pal see in the * town, then he was archbishop over all king Æthelberht's kingdom, as is read in * Historia Anglorum . . . . . make a see by the king's aid in . . . . . was begun by the old Romans, and to sprout forth. In that company the foremost were Mellitus, Justus, Paulinus, Rufianus. By these the blessed pope sent a pall, and therewith a letter, and direc- 'ion how he should hallow a bishop, and in which places in

An. DCCCC.XCVI. In this year Ælfric was hallowed arch-   244, 245.
bishop at Christchurch.   In this year Wulfstân was ordained
bishop of London.

An. DCCCC.XCVII.   In this year the army went about Devon-   246, 247.
shire into the mouth of the Severn, and there harried, as well
in Cornwall as in North Wales and in Devonshire ; and then
landed at Watchet, and there wrought great evil in burning
and in man-slayings ; and after that returned round the Land's
End, on the south side, and wended into the mouth of the
Tamar, and then went up until they came to Lidford, and
burnt and slew everything they found ; and burned Ordulf's
monastery at Tavistock, and brought unspeakable booty with
them to their ships.   In this year archbishop Ælfric went to
Rome after his arch-pall.

Britain he should set them.   And to the king . . . he sent
letters and many temporal gifts of various things.   And the
churches which they had prepared he ordered to be hallowed
in the name of our Lord Jesus Christ and St. Mary ; and for
himself and all his after-followers he should there fix a
dwelling-place ; and that he should place therein men of the
same order that he had sent to the land thither, and of which
he himself was; and also that each . . . . man of monkish order who should occupy the archiepiscopal chair at
Canterbury ; and that should be ever observed by God's leave
and blessing, and by St. Peter's, and by all theirs who come after
him.   When this deputation came again to king Æthelberht
and to Augustine, they were very joyful through such indica-
tion.   And the archbishop then hallowed the monastery in the
name of Christ and St. Mary, on the day which is called the
mass-day of the two martyrs, Primus and Felicianus (Jun. 9th),
and therein placed monks, all as St. Gregory commanded.
And they performed God's service purely ; and from the same
monks were taken bishops for every . . . . as thou
mayest read in * Historia Anglorum."   Then was archbishop * Beda, II. 3.
Ælfric very joyful that he had so many witnesses who stood
best at that time with the king.   Besides, the same ' witan,'
who were with the archbishop, said : "Thus also we . . . . . .
have continued monks at Christ-church, in Augustine's day,
and in Laurentius', Mellitus', Justus', Honorius', Deusdedit's,

An. DCCCC.XCVIII. In this year the army again wended east-ward into the mouth of the Frome, and everywhere there went up as far as they would into Dorsetshire. And a great force was often gathered against them ; but as soon as they should come together, then was there ever, through something, flight determined on ; and in the end they ever had the victory. And then another while they quartered themselves in Wight, and provisioned themselves the while from Hampshire and from Sussex.

248, 249.

Theodore's, Brihtwold's, Tatwine's, Nothelm's, Cuthberht's, Bregwine's, Ianberht's, ... Æthelheard's, Wulfred's, Felo-gild's. But the (first) year, when Ceolnoth came to the arch-bishopric, there was such a mortality, that in Christchurch there remained but five monks. In all his time there was strife and sorrow in this land, so that no man could think about anything but . . . . . Now, thanks to God, it is in this king's power, and in thine, whether they may longer be there within ; because they might never better be brought thereout than they may now be, if it be the king's will and thine." The archbishop then, without any letting, went with these men anon to the king, and made known to him all as we have here before told. Then was the king very joyful at this tiding, and said to the archbishop and to the others : "It seems to me advisable that thou first of all things shouldst go to Rome after thy [pall, and] that thou make known all this to the pope ; and afterwards proceed by his counsel." And they all answered, that that was the best counsel. When (the clerks) heard this, they advised that they should take two from themselves and send to the pope, and should offer him great treasure and silver, on condition that he should give them the arch-pall. But when they came to Rome,. the pope would not do that, because they had brought no letter, either from the king or from the people, and commanded them to go where they would. As (soon) as the clerks had gone thence, came the archbishop Ælfric to Rome, and the pope received him with great worship, and commanded him on the morrow to celebrate mass at St. Peter's altar ; and the pope himself put on him his own pall, and greatly honoured him. When this was done, the archbishop began to tell the pope all about the clerks, how it had fared, and how they were within the

An. DCCCC.XCIX. In this year the army again came about into the Thames, and then went up along the Medway, and to Rochester. And then the Kentish force came against them, and they stoutly engaged together, but alas! that they too quickly gave way and fled ; because they had not the support which they should have had. And the Danish had possession of the place of carnage ; and then took horses and rode whithersoever they themselves would, and ruined and plundered almost all the West Kentish. Then the king with his ' witan' resolved that they should be opposed with a naval force, and also with a land force. But when the ships were ready, then they delayed from day to day, and harassed the poor people who lay in the ships ; and ever as it should be forwarder, so was it later, from one time to another ; and ever they let their foes' army increase, and ever they receded from the sea, and ever they went forth after them. And then in the end neither the naval force nor the land force was productive of anything but the people's distress, and a waste of money, and the emboldening of their foes.

monastery at his archbishopric. And the pope in return related to him how the priests had come to him, and offered great treasure, on condition that he would give them the pall. " But," said the pope, " go now to England again, with God's blessing, and St. Peter's, and mine, and when thou comest home, put into thy monastery men of that order which the blessed Gregory commanded Augustine therein to place, by God's command, and St. Peter's, and mine." The archbishop then with this returned to England. As soon as he came home, he occupied his archiepiscopal chair, and afterwards went to the (king) : and the king and all his people thanked God for his return, and that he had so succeeded as was most pleasing to all. He then went again to Canterbury, and drove the clerks out of the monastery, and therein placed monks, all as the pope had commanded him.[a][1]

---

[1] For the Latin of the foregoing, see vol. I. p. 245.

---

[a] F.

An. M. In this year the king went to Cumberland, and ravaged it very nigh all. And his ships went out about Chester, and should have come to meet him, but they could not : they then ravaged Man. And the hostile fleet was this summer gone to * Richard's dominions.

* Normandy.

An. M.I. In this year the army came to the mouth of the Ex, and then went up to the town, and were there stoutly fighting ; but they were very firmly and boldly withstood. They then went over the land, and did as was their wont, slew and burned. Then was collected an immense force of the Devonshire people, and of the Somersetshire people; and they then came together at Penhoe. And as soon as they came together the people gave ground ; and they there made great slaughter, and then rode over the land : and ever was their last incursion worse than the preceding ; and they then brought great booty with them to their ships. And thence they went to Wight, and there went about as they themselves would ; and nothing withstood them ; nor durst approach them a naval force by sea, nor a land force, went they ever so far up. It was then in every wise sad, because they never ceased from their evil.[1]

250, 251.

---

[1] An. M.I. In this year there was much hostility in the land of the Angle race through the naval force, and everywhere they harried and burned, so that in one course they went forward until they came to Æthelinga dene (Alton ?) ; and then came there against them the men of Hampshire, and fought against them. And there were Æthelweard the king's high reeve slain, and Leofric of Whitchurch, and Leofwine the king's high reeve, and Wulfhere the bishop's thane, and Godwine of Worthy, bishop Ælfsige's son, and of all the men one and eighty ; and of the Danish many more were slain, though they had possession of the place of carnage. And then they went thence west until they came to Devonshire, and there came Pallig to meet them with the ships that he could gather ; because he had fled from king Æthelred, against all the assurances which he had given him : and the king had also well gifted him with vills, and with gold and silver. And they burned Teignton, and also many other good vills which we cannot name ; and peace was afterwards there made with

An. M.II. In this year the king and his 'witan' resolved that tribute should be paid to the fleet, and peace made with them, on condition that they should cease from their evil. Then the king sent the aldorman Leofsige to the fleet, and he, according to the word of the king and his 'witan,' settled a peace with them, and that they should receive food and tribute. And that they then accepted, and were then paid twenty-four thousand pounds. Then in the meanwhile the 252, 253. aldorman Leofsige slew Æfic the king's high reeve, and the king banished him from the country. And then in the same autumn came the lady, *Richard's daughter, Emma Ælfgifu, *count of Normandy. hither to land; and in the same summer* archbishop Ealdulf *of York. died. And in that year the king commanded all the Danish men who were in England to be slain. This was done on the mass-day of St. Bricius; because it had been made known to the king, that they would plot against his life, and afterwards those of all his 'witan;' and then have his realm without any gainsaying.

An. M.III. In this year Exeter was taken by storm, through the French *count Hugo, whom the †lady had appointed her *comes, Fl. reeve; and the army then totally ruined the town, and took Wigorn. great booty there. And in the same year the army went up +Emma. into Wiltshire. Then was gathered a very large force from

them. And then they went thence to the mouth of the Ex, so that they went up, in one course, until they came to Penhoe; and there were Kola the king's high reeve, and Eadsige the king's reeve, opposed to them with the force which they could gather: and they were there put to flight, and many were there slain, and the Danish had possession of the place of carnage. And the morning they burned the vill at Penhoe and at Clist, and also many good vills which we cannot name; and then went again eastward, until they came to Wight; and the morning after, they burned the vill at Waltham, and many other hamlets; and soon after this they were treated with and made peace.ᵃ

ᵃ A. W.

Wiltshire and from Hampshire, and very unanimously marched towards the army.   Then should the aldorman Ælfric have led the force ; but he drew forth his old artifices ; as soon as they were so near that one army could look on the other, he feigned himself sick, and began retching to vomit, and said that he was sick, and so turned back (deceived) the people that he should have led ; as it is said : ' When the leader is faint-hearted, there will all the army be greatly hindered.' When Svein saw that they were not unanimous, and that they all dispersed themselves, he led his army to Wilton, and they plundered and burned the town ; and he went thence to Sarum, and thence again went to the sea, where he knew his wave-horses were.

An. M.IV. In this year Svein came with his fleet to Norwich, and plundered and burned all that town.   Then Ulfkytel

254, 255.

with the ' witan ' of East Anglia resolved, that it were better that peace should be purchased of the army, before they did over much harm in the country ; because they had come unawares, and he had not had time that he might gather his force.   Then during the peace which should have been between them, the army stole up from their ships, and wended their way to Thetford.   When Ulfkytel perceived that, he sent to have the ships hewn in pieces ; but they whom he trusted in failed him, and he then secretly gathered his force, as he best might.   And the army then came to Thetford within three weeks from the time of their having before plundered Norwich, and were one night there within, and plundered and burned the town.   And then in the morning, when they would go to their ships, came Ulfkytel with his army, that they might there engage together ; and they there together stoutly engaged, and a great slaughter was made on each side.   There were the chief of the East Angles' folk slain ; but if the full power had been there, they would never again have gone to their ships ; as they themselves said, that they never met with a worse hand-play in England than Ulfkytel had brought them.

An. M.V. In this year was the great famine throughout England, such that no man ever before remembered one so destructive.   And the fleet went this year from this country to Denmark, and let be but a little space until it came again.

An. M.VI. In this year died *archbishop Ælfric, and after him Ælfheah succeeded to the archbishopric, and bishop Brihtwold succeeded to the *bishopric of Wiltshire. And in the same year from Wulfgeat was all his property taken ; and Wulfeah and Ufegeat were blinded, and the aldorman Ælfelm was slain ; and *bishop Kênulf died. And then after Midsummer came the great fleet to Sandwich, and did all as was before their wont, harried, and burned, and slew as they went. Then the king commanded all the population of Wessex and of Mercia to be called out ; and they then lay all the autumn in readiness against the army ; but it came to naught more than it had often done before. But for all this the army went as itself would ; and the armament did every harm to the country people ; so that neither did good to them, neither the in-army nor the out-army. When winter drew nigh, the force went home, and the army then came after St. Martin's mass (Nov. 11th) to their asylum in Wiht, and procured everywhere there what they required. And then at Midwinter they went to their ready quarters, out through Hampshire into Berkshire to Reading : and they did according to their old wont, kindled their war-beacons as they went. They then went to Wallingford, and burned it all down ; and were then one night at Cholsey, and then went along Ashdown to Cwichelms hlæw (Cuckamsley hill), and there tarried out of threatening vaunt, because it had often been said, if they came to Cwichelms hlæw, they would never go to the sea. They then went home by another way. A force was then assembled at Kennet, and they there engaged together, and they soon brought that army to flight, and then conveyed their booty to the sea. But there might the people of Winchester see an insolent and fearless army, as they went by their gate to the sea, and fetched them food and treasures over fifty miles from the sea. The king had then gone over the Thames into Shropshire, and there taken his abode in the Midwinter's tide. Then was there so great awe of the army, that no one could think or devise how they should be driven from the country, or this

*of Canterbury.

* Sherborne.

256, 257.

*of Winton.

258, 259.

An. M.VI. In this year Ælfheah was hallowed archbishop.ᵃ

ᵃ A.

country held against them ; because they had cruelly marked every shire in Wessex with burning and with harrying. The king then began with his 'witan' earnestly to consider what might seem most advisable to them all, so that this country might be protected, ere it was totally fordone. The king then and his 'witan' decreed, for the behoof of all the nation, although it was hateful to them all, that they must of necessity pay tribute to the army. Then the king sent to the army, and commanded it to be made known to them, that he desired that there should be peace between them, and that tribute should be paid, and food given them. And they then accepted all that; and then they were provisioned from throughout the English nation.

An. M.VII. In this year the tribute was paid to the army : that was six and thirty thousand pounds. In this year also was Eadric set as aldorman over the Mercians' kingdom. In this year bishop Ælfeah went to Rome after his pall.

An. M.VIII. In this year the king commanded that ships should be strenuously built over all England : that is to wit, from three hundred and ten hides one [1] long ship ; and from eight hides, a helmet and corselet.

An. M.IX. In this year the ships, about which we before spoke, were ready ; and there were so many of them as never before, from what books tell us, had been in England in any king's day. And they were all brought together at Sandwich, and were there to lie and hold this country against every foreign army. But we had not yet the happiness nor the honour, that the naval force should be useful to this country, more than it had often before been. It befel then, at this same time, or a little before, that Brihtric, the aldorman Eadric's brother, accused Wulfnoth child, the South Saxon, father of earl Godwine, to the king ; and he (Wulfnoth) then went out, and enticed ships to him, until he had twenty ; and he then ravaged everywhere by the south coast, and wrought every kind of evil. Then it was made known to the naval force, that they might easily be surrounded, if they would go about it. Then Brihtric took to him eighty ships, and

260, 261.

---

[1] Sceg%. (O.N. skéi%), " navigii longioris quoddam genus velocis vete-
" rum." Bj. Haldorsen, Lex. Isl.

thought that he should make himself much talked of, that he should get Wulfnoth alive or dead. But as they were thitherward, such a wind came against them as no man before remembered, and beat and thrashed all the ships to pieces, and cast them upon the land ; and immediately came Wulfnoth and burned the ships. When this was thus known to the other ships where the king was, how the others had fared, it was as if all counsel was at an end, and the king, and the aldormen, and the high 'witan' went home, and thus lightly left the ships ; and the people then that were in the ships brought the ships again to London ; and they let the toil of all the nation thus lightly perish ; nor was the victory better, for which all the Angle race had hoped. When this naval force had thus ended, then soon after Lammas (Aug. 1st) came the immense hostile army, which we have called Thorkell's army, to Sandwich, and soon went their way to Canterbury, and would soon have subdued the town, if they the more speedily had not craved peace of them. And all the East Kentish made peace with the army, and gave them three thousand pounds. And then, soon after that, the army went until it came to Wight ; and thence everywhere in Sussex, and in Hampshire, and also in Berkshire, harried and burned, as is their wont. Then the king commanded all the nation to be called out, that they might be resisted on every side ; but lo ! they went, nevertheless, how they would. Then on one occasion the king had got before them with all his force, when they would go to their ships, and all the people were ready to attack them ; but it was then prevented through the aldorman Eadric, as it ever yet had been. Then, after St. Martin's mass (Nov. 11th), they went again to Kent, and took them winter-quarters on the Thames, and sustained themselves from Essex, and from the shires which were there nearest, on both sides of the Thames. And they often fought against the town of London, but to God be praise that it yet stands sound ; and they there ever fared ill. And then, after Midwinter, they took an upward course, out through Chiltern, and so to Oxford, and burned that town, and then took their way, on both sides of the Thames, towards their ships. They were then warned that there was a force gathered against them at London ; they then went over at Staines ; and thus went all the winter, and that Lent they were in Kent, and repaired their ships.

262, 263.

An. M.X. In this year, after Easter (Apr. 9th), the before-mentioned army came to East Anglia, and landed at Ipswich, and went forthwith to where they understood Ulfkytel was with his force. This was on the day Prima Ascensio Domini (May 18th). And then the East Anglians immediately fled. Then Cambridgeshire stood firmly against them. There were slain Æthelstân, the king's son-in-law, and Oswig and his son, and Wulfric Leofwine's son, and Eadwig Æfic's brother, and many other good thanes, and people out of number. The flight first began Thurkytel Mare's-head. And the Danes had possession of the place of carnage, and were there horsed, and after that held sway over the East Angles, and for three months harried and burned, ay even into the wild fens they went, and there slew men and cattle, and burned throughout the fens; and Thetford they burned, and Cambridge. And afterwards went again southward to the Thames; and the horsed men rode towards the ships; and then again quickly turned westward to Oxfordshire, and thence to Buckingham-shire, and so along the Ouse till they came to Bedford, and so forth as far as Tempsford, and ever burned as they went: went then again to their ships with their booty. And when they had gone to their ships, then should the force have again gone out to oppose them if they would land: then the force went home; and when they were east, then was the force held west; and when they were south, then was our force north. Then were all the 'witan' summoned to the king, and they should then advise how this country could be defended. But though something was then resolved, it stood not even for a month: at last there was not a chief man who would gather a force, but each fled as he best might; nor even at last would any shire assist another. Then before St. Andrew's mass-day (Nov. 30th), the army came to Northampton, and speedily burned that town, and took there-about as much as they themselves would; and thence went over the Thames into Wessex, and so by Canegan-mersc (All-Cannings?), and burned all that. When they had gone as far as they would, they came at Midwinter to their ships.

An. M.XI. In this year the king and his 'witan' sent to the army and desired peace, and promised them tribute and food, on condition that they would cease from their plundering. They had then overrun, 1st East Anglia, and 2ndly Essex, and 3rdly Middlesex, and 4thly Oxfordshire, and 5thly

264, 265.

266, 267.

Cambridgeshire, and 6thly Hertfordshire, and 7thly Buckinghamshire, and 8thly Bedfordshire, and 9thly half of Huntingdonshire, and 10thly much in Northamptonshire; and south of the Thames, all Kent, and Sussex, and Hastings, and Surrey, and Berkshire, and Hampshire, and much in Wiltshire. All these calamities befel us through evil counsels, that tribute was not offered them in time, or they were not fought against; but when they had done the most evil, then a truce and peace were made with them. And, nevertheless, for all this, peace and tribute, they went everywhere in flocks, and harried our miserable people, and robbed and slew them. And then, in this year, between the Nativity of St. Mary (Sept. 8th) and St. Michael's mass (Sept. 29th), they besieged Canterbury and entered it, through treacherous wiles, for ·Ælfmær betrayed it, whose life the archbishop Ælfeah had before saved. And they there took the archbishop Ælfeah, and Ælfweard the king's reeve, and the *abbess Leofrûn, and *of St.Mildred's. *bishop Godwine. And the †abbot Ælfmær they let go away; * of Rochester. and they took there within all the men in orders, and men † of St. Augustine's. and women. It was not to be told to any man how many people there were. And in the town they were after that as long as they would; and when they had searched all the town, they went to their ships, and led the archbishop with them.[1]

Was then a captive	where oft before	
he who was ere a head	was seen bliss,	
of the Angle race,	in that poor city,	268, 269.
and of Christendom.	whence to us came first	
There might then	Christianity and bliss	
be misery seen,	'fore God and 'fore the world.	

And they had the archbishop with them as long as to the time when they martyred him.

An. M.XII. In this year came the aldorman Eadric and all the highest 'witan,' ordained and lay, of the Angle race to London, before Easter; then was Easter day on the date Ides of April (Apr. 13th); and then they were there so long after Easter as until all the tribute was paid; that was eight and forty thousand pounds. [Then on the Saturday the army was

---

[1] Florence of Worcester (I. p. 164) gives a more circumstantial account of these atrocities.

greatly excited against the bishop, because he would not promise them any money, but forbade that anything should be
given for him.   They were also very drunken, for wine had
been brought thither from the South.   They then took the
bishop, led him to their 'husting,' on the Sunday eve, the
octaves of Easter, that was on the xiiith of the Kal. of May
(Apr. 19th) ; and there they then shamefully murdered him ;
they pelted him with bones and with the heads of oxen ; and
one of them then struck him on the head with an axe-iron, so
that with the dint he sank down, and his holy blood fell on the
earth, and his holy soul he sent forth to God's kingdom.   And
on the morrow the body was borne to London, and the bishops

* of Dorchester. • Eadnoth and †Ælfhûn, and the townsfolk received it with all
† of London.   veneration, and buried it in St. Paul's monastery.] And there
God [1] now manifests the holy martyr's miracles.   When the
tribute was paid, and peace-oaths were sworn, the army

270, 271.   separated as widely as it had before been gathered.   Then
submitted to the king, from the army, five and forty ships,
and promised him that they would defend this country ; and
he was to feed and clothe them.

       An. M.XIII.   In the year after that in which the archbishop
* of Wells.   Ælfeah was martyred, the king appointed * bishop Lyfing to
the archiepiscopal chair of Canterbury.   And in this same
year, before the month of August, came king Svein with his
fleet to Sandwich ; and went then very soon about East
Anglia into the mouth of the Humber, and so upward along
the Trent until he came to Gainsborough.   And then straightways earl Uhtred and all the Northumbrians submitted to him,
and all the people in Lindsey; and after that, the people in the
Five burghs, and shortly afterwards, all the army north of
Watling Street ; and hostages were given him from every
shire.   After he understood that all the people were submis-
sive to him, he commanded that his army should be victualled
and horsed ; and he then afterwards went southward with his
full force, and committed the ships and the hostages to his son
Cnut.   And after he came over Watling Street, they wrought
the greatest evil that any army could do.   He then went to
Oxford, and the townsmen immediately submitted and gave

---

[1] Hence it would appear that this
was written shortly after the event,
as the archbishop's body was in
1023 removed from St. Paul's to
Canterbury.

hostages ; and thence to Winchester, and they did the same. Then he went thence eastward to London, and many of his people were drowned in the Thames, [1] because they kept to no bridge. When he came to the city, the townsmen would not submit, but withstood with full war against him, because king Æthelred was therein, and Thorkell with him. Then went king Svein thence to Wallingford, and so over the Thames westward to Bath, and sat there with his force. And thither came the *aldorman Æthelmær, and the western thanes with [* of Devon.] him, and they all submitted to Svein, and gave him hostages. When he had thus fared he went northward to his ships, and all [272, 273.] the nation considered him then as full king. And after that the townsmen of London submitted and gave hostages ; for they dreaded that he would fordo them. Svein then commanded a full contribution, and provisions for his army during the winter ; and Thorkell ordered the same for the army that lay at Greenwich ; and for all that, they harried as often as they would. Then nothing profited this people, neither from south nor north. Then was king Æthelred a while with the fleet which lay in the Thames ; and the *lady went over sea [* Emma.] to her brother Richard, and Ælfsige, abbot of Peterborough, with her. And the king sent *bishop Ælfhûn with the [* of London.] æthelings Eadweard and Ælfred over sea, that he might have care of them. And the king then went from the fleet at Midwinter to Wight, and was there during that tide ; and after that tide he went over the sea to Richard, and was there with him until the time when Svein was dead.[2]

---

[2] And while the lady was with her brother beyond sea, abbot Ælfsige of Peterborough, who was there with her, went to the monastery which is called Bonneval, where St. Florentine's body lay. He there found a poor place, a poor abbot, and poor monks ; for they had been plundered. He then bought there of the abbot and of the monks St. Florentine's body, all but the head, for five hundred pounds ; and when he came back, he offered it to Christ and St. Peter.[a]

---

[1] " quia nunquam pontem neque vadum quærere voluerunt." Fl. Wigorn.

---

[a] E.

✓ An. M.XIV. In this year king Svein ended his days at Candlemas, on the IIIrd of the Nones of February (Feb. 3rd). And in the same year Ælfwig was ordained bishop of London at York, on St. Juliana's mass-day (Feb. 16th.) And then all the fleet chose Cnut for king. Then resolved all the ' witan ' who were in England, ordained and lay, that king Æthelred should be sent after ; and said, that to them no lord was dearer than their natural lord, if he would govern them more justly than he did before. Then the king sent his son Eadweard hither with his messengers, and bade them greet all his people, and said, that he would be to them a kind lord, and amend all the things which they all eschewed, and all the things should be forgiven which had been done or said to him, on condition, that they all, unanimously without treachery, would turn to him. ι And they then confirmed full friendship, with word and with pledge, on each side, and pronounced every Danish king an outlaw from England for ever. Then came king Æthelred, during Lent, home to his own people, and he was gladly received by all. Then after Svein was dead, Cnut sat with his army at Gainsborough until Easter (Apr. 17th) ; and it was agreed between him and the people of Lindsey, that they should supply him with horses, and afterwards all should go together and harry. Then came king Æthelred thither to Lindsey, with a full force, before they were ready ; and they then harried, and burned, and slew all of human race whom they could reach. And Cnut went away out with his fleet, and the miserable people were thus deceived through him ; and he then went southward, until he came to Sandwich, and ·then caused the hostages that had been given to his father to be landed, and cut off their hands, and ears, and noses. And besides all these evils, the king commanded one and twenty thousand pounds to be paid to the army which lay at Greenwich. And in this year, on St. Michael's mass eve (Sept. 28), came the great sea-flood widely through this country, and ran ·'so far up as it never before had done, and drowned many vills, and of mankind a countless number.

An. M.XV. In this year was the great meeting at Oxford ; and there the aldorman Eadric insnared Sigeferth and Morkere, the chief thanes in the Seven Burghs. He enticed them into his chamber, and therein they were foully slain. And the king then took all their possessions, and ordered Sigeferth's

274, 275.

276, 277.

relict to be taken and brought to Malmesbury. Then after a little space, Eadmund ætheling went thither, and took the woman against the king's will, and had her for his wife. Then, before the Nativity of St. Mary (Sept. 8th), the ætheling went thence from the west, north to the Five Burghs, and immediately took possession of all Sigeferth's and Morkere's property, and all the folk submitted to him. And then, at the same time, king Cnut came to Sandwich, and then immediately went about Kent to Wessex, until he came to the mouth of the Frome, and then harried in Dorsetshire, and in Wiltshire, and in Somersetshire. Then lay the king sick at Cosham (Corsham). Then the aldorman Eadric gathered a force, and the ætheling Eadmund one in the north. When they came together, the aldorman would deceive the ætheling, but he could not ; and then, on that account, they parted without a battle, and gave way to their foes. And the aldorman Eadric then enticed forty ships from the king, and then submitted to Cnut. And Wessex submitted, and gave hostages, and supplied the army with horses ; and it was there till Midwinter.

v An. M.XVI. In this year Cnut came with his army, and the aldorman Eadric with him, over the Thames into Mercia at Cricklade. And then they went to Warwickshire, during the Midwinter's tide, and harried, and burned, and slew all that they came to. Then the ætheling Eadmund began to gather a force. When the force was assembled, they were not content with it, unless it were that the king should be with them, and they had the support of the citizens of London ; they withdrew then from the expedition, and each man went home. Then, after that *tide, a force was ordered, on pain of full penalty, so that every man who was able to go should turn out : and they sent to the king at London, and prayed him that he would come to join the force with the aid that he might gather. When they all came together, it availed naught the more than it had often before done. Then it was made known to the king that they would be treacherous to him who should be a support to him. He then left the force and returned to London. Then the ætheling Eadmund rode to Northumbria to earl Uhtred, and every man imagined that they would collect a force against king Cnut. They then marched into Staffordshire, and into Shropshire, and to Chester ; and they harried on their part, and Cnut on his

* Midwinter.

278, 279.

part. He went out through Buckinghamshire into Bedfordshire, and thence to Huntingdonshire, and so into Northamptonshire along the fens to Stamford, and then into 'Lincolnshire; then thence to Nottinghamshire, and so to Northumbria towards York. When Uhtred was apprized of this,
he abandoned his harrying and hastened northwards, and
then from necessity submitted, and all Northumbria with him;
and he gave hostages; and, notwithstanding, they slew him,
(through the counsel of the aldorman Eadric, and Thorkytel
son of Nafena with him.) And then, after that, king Cnut
appointed Eric as his earl in Northumbria, as Uhtred had
been; and afterwards went south, by another way, all to the
west; and then all the army before Easter (Apr. 1st) came to
their ships. And the ætheling Eadmund went to London to
his father. And then, after Easter, king Cnut went with all his
ships towards London. Then it befel that king Æthelred died
before the ships came. He ended his days on St. George's
mass-day (Apr. 23rd): and he held his kingdom with great
toil and difficulty, while his life lasted. And then, after his

280, 281.   end, all the 'witan' that were in London, and the townsmen,
chose Eadmund for king; and he boldly defended his kingdom while his time was. Then came the ships to Greenwich
in the Rogation days (May 7th); and within a little space
they went to London, and they then dug a great ditch on the
south side, and dragged their ships to the west side of the
bridge, and afterwards ditched the town without, so that no
one could pass either in or out; and they repeatedly fought
against the town, but they boldly withstood them. Then
before that, king Eadmund had gone out; and he rode over
Wessex, and all the folk submitted to him. And shortly
after that, he fought against the army at Pen by Gillingham.
And a second battle he fought after Midsummer at Sherston
(Scoorstân), and there was great slaughter made on each side,
and the armies of themselves separated. In that battle the
aldorman Eadric (and Ælmær Dyrling) gave aid to the army
against king Eadmund. And then a third time he gathered a
force and went to London, all north of the Thames, and so
out through Clayhanger, and saved the townsmen, and drove

---

¹ Stamford was then included in Northamptonshire.

the army in flight to their ships. And then, two nights after, the king went over at Brentford, and then fought against the army, and put it to flight; and there were drowned a great many of the English folk, by their own carelessness, those who went before the force, and would take booty. And after that, the king went into Wessex, and collected his force. Then the army went forthwith to London, and beset the city around, and obstinately fought against it, both by water and by land. But Almighty God saved it.

The army then, after that, went from London with their ships into the Arewe (Orwell), and there landed, and went into Mercia, and slew and burned whatever they overran, as is their wont; and provided themselves with food: and they 282, 283. drove both their ships and their droves into the Medway. Then a fourth time king Eadmund collected all his force, and went over the Thames at Brentford, and went into Kent; and the army fled before him, with their horses, to Shepey: and the king slew as many of them as he could overtake. [1] And the aldorman Eadric then went to meet the king at Aylesford. Never was greater evil counsel counselled than that was. VThe army turned again up into Essex, and went into Mercia, and destroyed all that it passed over. When the king learned that the army was gone up, he, for the fifth time, assembled all the English nation, and went after them, and overtook them in Essex, at the hill which is called Assandûn (Assingdon), and there they boldly engaged together. Then did the aldorman Eadric as he had often before done; first began the flight with the men of Worcestershire and Herefordshire, and so betrayed his royal lord and all the people of Angle race. There Cnut had the victory, and won him all the English nation. There were bishop *Eadnoth slain, and * of Dorchester. abbot Wulfsige, and the aldorman Ælfric, and Godwine the aldorman of Lindsey, and Ulfkytel of East Anglia, and Æthelweard son of the aldorman Æthelwing; and all the flower of the Angle race was there destroyed. Then, after this battle,

---

[1] " Et nisi perfidus dux Edricus
" Streona, suis insidiis et insiliis,
" eum apud Eagelesford, ne suos
" persequeretur hostes, retineret,
" eo die plena potiretur victoria."

Fl. Wigorn. " Sed cum perve-
" nisset rex ad Ægelesford, dux
" Eadricus per dolum fecit exerci-
" tum Anglorum redire." F. *Lat.*

king Cnut, with his army, went up into Gloucestershire, where he had learned that king Eadmund was.

Then the aldorman Eadric and the 'witan' who were there advised that there should be a reconciliation between the kings; and they gave hostages between them. And the kings came together at Olney (by Deerhurst) 'and there confirmed their friendship,' both with pledge and with oath; and fixed the contribution for the army. And they then separated with this agreement: and Eadmund took to Wessex, and Cnut to Mercia. And the army then went to their ships with the things that they had taken. And the Londoners made a truce with the army, and bought themselves peace; and the army brought their ships to London, and took them winter-quarters therein. Then, on St. Andrew's mass-day (Nov. 30th), king Eadmund died; and his body lies at Glastonbury with his grandfather Eadgar. [And in the same year died Wulfgar, abbot of Abingdon; and Æthelsige succeeded to the abbacy.]

✓ An. M.XVII. In this year king Cnut succeeded to all the kingdom of the Angle race, and divided it into four: to himself Wessex, and to Thorkell East Anglia, and to Eadric Mercia, and to Eric Northumbria. And in this year the aldorman Eadric was slain in London very rightly, and Northman son of Leofwine the aldorman, and Æthelweard son of Æthelmær *the Great, and Brihtric son of Ælfeah in Devonshire. And king Cnut drove out Eadwig the ætheling, and afterwards commanded him to be slain, and Eadwig king of the churls. And then before the Kal. of August (Aug. 1st), the king commanded the relict of king Æthelred, Richard's daughter to be fetched for him to wife (that was Ælfgifu in English, Ymma in French).

✓ An. M.XVIII. In this year the tribute was paid over all the Angle race: that was in all two and seventy thousand pounds, exclusive of what the townsmen of London paid, which was

---

'' and became fellows and sworn brothers, and confirmed it.[a]

An. M.XVII. In this year Cnut was chosen king.[b]

284, 285.

* dux. Fl. Wigorn.

[a] D.   [b] A.

ten and a half thousand pounds. And some of the army then
went to Denmark, and forty ships remained with king Cnut. 286, 287
And the Danes and the Angles were unanimous at Oxford for
Eadgar's law. And in this year abbot Æthelsige died at
Abingdon, and Æthelwine succeeded.]

An. M.XIX. In this year king Cnut went with forty ships
to Denmark, and there abode all the winter.[1]

An. M.XX. In this year died *archbishop Lyfing : and king * of Canterbury.
Cnut came again to England. And then at Easter (Apr. 17th)
there was a great council at Cirencester, when the aldorman
Æthelweard and Eadwig king of the churls were outlawed.
And in this year the king went to Assingdon,[2] and *arch-   * of York.
bishop Wulfstân, and earl Thorkell, and many bishops and also
abbots, and many monks with them, and hallowed the monastery
at Assingdon. And Æthelnoth the monk, who was dean of
*Christchurch, was in the same year, on the Ides of November * Canterbury.
(Nov. 13th), hallowed bishop at Christchurch by archbishop
Wulfstân.

An. M.XXI. In this year, at Martinmas (Nov. 11th), king
Cnut outlawed earl Thorkell. And *bishop Ælfgar the   * of Elmham.
alms-giver died on Christmas dawn.

An. M.XXII. In this year king Cnut went out with his
ships to Wight. And archbishop Æthelnoth went to Rome,
and was there received by *Benedict, the venerable pope, * VIII.
with great worship ; and he with his own hands, placed his
pall upon him, and very honourably hallowed him archbishop,
and blessed him, on the Nones of October (Oct. 7th). And

An. M.XIX. [1]And in this year died archbishop Ælfstân, who
was named Lyfing, and he was a sagacious man, both before
God and before the world.[a]

An. M.XX. [2]— and caused to be built there a monastery
of stone and lime, for the souls of the men who were there
slain, and gave it to one of his priests, whose name was
Stigand.[b]

---

* D. in continuation. | ᵇ F. in continuation.

the archbishop therewith immediately, on that same day, sang mass; and then after, with the pope himself, honourably took refection, and also of himself took the pall from St. Peter's altar, and then joyfully went home to his own country.' And abbot Leofwinê, who had been unjustly driven from Ely, was his companion ; and he cleared ⁊imself of everything that was said against him, as the pope instructed him, with the witness of the archbishop, and of all the company that was with him.

288.   An. M.XXIII. In this year king Cnut came again to England, and Thorkell and he were reconciled; and he intrusted Denmark and his son to the guardianship of Thorkell; and the king took Thorkell's son with him to
* of York.   England.' In this year died * archbishop Wulfstân ; and
289.   *Ælfric succeeded; and archbishop Æthelnoth blessed him at
* Puttuo.
Fl. Wigorn.   Canterbury.' In this year king Cnut, within London, in St. Paul's monastery, gave full leave to archbishop Æthelnoth
* of Sherborne.   and *bishop Bryhtwine, and to all God's servants who were with them, that they might take up from the burial place the archbishop St. Ælfheah. And they then did so, on the VIth of the Ides of June (June 8th). And the renowned king, and the archbishop, and suffragan bishops, and earls, and very many men in orders, and also laymen, conveyed in a ship his holy body over the Thames to Southwark, and there delivered the holy martyr to the archbishop and his companions; and they then, with an honourable band and win-

---

An. M.XXII. '— And afterwards with the pall he there celebrated mass, as the pope directed him : and he took refection after that with the pope; and afterwards with a full blessing went home.ᵃ

An. M.XXIII. '—And he caused the remains of St. Ælfheah to be borne from London to Canterbury.ᵇ

An. M.XXIII. '— And the same year archbishop Æthelnoth conveyed the remains of St. Ælfeah to Canterbury from London.ᶜ

ᵃ E. F. in continuation.
C.

E. F. in continuation.

some joy, conveyed him to Rochester. Then, on the third day, came Emma the lady, with her royal child Harthacnut; and they then all, with great magnificence and bliss, and song of praise, conveyed the holy archbishop into Canterbury, and so honourably brought him to Christchurch, on the, IIIrd of the Ides of June ¶(June 11th). Again, after that, on the eighth day, on the XVIIth of the Kal. of July (June 15th), archbishop Æthelnoth and *bishop Ælfsige, and bishop *of Winton. Bryhtwine, and all those who were with them, deposited St. Æfheah's holy body on the north side of Christ's altar, to the glory of God, and the honour of the holy archbishop, and to the eternal health of all who there with devout heart, and with all humility, daily seek his holy body. May God Almighty have mercy on all Christian men through St. Ælfheah's holy merits !

An. M.XXIV. Robert, count of Normandy, succeeds Richard.

An. M.XXV. In this year king Cnut went to Denmark with ships to the Holm at the river Helgo. And there came against him 'Ulf and Eylaf, and a very large army, both a land force and a naval force, of Swedes. And there very many men perished on king Cnut's side, both Danish men 290, 291. and English; and the Swedes had possession of the place of carnage.

An. M.XXVI. In this year *bishop Ælfric went to Rome, *abp. of York. and received the pall from pope *John, on the IInd of the *XIX. Ides of November (Nov. 12th).

An. M.XXVII.

---

¹ The Ulf here mentioned must not be confounded with Ulf jarl, who married Astrith (Estrith), the sister of Cnut, and by her was progenitor of a long line of Danish sovereigns, the last male of whom, Valdemar Atterdag, father of queen Margaret, died in 1375. This Ulf accompanied Cnut in the abovementioned expedition. The brothers Ulf and Eylaf were sons of Rögnvald, jarl of West Gothland, and of Ingeborg, a daughter of king Olaf Tryggvason. The 'halge eá' of the Saxon text (literally the holy river) is the ' Helga amnis ' of Saxo Grammaticus, at the foot of the mountain Stanga ; and is the modern Helgo, in the government of Christianstad, in the south of Sweden. See Saxo Gramm. p. 518, ed. Müller ; Olafs Saga hins Helga in Snorri, c. 161., Ann. Isl. a. 1027, ap. Langebek, t. III., and Suhm, Hist. of Danm. III. p. 634.

An. M.XXVIII. In this year king Cnut went from England, with [1] fifty ships of English thanes, to Norway, and drove king Olaf from the land, and possessed himself of all that land.

An. M.XXIX. In this year king Cnut came again to England; and as soon as he came again to England, [2] he gave to Christchurch at Canterbury the haven at Sandwich, and all the dues that arise therefrom, from each side of the haven; so that when the flood is of all the highest, and of all the fullest, be a ship floating so nigh the land as it nighest may, and there be a man standing in the ship, and have a [3] ' taper axe ' in his . . . . . .

An. M.XXX. In this year king Olaf was slain in Norway by his own people, and was afterwards sainted. And in this year, before that, died [4] Hakon, the doughty jarl, at sea.

An. M.XXXI. In this year king Cnut [5] went to Rome ; and as soon as he came home, he went to Scotland, and the Scots' king Malcolm submitted to him, and became his man ; [6] but held that only a little while ; and two other kings, Mælbæthe and Iehmarc. And Robert count of Normandy went to Jerusalem, and there died ; and William, who was afterwards king of England, succeeded to Normandy, though he was a child.

An. M.XXXII. In this year appeared the wildfire, such as no man before remembered; and moreover it did harm in many places. And in the same year died bishop Ælfsige at Winchester; and Ælfwine the king's priest succeeded to the see.

292, 293.

An. M.XXX. In this year king Olaf came again to Norway ; and the people gathered against him, and fought against him, and he was there slain.[a]

---

[1] " L. navibus magnis." Flor. Wigorn.

[2] See the entire charter in Cod. Diplom. IV. No. 737, VI. No. 1328.

[3] Tapar-öxi, securis malleata. Bj. Haldorsen.

[4] He was the son of Eric, jarl of Norway, by Gytha the sister of Cnut.

[5] See his letter to the clergy and magnates of the land in Fl. Wigorn. I. p. 185, edit. E. H. S.

[6] He died three years after.

D. E.

An. M.XXXIII. In this year died *bishop Leofsige, and his * of Worcester.
body rests at Worcester; and Brihteh was raised to his see.
In this year died Merehwit, bishop of *Somerset ; and he is * Wells.
buried at Glastonbury.

An. M.XXXIV. In this year died *bishop Ætheric, and he lies * of Dorchester.
at Ramsey. And in that same year died Malcolm, king of
Scotland.

An. M.XXXV. In this year died king Cnut ; and Harold his
son succeeded to the kingdom. He departed at Shaftesbury
on the IInd of the Ides of November (Nov. 12th) ; and
they conveyed him thence to Winchester, and there buried
him. And Ælfgyfu Emma, the lady, sat then there within :
and Harold, who said that he was the son of Cnut and of the
other Ælfgyfu, though it was not true, sent thither, and caused
to be taken from her all the best treasures, which she could
not withhold, that king Cnut had possessed ; and yet she sat
there within, the while she might.

An. M.XXXVI. In this year the innocent ætheling Ælfred,
son of king Æthelred, came hither, and would go to his
mother, who sat in Winchester ; but that earl Godwine
would not permit, nor other men also, who could exercise
much power ; because the public voice was then greatly   294.
in favour of Harold ; though it was unjust. But Godwine
then impeded him, and in durance set him, and his companions he dispersed ; and diversely some slew ; some they
for money sold, some cruelly killed, some they bound, some

An. M.XXXVI. In this year died king Cnut at Shaftesbury,
and he is buried at Winchester, in the Old monastery : and he
was king over all England very nigh twenty winters. And
immediately after his decease, there was a great assembly of all
the 'witan' at Oxford ; and earl Leofric and almost all the thanes
north of the Thames, and the ' 'lithsmen' of London, chose
Harold to the government of all England, him and his brother
Harthacnut, who was in Denmark. And earl Godwine and all
the chief men of Wessex, opposed it as long as they could, but
they could not prevail aught against it. And it was then resolved that Ælfgyfu, Harthacnut's mother, should dwell at

_____

¹ *Sailors, from liỡ, a ship.*

* or hamstrung. they blinded, some *mutilated, some scalped. No bloodier deed
was done in this country since the Danes came, and here made
peace. Now is our trust in the beloved God, that they possess
bliss joyfully with Christ, who were without guilt so miserably
slain. The ætheling yet lived, every evil they vowed him,
until it was resolved that he should be led to Ely, thus bound.
As soon as he was near the land, in the ship they blinded him ;
and him thus blind brought to the monks ; and he there abode
the while that he lived. After that, he was buried, as to him
was befitting, full honourably, as he was worthy, at the west
end, to the steeple full nigh, in the south porch. His soul is
with Christ.

    An. M.XXXVII. In this year Harold was chosen over all for
king, and Harthacnut rejected, because he was too long in
Denmark. And then then they drove out his mother Ælfgyfu
the queen, without any mercy, against the stormy winter ;
and she came then to Bruges beyond sea, and count Baldwine
there well received her, and held her there while she had need.
And before, in this year, died Æfic, the noble dean at Evesham.

    An. M.XXXVIII. In this year died Æthelnoth, the good
* of Canterbury. *archbishop, and Æthelric, bishop of the †South Saxons, who
† Belsey.

Winchester with the king her son's [1] 'hûscarls,' and hold all
Wessex under his authority. And earl Godwine was their
most devoted man. Some men said of Harold, that he was the
son of king Cnut and of Ælfgyfu, the daughter of Ælfhelm the
aldorman ; but it seemed very incredible to many men ; and
he was, nevertheless, full king over all England.[a]

295.   An. M.XXXVII. In this year Ælfgyfu, king Cnut's relict,
was driven out : she was king Harthacnut's mother : and she
then sought the protection of Baldwine, south of the sea; and
he gave her an abode at Bruges, and he protected and maintained her the while that she was there.[a]

    An. M.XXXVIII. In this year died Æthelnoth, the good
archbishop, on the Kal. of November (Nov. 1st) ; and a little

---

[1] The Danish body guard, though retained till the time of the Conquest.

---

[a] E. F.

desired of God that he would not let him live any while after
his beloved father Æthelnoth : and within seven nights after,   296.
he also departed; and bishop Ælfric of * East Anglia, and * Elmham.
bishop Byrhteh of Worcestershire, on the xiiiith of the Kal.
of January (Dec. 20th) ; and then [1] bishop Eadsige suc-   297.
ceeded to the archbishopric; and Grymkytel to the bishopric
of the South Saxons ; and * bishop Lyfing to Worcestershire * of Crediton.
and to Gloucestershire.

An. M.XXXIX. In this year was the great wind; and bishop
Byrhtmær died at Lichfield.   And the Welsh slew Eadwine,
the brother of earl Leofric, and Thorkell, and Ælfgeat, and
very many good men with them.   And in this year also came
Harthacnut to Bruges, where his mother was.

---

after, Æthelric, bishop of the South Saxons ; and then before
Christmas, Brihteh, bishop of Worcestershire ; and shortly
after Ælfric, [a]bishop of the East Angles.   * of Elmham.

An. M.XXXIX. [2]In this year king Harold died at Oxford,
on the xviith of the Kal. of April (Mar. 17th), and he was
buried at Westminster.   And he ruled England four years and
sixteen weeks.   And in his days, to sixteen ships eight marks
were paid for every rower, as had before been done in king
Cnut's days.   And in this same year king Harthacnut came to
Sandwich, seven nights before Midsummer.   And he was immediately received both by Angles and by Danes ; though his
counsellors afterwards cruelly requited it, when they counselled, that to sixty-two ships should be paid, for each rower,
eight marks.   And in this same year the 'sester' of wheat
went to fifty-five pence, and even further.[a]

---

[1] This appears to be an error. In
F. he is styled "þæs cinges preost,"
and in F. _Lat._ and Florence, "regis
"capellanus."
   [2] From this time the dates in E.
and F. are often faulty. Harold is
here said to have reigned four years

and sixteen weeks, although Cnute's
death, Nov. 12, is placed under the
year 1036, and the death of Harda-
cnute, and the coronation of Edward, which belongs unquestionably
to the year 1043, are in like manner
misdated.—R.P.

[a] E. F.

I 2

An. M.XL. In this year king Harold died. Then was Harthacnut sent after, at Bruges : it was imagined to be well done.
And he then came hither with sixty ships before Midsummer,
and imposed a very heavy contribution ; so that it was borne
with difficulty: that was eight marks for each rower : and then
was every one unfavourable to him who had before desired
him ; nor did he perform aught kingly while he reigned. He
caused the dead Harold to be dragged up, and had him cast
into a fen. In this year archbishop Eadsige went to Rome.

An. M.XLI. In this year Harthacnut caused all Worcestershire to be ravaged, for the sake of his two 'hûscarls,' who
announced the heavy impost, when the people slew them within
the town, in the monastery. And in this year, shortly after,
came his maternal brother Eadward, the son of king Æthelred,
from beyond sea, who before, for many years, had been driven
from his country ; and yet was sworn king ; and he then
dwelt so in his brother's family while he lived. And also in
this year Harthacnut betrayed *earl Eadulf while under his
safeguard ; and he was then a belier of his pledge. And in this
year *bishop Ægelric was ordained at York, on the IIIrd of
the Ides of January (Jan. 11th).

298.

* of North-
umbria.

* of Durham.

An. M.XLII. In this year died Harthacnut, as he stood at
his drink, and he suddenly fell to the earth with a terrible
struggle ; and then they who were nigh took hold of him ; and

---

An. M.XL. In this year the military contribution was paid ;
that was twenty-one thousand and ninty-nine pounds. And
after that, there were paid to thirty-two ships, eleven thousand
and forty-eight pounds. And in this same year came Eadward,
king Æthelred's son, hither to land from Normandy. He was
king Harthacnut's brother : they were both sons of Ælfgifu,
who was count Richard's daughter.*

299.

An. M.XLI. In this year king Harthacnut died at Lambeth,
on the VIth day of the Ides of June (June 8th). And he was
king over all England two years less ten nights ; and he is
buried in the Old monastery at Winchester with king Cnut his
father. And his mother, for his soul, gave to the New monastery the head of St. Valentine the martyr. And before he

---

* .F.

he afterwards spoke not a word ; and he died on the VIth of
the Ides of June (June 8th). And all the people then received
Eadward for king, as was his natural right.

An. M.XLIII. (M.XLII.) In this year Eadward was hallowed
king at Winchester, on the first Easter-day, with great worship;
and then was Easter on the IIIrd of the Nones of April (April
3rd). Archbishop Eadsige hallowed him, and before all the
people well instructed him, and for his own and all the people's
need, well exhorted him. And Stigand the priest was blessed
bishop of the *East Angles. And shortly after the king caused * of Elmham.
all the lands which his mother possessed to be seized into his 300, 301.
hand ; and took from her all that she possessed in gold, and in
silver, and in unspeakable things ; because she had before held
it too strictly towards him. And soon after, Stigand was
deposed from his bishopric, and all that he owned was seized
into the king's hand ; because he was closest in his mother's
counsel, and she went as he advised her, as it was supposed.

---

was buried all the people chose Eadward king in London.
May he hold it while God shall grant it him ! And all that
year it was very sad in many and various things, both in tempests and in earth-fruits. And so much cattle perished in this
year as no man before remembered, both through various
diseases and through bad weather. And at this same time
died Ælfsine, abbot of Peterborough ; and then Arnwi, a
monk, was chosen abbot ; because he was a very good man
and very meek.[a]

An. M.XLIII. In this year Eadward was hallowed king at
Winchester on the first Easter-day (April 3rd). And in this
year, fourteen nights before St. Andrew's mass (Nov. 16th),
the king was so advised that he and earl Leofric, and earl
Godwine, and earl Siward, with their attendants, rode from
Gloucester to Winchester unawares upon the *lady, and they * Emma.
bereaved her of all the treasures which she owned, which were
not to be told ; because she had before been very hard to the
king her son, inasmuch as she had done less for him than he
would, before he was king, and also since then. And after
that they let her reside therein.[b]

---

[a] E. F. [b] D.

* of Canterbury.   An. M.XLIV. (M.XLIII.) In this year *archbishop Eadsige resigned the bishopric, on account of his infirmity, and blessed thereto Siward abbot of Abingdon, as bishop, by the king's leave and counsel, and earl Godwine's; it was else known to few men before it was done; because the archbishop thought that some other man would obtain it by solicitation, or buy it, whom he less trusted and liked, if more men knew of it. And in this year there was a very great famine over all England, and corn so dear as no man before remembered, so that the 'sester' of wheat went to sixty pence, and even further. And in the same year the king went out to Sandwich with thirty-five ships; and Æthelstân the church-ward succeeded to the abbacy at Abingdon ; and Stigand obtained his bishopric. And in the same year king Eadward took Eadgyth, earl Godwine's daughter, to wife, ten nights before Candlemas (June 23rd).

* of Sherborne.   An. M.XLV. In this year * bishop Bryhtwold died, on the
302.   xth of the Kal. of May (April 22nd), and king Eadward gave the bishopric to Hereman his priest. And in the same summer king Eadward went out with his ships to Sandwich ; and there so great a force was gathered, that no man had seen any greater naval force in this land. And in this same year
* of Crediton.   died * bishop Lyfing, on the xiiith of the Kal. of April (Mar. 20th) ; and the king gave the bishopric to Leofric his priest.
303.   In this year died Ælfward, bishop of London, on the viiith of the Kal. of August (July 25th). He was first abbot of

---

An. M.XLIII. (M.XLIV.) In this year king Eadward took the daughter of earl Godwine for his queen. And in this same year bishop Brihtwold died : and he held the bishopric thirty-eight years, that was the bishopric of Sherborne; and Hereman the king's priest succeeded to the bishopric. And in this year Wulfric was hallowed abbot of St. Augustine's at Christmas, on St. Stephen's mass-day (Dec. 26th), by the king's leave, and abbot Ælfstân's, on account of his (Ælfstân's) great infirmity.*

An. M.XLVI. In this year bishop Brihtwold died in Wiltshire, and Hereman was placed in his see. In that year king Eadward gathered a great naval force at Sandwich, on

---

Evesham, and greatly advanced that monastery, while he was there. He then went to Ramsey, and there gave up his life.[1] And Manni was chosen *abbot, and ordained on the ivth of * of Evesham. the Ides of August (Aug. 10). And in this year the noble woman Gunnhild, king Cnut's [2] kinswoman, was banished ; and afterwards she long resided at Bruges, and then went to Denmark.

account of the threatening of Magnus of Norway ; but his (Magnus') and [3] Svein's war in Denmark hindered him from coming hither.[a]

An. M.XLIV. (M.XLV.) In this year *bishop Lyfing died in * of Crediton. Devonshire, and Leofric succeeded to his see ; he was the king's priest. And in this same year Ælfstân, abbot of * St. * at Canterbury. Augustine's, died, on the iiird of the Nones of July (July 5th). And in this same year Osgod Clapa was driven out.[b]

An. M.XLVII. In this year died Lyfing, the eloquent bishop, on the xth of the Kal. of April (Mar. 23rd) ; and he had three bishoprics, one in Devonshire, and one in Cornwall, and one in Worcester. Then Leofric succeeded to Devonshire and to Cornwall, and bishop Aldred to Worcester. And in this year Osgod the *constable was outlawed ; and † Magnus won * stallere. Denmark.[a]   † k. of Norway.

[1] Florence of Worcester is more explicit on the subject of bishop Ælfward : "Ælfwardus Lundoni- "ensis præsul, qui et ante episcopa- "tum et in episcopatu, abbatis jure, "Eoveshamnensi cœnobio præfuit, "cum pontificatum administrare pro "sua infirmitate minus sufficeret, "Eoveshammi residere voluit, sed "fratres loci illius id omnino con- "sentire noluerunt. Quapropter, "ablatis ex maxima parte libris et "ornamentis, quæ ipse eidem con-

"tulerat loco, et quædam, ut fertur, "quæ alii contulerant, ad monas- "terium Ramesege secessit." The monks of Evesham would not admit him because he was afflicted with leprosy. Hist. Rames. c. XIV.

[2] She was his niece, being the daughter of his sister Gytha, married to Wyrtgeorn, king of the Wends, and was wife of Hakon jarl. Flor. Wigorn.

[3] Svein Estrithson, the son of Cnut's sister Astrith, by Ulf jarl.

a D.   b E. F.

An. M.XLVI. In this year [1] earl Swegen went into Wales, and Griffith, the * Northern king, went forth with him ; and hostages were given him. When he was homeward, he ordered the abbess of Leominster to be fetched to him, and had her while it listed him, and then let her go home. And in this same year Osgod Clapa was outlawed before Midwinter. And in this same year, after Candlemas (Feb. 2nd), came the severe winter, with frost and with snow, and with all kinds of bad weather, so that there was no man alive who could remember so severe a winter as that was, both through mortality of men and murrain of cattle ; both birds and fishes perished through the great cold and hunger.

* of N. Wales.

An. M.XLVII. In this year died bishop Grimkytel ; he was * bishop in Sussex, and he lies in Christchurch at Canterbury; and king Eadward gave the bishopric to Hecca his priest. And in this same year died * bishop Ælfwine, on the IVth of the Kal. of September (Aug. 29th); and king Eadward gave the bishopric to * bishop Stigand. And Æthelstân, abbot of

* of Selsey.
* of Winton.
* of Elmham.

An. M.XLVIII. In this year was the hard winter ; and in this year died Ælfwine, bishop of Winchester ; and bishop Stigand was raised to his see. And before that, in the same year, died Grymkytel, bishop of the * South Saxons, and Heca the priest succeeded to the bishopric. And * Svein also sent hither, praying for aid against Magnus, king of Norway; that fifty ships should be sent to his aid. But it seemed unadvisable to all people; and then it was prevented, by reason that Magnus had a great naval force. And he then ousted Svein, and with great slaughter won the land ; and the Danes paid him much money, and received him for king. And in that same year Magnus died. [a]

* Selsey.
* k. of Denmark.

An. M.XLV. (M.XLVI.) In this year died Grimkytel, bishop of the South Saxons, and Heca the king's priest succeeded to the bishopric. And in this year died Ælfwine, bishop of Winchester, on the IVth of the Kal. of September (Aug. 29th),

---

[1] One of Godwine's sons.

---

[a] D.

Abingdon, died in the same year, on the ɪᴠth of the Kal. of April (Mar. 29th): then was Easter-day on the ɪɪɪrd of the Nones of April (April 3rd). And there was over all England a very great mortality in the same year.

An. ᴍ.xLvɪɪɪ. In this year there was a great earthquake   304. widely throughout England. And in the same year Sandwich and Wight were ravaged, and the best men who were there, slain. And after that king Eadward and the carls

---

and Stigand, * bishop in the north, succeeded to the bishopric. * of Elmham. And in the same year earl Swegen went out to Baldwine's land, to Bruges, and abode there all the winter ; and then in   305. summer he went out.ᵃ

An. ᴍ.xLvɪ. (ᴍ.xLvɪɪ.) In this year died Æthelstân, abbot of Abingdon, and Spearhafoc, a monk of St. Edmundsbury, succeeded. And in this same year died bishop Siward, and archbishop Eadsige again succeeded to all the * bishopric. And in * Canterbury. this same year ¹Lothin and Erling came with twenty-five ships to Sandwich, and took there unspeakable booty, in men, and in gold, and in silver, so that no man knew how much it all was. And they then went about Thanet, and would there do the like; but the country folk boldly withstood them, and refused them both landing and water, and completely drove them thence. And they went thence to Essex, and there harried, and took men, and property, and whatever they could find ; and then went east to *Baldwine's land, and there sold what they had * Flanders. plundered ; and afterwards went east frcm thence to whence they before came.ᵃ

---

¹ This predatory expedition, assigned here to the year 1046, is of a much earlier date. Lothin was a wealthy Norwegian of rank, who, as was not unusual in those days, united with the profession of commerce that of piracy. He was stepfather to king Olaf Tryggvason, having married his mother Astrith, who had been captured by pirates, and whom he found exposed for sale in a slave market in Esthonia. Er. ling was Olaf's brother-in-law, having married his sister, also named Astrith. Olaf Tryggvason fell in the year 1000. See Saga Olafs Tryggvasonar, pp. 185, 298. edit. 1826, and his Saga in Snorri, cc. 1, 58, 62.

ᵃ E. F.

went out with their ships. And in the same year bishop
Siward resigned the *bishopric, on account of his infirmity,
and went to Abingdon; and archbishop Eadsige again succeeded to the bishopric; and *he died within eight weeks after,
on the xth of the Kal. of November (Oct. 23rd).

An. M.XLIX. In this year the emperor gathered a countless
force against * Baldwine of Bruges, because he had destroyed
the palace at Nymegen, and also of many other injuries that he
had done him. The force was not to be told that he had
gathered. There were Leo the pope of Rome, and many great
men of many nations. He (the emperor) sent also to king
Eadward, and craved naval aid from him, that he would
not allow him to escape from him by water. And he (king
Eadward) went then to Sandwich, and there continued to lie
with a great naval force, until the emperor had from Baldwine
all that he would. Thither came earl Swegen back again to
king Eadward, and craved land of him, that he might sustain
himself thereon. But Harold his brother and Biörn declared
that they would not restore to him anything of what the king
had given them. He came hither with guile, said that he
would be his man, and prayed earl Biörn that he would support
him. But the king refused him everything. Swegen then
went with his ships to Bosham ; and earl Godwine went from

*Canterbury.

* Siward.

308.

* count of
Flanders.

306.   An. M.XLIX. [1] In this year Svein came again to Denmark,
and Harold, the paternal uncle of Magnus, went to Norway,
after that Magnus was dead, and the Normen received him ;
and he sent hither to this country about peace. And Svein
also sent from Denmark, and prayed king Eadward for naval
support, that should at least be fifty ships ; but all the people
refused. And in this year was also an earthquake, on the
Kal. of May (May 1st), in many places, at Worcester, at
Wick, and at Derby, and elsewhere ; and there was also a
great mortality among men, and a murrain among cattle ; and
the wildfire also did much evil in Derbyshire and elsewhere.[a]

---

[1] The narratives now, under the
same date in the manuscripts, differ
so widely in subject from each other,
that it is no longer possible to note
their discrepancies.

---

* D.

Sandwich with forty-two ships to Pevensey, and earl Biörn along with him ; and then the king allowed all the Mercians to go home, and they did so. Then it was announced to the king that Osgod lay at Wulpe with thirty-nine ships. The king then sent after those ships which he could send off, which lay within Northmouth. But Osgod fetched his wife from Bruges, and came back again with six ships ; and the others went to Essex, to Eadulfsness (Walton on the Naze), and there did harm, and went again to their ships. Then lay earl Godwine and earl Biörn at Pevensey, with their ships. Then came earl Swegen with guile, and prayed earl Biörn that he would be his companion to the king at Sandwich, saying that he would swear oaths to him, and be faithful to him. Then Biörn fancied that, on account of their kinship, he   310.

An. M.XLVI. In this year was the great synod at Rheims. Thereat were Leo the pope, and the archbishop of * Burgundy, * Lyons. and the archbishop of Besançon, and the archbishop of Treves, and the archbishop of Rheims, and many a man besides, both ecclesiastical and lay. And king Eadward sent thither * bishop Dudoc, and Wulfric, abbot of St. Augustine's, and * of Wells. * abbot Ælfwine, that they might make known to the king * of Ramsey what should be there determined for Christendom. And in   307. this same year king Eadward went out to Sandwich with a great naval force ; and earl Swegen, earl Godwine's son, came into Bosham with seven ships, and made his peace with the king ; and it was promised him that he should be held [1] worthy of all the things that he before possessed. Then earl Harold his brother and [2] earl Biörn said in opposition, that he should not be worthy of any of the things which the king had granted him ; but a safeguard of four nights was fixed to him for his ships. Then it was, during that time, that word came to the king that hostile ships lay westward and harried. Then went earl Godwine west about with two of the king's ships, the one commanded by earl Harold, and the other by his brother Tostig, and forty-two ships of the country people.

[1] That is *law*-worthy, or legally entitled to.
[2] Biörn was a son of Ulf jarl and Astrith, sister of Cnut, and brother of Svein, king of Denmark.

would not deceive him. He then took three companions with him, and they rode to Bosham, as if they would go to Sandwich, where Swegen's ships lay. And they immediately bound him and led him to a ship, and then went to Dartmouth, and there he caused him to be slain and deeply buried. But his kinsman Harold fetched him thence, and conveyed him to Winchester, and there buried him by king Cnut his uncle. And the king then, and all the army declared Swegen a [1] 'nithing.' He had eight ships before he murdered Biörn ; after that all but two forsook him. And he then went to Bruges, and there abode with Baldwine. And in this year died Eadnoth, the good * bishop, in Oxfordshire ; and Oswig, abbot of Thorney, and Wulfnoth, abbot of Westminster : and king Eadward gave the bishopric to [2] Ulf his priest, and ill bestowed it. And in this same year king Eadward discharged nine ships from pay, and

of Dorchester.

---

[*] Then was earl Harold moved up to the king's ship which earl Harold before commanded.' They then went west to Pevensey, and lay there weather-bound. Then two days after this, earl Swegen came thither, and spoke with his father and with earl Biörn, and prayed Biörn that he would go with him to the king at Sandwich, and aid him to the king's friendship, and he thereto assented. They then went as if they would go to the king. Then, while they were riding, Swegen begged of him that he would go with him to his ships, saying that his shipmen would go from him, unless he the more speedily came. They then went both to where his ships lay. When they came thither, earl Swegen prayed him that he would go with him on shipboard. He refused vehemently, so long until his shipmen seized him, and threw him into the boat, and bound him, and rowed to the ship, and put him therein ; then hoisted their sails, and ran west to Exmouth, and had him with them until they slew him : and they took the body, and buried it in a church. And then came his friends and sailors from London and took him up, and conveyed him to Winchester, to the Old monastery, and he is there buried by king Cnut his uncle.

---

[1] a wretch, outlaw.
[2] " genere Nortmannus." Flor. Wigorn.

[3] This passage I am unable to explain : it is apparently corrupt or defective.

they went away ships and all ; and five ships remained behind, and the king promised them twelve months' pay. And in the same year bishop Hereman and bishop Ealdred went to Rome to the pope, on the king's errand.

An. M.L. In this year, the bishops came home from Rome ; 312. and earl Swegen was inlawed. And in this same year died archbishop Eadsige, on the ivth of the Kal. of November

---

And Swegen then went east to Baldwine's land, and resided there all the winter, at Bruges, with his full protection. And in the same year died . bishop Eadnoth in the north, and Ulf * of Dorchester. was appointed bishop.ᵃ

An. M.L. —¹ Thither came also earl Swegen, who had before gone from this land to Denmark, and had there ruined himself with the Danes. He came hither with guile, saying that he would again submit to the king. And earl Biörn promised him that he would support him. Then after the reconciliation was of the emperor and Baldwine, many of the ships went home, and the king remained behind at Sandwich with a few ships : and earl Godwine also went with forty-two ships from Sandwich to Pevensey, and earl Biörn went with him. Then it was made known to the king that Osgod lay at Wulpe with thirty-nine ships ; and the king sent after the ships, which he could send off, which had before gone home. And Osgod fetched his wife from Bruges, and they went back again with six ships. And the others went to 'Sussex, to Eadulfsness, * Essex. and there did harm, and returned to their ships : and then a strong wind came against them, so that they were all destroyed but four, the crews of which were slain beyond sea. While earl Godwine and earl Biörn lay at Pevensey, earl Swegen came, and with guile prayed earl Biörn, who was his uncle's son, that he would be his companion to the king at Sandwich, and better his affairs with him. He went then, on account of their kinship, with three companions, and he led him towards Bosham, where his ships lay ; and then they bound him, and led him on shipboard, then went thence with him to Dart-

---

¹ Continued from l. 16. p. 138.

ᵃ E. F. M.XLVIII. F.

(Oct. 29th); and also, in this same year, died Ælfric, archbishop of York, on the xɪth of the Kal. of February
(Jan. 22nd); and his body lies at Peterborough. Then king
Eadward held a 'witena-gemôt' in London at Midlent, and
appointed Robert archbishop of Canterbury, and abbot Spearhafoc to London; and gave to bishop Rothulf, his kinsman,
the abbacy of Abingdon. And in the same year he discharged
all the 'lithsmen' from pay.

----

mouth, and there ordered him to be slain, and deeply buried.
He was afterwards found, and conveyed to Winchester, and
buried by king Cnut his uncle. A little before that, the men
of Hastings and thereabouts won two of his ships with their
ships, and slew all the men, and brought the ships to Sandwich to the king. He had eight ships before he inveigled
Biörn; after that all forsook him but two. In the same year
arrived in the Welsh Axe (Usk?) thirty-six ships from Ire-
* of S. Wales. land, and thereabouts did harm, with the aid of * Griffith, the
Welsh king. People were then gathered against them, there
* of Worcester. was also * bishop Ealdred with them; but they had too little
support; and they came unawares upon them at quite early
morn, and there slew many good men, and the others escaped
along with the bishop; this was done on the ɪvth of the Kal. of
August (July 29th). In this year died in Oxfordshire Oswig,
abbot of Thorney, and Wulfnoth, abbot of Westminster; and
Ulf the priest was placed as pastor to the bishopric that
Eadnoth had held; but he was afterwards driven away,
because he performed nothing bishoplike therein, so that it
shames us now to tell more. And ¹ bishop Siward died; he
lies at Abingdon. And in this year was hallowed the great
* IX. monastery at Rheims; there were the pope * Leo, and the
* Henry III. * emperor; and they had a great synod there concerning
God's service. At that synod presided the pope St. Leo. It is
difficult to know (the names) of the bishops who came thither,
and certainly of the abbots; and from this land two were
* at Canterbury. sent, from * St. Augustine's and from Ramsey.ᵃ

----

¹ " Edsii Dorubernensis archiepiscopi corepiscopus." Flor. Wigorn.

ᵃ D.

An. M.LI. In this year archbishop Robert came hither over sea with his pall. And in this same year earl Godwine and

---

An. M.LI. In this year died Eadsige, archbishop of Canter bury, and the king gave the archbishopric to Robert the Frenchman, who had before been bishop of London. And Spearhafoc, abbot of Abingdon, succeeded to the bishopric of London; and it was afterwards taken from him ere he was ordained. And bishop Hereman and bishop Ealdred went to Rome.[a]

An. M.XLVII. (M.XLIX.) In this year there was a great council at London at Midlent, and nine ships of 'lithsmen' were discharged, and five remained behind. And in this same year earl Swegen came to England. And in this same year was the great synod at Rome; and king Eadward sent thither bishop Hereman and bishop Ealdred; and they came thither on Easter-eve. And afterwards the pope had a synod at Vercelli, and bishop Ulf came thereto; and they were very near breaking his staff, if he had not given the greater treasures, because he could not do his offices so well as he should. And in this year died archbishop Eadsige, on the IVth of the Kal. of November (Oct. 29th).[b]   309.

An. M.XLVIII. In this year king Edward appointed Robert of London archbishop of Canterbury, in Lent. And in the same Lent he went to Rome after his pall. And the king gave the bishopric of London to Spearhafoc, abbot of Abing-don; and the king gave the abbacy of Abingdon to bishop Rothulf, his kinsman. Then came the archbishop from Rome, one day before St. Peter's mass-eve, and occupied his archi-episcopal chair on St. Peter's mass-day (June 29th); and im-mediately after went to the king. Then came abbot Spear-hafoc to him, with the king's letter and seal, to the end that he should ordain him bishop of London. Then the archbishop refused, and said, that the pope had forbidden it him. Then the abbot again applied to the archbishop for that purpose, and then claimed episcopal ordination, and the archbishop   313.

---

all his sons were banished from England. And he and his
wife, and his three sons, Swegen, and Tostig, and Gyrth, went

---

firmly refused him, and said, that the pope had forbidden it him.
The abbot then went to London, and resided in the bishopric,
which the king had before given him, with his full leave, all
the summer and the autumn. [And then came * Eustace from
beyond sea immediately after the bishop, and went to the king,
and spoke with him that which he wished, and then went
homewards. When he came east to Canterbury, he and his
men took refection there, and went to Dover. When he was
a few miles or more on this side of Dover, he put on his coat
of mail, and all his companions, and went to Dover. When
they came thither, they would lodge themselves where it
pleased them. Then came one of his men, and would quarter
himself in the house of an inhabitant, against his will,· and
wounded the inhabitant ; and the inhabitant slew the other.
Then Eustace mounted upon his horse, and his companions
upon theirs, and slew him within his own home ; and then
went towards the town, and slew, both within and without,
more than twenty men. And the townsmen, on the other
side, slew nineteen men, and wounded they knew not how
many. And Eustace escaped with a few men, and went again
to the king, and made known to him in part how they had
fared. And the king became very furious against the townsmen. And the king sent off earl Godwine, and bade him go
into Kent with hostility to Dover ; for Eustace had declared
to the king that it had been more the sin of the townsfolk than
his: but it was not so. And the earl would not agree to the
inroad, because he was loath to injure his own followers.
Then the king sent after all his 'witan,' and bade them come
to Gloucester near the after-mass of St. Mary (Sept. 8th).
The Welshmen had then built a castle in Herefordshire,
among the followers of earl Swegen, and wrought every kind
of harm and insult to the king's men thereabout that they
could. Then came earl Godwine, and earl Swegen, and earl
Harold, together at Beverston, and many men with them, in
order that they might go to their royal lord and to all the
'witan' who were gathered with him, that they might have

*count of
Boulogne.

315.

to Bruges; and Harold and Leofwine went to Ireland, and there dwelt the winter. And in this same year died the old lady, king Eadward's and Harthacnut's mother, named Emma,

---

the counsel and support of the king and of all the 'witan,' how they might avenge the insult to the king and to all the nation. Then were the Welshmen beforehand with the king, and accused the earls, so that they might not come within his eyesight, for they said that they would come thither to betray the king. Thither had come * earl Siward, and earl † Leofric, * of Northumbria. and many people with them from the north, to the king; † of Mercia. and it was made known to earl Godwine and his sons, that the king and the men who were with him would resolve concerning them, and they arrayed themselves firmly on the other hand; though it was hateful to them that they should stand against their royal lord. Then the 'witan' decreed, that on each side every kind of evil should cease, and the king gave God's peace and his full friendship to each side. Then the 316. king and his 'witan' decreed that, for the second time, a 'gemôt' of all the 'witan' should be held in London at the autumnal equinox; and the king ordered the army to be called out, both south of Thames and north; [1] all that ever was best. Swegen was then declared an outlaw, and earl Godwine and earl Harold were summoned to the 'gemôt,' as speedily as they could come to it. When they had come * thither, they * to London. were summoned to the 'gemôt;' then he desired a safe-conduct and hostages, so that he might come securely into the 'gemôt' and out of the 'gemôt.' Then the king required all the thanes whom the earls before had, and they gave them all into his hand. Then the king sent again to them, and commanded them that they should come with xii. men to the king's council. Then the earl again desired a safe-conduct and hostages, that he might clear himself of each of the things that he was charged with. Then the hostages were refused him, and he was decreed a safe-conduct for five nights to go out of the land. 317. And earl Godwine and earl Swegen then went to Bosham, and

---

[1] " qui meliores in sua et illorum parte erant." Flor. Wigorn.

on the IInd of the Ides of March (Mar. 14); and her body lies
in the Old monastery by king Cnut.

√ **An. M.LII.** In this year earl Harold came from Ireland
with ships to the mouth of the Severn, near to the boun-
daries of Somersetshire and Devonshire, and greatly ravaged
there; and the country people gathered against him, both
from Somersetshire and Devonshire, and he put them to flight,
and slew there more than thirty good thanes, besides
other people; and immediately after that he went about-
Penwithsteort (the Land's End). And then king Eadward
caused forty smacks to be equipped. They lay at Sandwich many weeks; they were to lie in wait for earl Godwine, who was in Bruges that winter, and yet he came hither

shoved out their ships, and went beyond sea, and sought Baldwine's protection, and dwelt there all the winter. And earl
Harold went west to Ireland, and was there all the winter under the king's protection. And shortly after this was, the king
forsook the lady who had been hallowed his queen, and caused
to be taken from her all that she owned, in land, and in gold,
and in silver, and in all things, and committed her to his sister
at Wherwell. And abbot Spearhafoc was then driven out of
the bishopric of London, and William, the king's priest, was
ordained thereto. And Odda was then set as earl over Devonshire, and over Somersetshire, and over Dorset, and over
Wales; and Ælfgar, son of earl Leofric, was set over the
earldom which Harold had before possessed.[a]

√ **An. M.LII.** In this year died Ælfric, archbishop of York,
a very venerable and wise man. And in the same year king
Eadward abolished the military contribution (heregyld) which
king Æthelred had before imposed : that was in the nine and
thirtieth year after he had begun it. That tax distressed all
the English nation during so long a space as is here above
written. That was always paid before other taxes, which
were variously paid, and with which people were manifoldly
distressed. In the same year [*]Eustace landed at Dover, who
had king Eadward's sister to wife. Then his men went

[a] E.

to land first, so that they did not know it. And in the time that he was here in the land he enticed to him all the Kentish men, and all the ''butse-carls' (shipmen) from Hastings, and everywhere there by the sea coast, and all the east end, and Sussex, and Surrey, and much else in addition thereto ; then all said that with him they would die and live. When the fleet which lay at Sandwich was apprized of God-wine's course they set out after him, and he escaped them ; he secured himself wherever he could, and the fleet went again to Sandwich, and so homeward to London. When Godwine learned that the fleet which had lain at Sandwich was gone home, he went again to Wight, and lay thereabouts by the sea-coast until earl Harold his son and he came together. And they did no great harm after they came together, except that they took provisions; but they enticed to them all the country-folk by the sea-coast, and also up in the country, and then went towards Sandwich, and collected ever on with them all the ' butse-carls ' that they met with, and then came to Sand-

318.

Foolishly after quarters, and one man of the town they slew, and another man of the town, their companion, so that there lay seven of his companions. And great harm was there done on each side, with horse and also with weapons, until the people gathered ; and they then fled, until they came to the king at Gloucester, and he gave them protection. When earl Godwine understood that such things should have hap-pened in his earldom, he began to gather people over all his earldom; and earl Swegen, his son, over his, and Harold, his other son, over his earldom; and they all gathered in Glou-cestershire, at Langtree, a great and countless force, all ready for war against the king, unless Eustace were given up, and his men delivered into their hands, and also the Frenchmen who were in the castle. This was done seven nights before the latter mass of St. Mary (Sept. 1st). King Eadward was then residing at Gloucester. He then sent after *earl Leofric, and north after *earl Siward, and required their followers. And

314.

* of Mercia.
* of Northum-bria.

---

¹ The first component of this word is, no doubt, our *buss*, as in *herring-* | *buss*; O. Nor. bússa, *a large boat*; Old High Ger. buso.

wich with an overwhelming army. When king Eadward
learned that, he sent up after more succour, but it came very
slowly; and Godwine with his fleet ever inclined towards
London, until he came to Southwark, and there waited some-
while until the flood came up. In that time he also arranged
with the townsfolk, so that they almost all would that which
he would. When he had settled all his proceedings, then came
the flood; and they then immediately drew up their anchors,
and steered through the bridge by the south shore; and the

they then came to him, first with a moderate aid, but when they .
knew how it was there in the south, they sent north over all
their earldoms, and caused a great force to be ordered out, for
the help of their lord ; and ¹ Ralph also, over his earldom;
and then they all came to Gloucester to the king's help, though
it was late. Then were they all so unanimous with the king,
that they would have sought Godwine's force, if the king had
willed it. Then some thought that it would be great folly
that they should engage, because there was most of what was
most illustrious in England in the two bodies; and thought
that they would expose the land to our foes, and cause great
destruction among ourselves. They then advised that hostages
should be mutually given, and a rendezvous appointed at
London; and thither the people were ordered out over all this
north end, in Siward's earldom, and in Leofric's, and also
elsewhere; and earl Godwine and his sons should come thither
with their defence. They came then to Southwark, and a
great multitude with them from Wessex; but his band waned
ever the longer the more. And they bound to the king by
surety all the thanes who were under his son, earl Harold ;
and they then outlawed earl Swegen, his other son. Then
it did not suit him to come with a defence to meet the king,
and to meet the army that was with him. He then went away
by night; and on the morrow the king had a 'witena-gemôt ;'
and, also all the army, declared him outlaw, him and all his
sons, and he went south to Thorney, and his wife, and his son

---

¹ He was the son of Eadward's sister Goda, married to Eustace of
Boulogne.

land-force came from above, and arrayed themselves along
the strand; and they then inclined with the ships towards the
north shore, as if they would hem in the king's ships. The
king had also a great land-force on his side, besides his shipmen ; but it was repugnant to almost all of them that they
should fight against men of their own race; for there was
little else there who could do anything great, except Englishmen on each side ; and also they would not that this country

---

Swegen, and Tostig and his wife, Baldwine of Bruges' kinswoman, and his son Gyrth. And earl Harold and Leofwine
went to Bristol, in the ship which earl Swegen had before
made ready and provisioned for himself. And the king sent
bishop * Ealdred from London with a body of men; and they * of Worcester.
were to overtake him ere he came on shipboard; but they
could not, or they would not. And he then went out from
the mouth of the Avon, and encountered such rigorous
weather, that he with difficulty got away; and he there sustained much damage. He then went on to Ireland, when
favourable weather came. And Godwine and those who were
with him went from Thorney to Bruges, to Baldwine's land, in
a ship, with as much treasure as they could possibly stow for
each man. It would have seemed wonderful to every man that
was in England, if any man before that had said that it would
so happen; for he had been before exalted to that degree, as if
he ruled the king and all England; and his sons were earls and
the king's darlings, and his daughter was wedded and married
to the king : she was brought to Wherwell, and committed to
the abbess. Then soon came count *William from beyond sea, *of Normandy.
with a great body of Frenchmen, and the king received him
and as many of his companions as it pleased him, and let him
go again. In this same year the bishopric of London was
given to William the priest, which had before been given to
Spearhafoc.ᵃ

An. M.LII. In this year died Ælfgyfu the lady, relict of
king Æthelred and king Cnut, on the IInd of the Nones of
March (Mar. 6th). In the same year Griffith, the Welsh king,

ᵃ D.

should be the more exposed to outlandish peoples, in consequence of their destroying each other. They then resolved
that wise men should be sent between them, and they settled a
peace on each side. And Godwine and his son Harold landed,
320.   and of their fleet as many as to them seemed good. And then
there was a 'witena-gemôt ;' and to Godwine was his earldom
clean given, as full and as free as he first possessed it ; and in

---

harried in Herefordshire until he came very near to Leominster ; and the men gathered against him, both the countrymen
and the Frenchmen from the castle ; and there were slain
very many good men of the English and also of the French.
* a. M.XXXIX.   That was on the same day thirteen years on which *Eadwine
was slain with his companions, etc.*

An. M.LII. In this year died Ælfgyfu Emma, the mother of
king Eadward and king Harthacnut; and in the same year the
king and his 'witan' resolved that ships should be sent out to
* of Devon.   Sandwich, and they set earl Ralph and *earl Odda as captains
thereto.   Then earl Godwine went out from Bruges with his
ships to Ysere (Ysendyk), and set sail one day before Midsummer's mass-eve, so that he came to Næss (Dungeness), which
is to the south of Romney.[1]   It then came to be known to the
earls out at Sandwich, and they went out after the other ships,
and a land-force was ordered out against the ships.   Then in
the meanwhile earl Godwine was warned, and betook himself
to Pevensey; and the weather was very violent, so that the
earls could not know how earl Godwine had fared.   And then
earl Godwine went out again until he came again to Bruges,
and the other ships betook themselves again to Sandwich.   And
it was then resolved that the ships should again return to
London, and that other earls and other chief officers should
be appointed to the ships.   It was then so long delayed that
the naval force all lagged behind, and all betook themselves

---

[1] See contination as in F., p. 153.

---

* D.

like manner to his sons, all tIfat they had before possessed ; and to his wife and his daughter, all as full and as free as they had before possessed. And they confirmed between them full friendship, and to all the people they promised good law.

---

home. Then was earl Godwine apprized of that, and, together with his fleet, hoisted his sails, and they at once betook themselves to Wight, and there landed, and there harried so long until the people paid them as much as they imposed on them. And then they went westward until they came to Portland, and there they landed and did whatever harm they could do. Harold was then come out from Ireland, with nine ships, and landed at Porlock, and there much people was gathered against him, but he failed not to procure him food ; then went up and slew a great number of people, and took to him in cattle, and in men, and in property, as it might happen. And he then betook himself eastward to his father ; and then they both betook themselves eastward until they came to Wight, and took there what they had before left behind them. And they then betook themselves thence to Pevensey, and got on with them as many ships as were there ready; and so on until he came to Næss (Dungeness); and got all the ships that were in Romney, and in Hythe, and in Folkestone, and went then east to Dover, and landed there, and there took them ships and hostages as many as they would, and so went to Sandwich, and did just the same ; and hostages were everywhere given them, and provisions wherever they desired. And then they betook themselves to Northmouth, and so towards London ; and some of the ships went. within Shepey, and there did great harm, and betook themselves to King's Middleton and burned it all, and then went to London after the earls. When they came to London, the king and all the earls lay against them with fifty ships. The earls then sent to the king, and craved of him that they might be [1] worthy

319.

321.

And they then outlawed all the Frenchmen who had before
raised up unjust law, and judged unjust judgments, and
counselled evil counsel in this country; except so many as they
resolved on that the king might like to have with him, who
were true to him and all his people. And archbishop Robert,
and bishopWilliam, and bishop Ulf, with difficulty escaped, with
the Frenchmen who were with them, and so went over sea.
And earl Godwine, and Harold, and the queen, resided on their
property.] Swegen had before gone to Jerusalem from Bruges,

---

of each of those things which had been unjustly taken from
them. Then the king, however, refused for some while ; so
long until the people who were with the earl were much
excited against the king and against his folk; so that the earl
himself with difficulty stilled the people. Then went bishop
Stigand to them, with God's support, and the wise men, both
within the town and without, and they resolved that hostages
should be fixed on each side, and it was so done. When
archbishop Robert and the Frenchmen were apprized of that,
they took their horses, and went, some to Pentecost's castle,
some north to Robert's castle. And archbishop Robert, with
bishop Ulf, and their companions, went out at East-gate and
slew and otherwise maltreated many young men, and straightways betook themselves to Eadulfsness (Walton-on-the-Naze);
and there lighted on a crazy ship, and he betook himself at
once over sea, and left his pall and all Christianity here in the
country, so as God willed it, as he had before obtained the
dignity, as God willed it not. Then a great 'gemôt' was
proclaimed without London, and all the earls and the best men
that were in this country were at the 'gemôt.' There Godwine brought forth his speech, and there declared before king
Eadward his lord, and before all the people of the land, that
he was guiltless of that which was laid to his charge, and to
Harold his son's, and all his children's. And the king gave to
the earl and his children his full friendship and full earldom,
and all that he had before possessed, and to all the men who
* Eadgyth.   were with him ; and the king gave to the *lady all that she
before owned. And archbishop Robert was without reserve

and died when homeward, at Constantinople, at Michaelmas. It was on the Monday after St. Mary's mass (Sept. 14th), that Godwine with his ships came to Southwark ; and the morning after, on the Tuesday, they were reconciled, as it here before stands. Godwine then sickened shortly after he landed and [1] re-embarked : but he made altogether too little reparation for the property of God which he had from many holy places. In the same year came the strong wind on Thomas' mass-night (Dec. 21st), and everywhere did much harm ; also was Rhys, the Welsh king's brother, slain.

---

declared an outlaw, and all the Frenchmen, because they had chiefly made the discord between earl Godwine and the king. And bishop Stigand succeeded to the archbishopric of Canterbury ; and at this same time Arnwi, abbot of Peterborough, left the abbacy in sound health, and gave it to Leofric, a monk, by leave of the king and of the monks ; and abbot Arnwi lived afterwards eight winters. And the abbot Leofric then so enriched the monastery that it was called the golden borough ; it then waxed greatly in land, and in gold, and in silver.[a]

An. M.LII. —and so went to Wight, and took there all the ships which might be of any value, and hostages, and so turned eastward. And Harold with nine ships was arrived at Porlock, and there slew many people, and took cattle, and men, and property, and went eastward to his father ; and they both went to Romney, to Hythe, to Folkestone, to Dover, to Sandwich ; and ever took all the ships that they found, which might be of any value, and hostages as they went, and then betook themselves to London, etc.[b]

---

[1] In the text 'eft gewyrpte,' which I do not understand ; my translation is consequently conjectural. It may be a nautical term.

---

[a] E. [b] F. in continuation, see p. 150.

322.

An. M.LIII. In this year the king was in Winchester, at Easter (April 11th), and earl Godwine with him, and Harold his son, and Tostig. Then on the second Easter-day he was sitting with the king at refection, when he suddenly sank down by the footstool, deprived of speech and of all his power ; and he was then removed into the king's chamber ; and it was thought that it would pass over, but it was not so ; but he continued so, speechless and powerless, until the Thursday, and then resigned his life ; and he lies there within the Old monastery. And his son Harold succeeded to his earldom, and resigned that which he before had, and Ælfgar succeeded thereto. In this same year died Wulfsige, bishop of Lichfield ; and Leofwine, abbot of Coventry, succeeded to the bishopric. And Ægelward, abbot of Glastonbury, died, and Godwine, abbot of Winchcombe. Also the Welshmen slew a great number of English folk of the wardmen, near Westbury. [1] In

An. M.LIII. In this year was the great wind on Thomas' mass-night (Dec. 21st) ; and also all the Midwinter there was much wind. And it was resolved that Rhys, the Welsh king's brother, should be slain, because he committed ravages, and his head was brought to Gloucester on Twelfth-day eve. And in this same year, before All-Hallows mass (Nov. 1st), died Wulfsige, bishop of Lichfield, and Godwine, abbot of Winchcombe, and Ægelward, abbot of Glastonbury, all within one month ; and Leofwine succeeded to the bishopric of Lichfield, *of Worcester. and *bishop Ealdred assumed the abbacy of Winchcombe ; and Ægelnoth succeeded to the abbacy of Glastonbury. And in the same year died Ælfric, Odda's brother, at Deerhurst, and his body rests at Pershore. And in the same year died earl Godwine, and he was taken ill where he was sitting with the king at Winchester. And Harold, his son, succeeded to the earldom, which his father had before had ; and earl Ælfgar succeeded to the earldom which Harold had before had.[a]

323.

[1] Stigand occupied the see of Robert, and had not received his | pall from the pope. Kinsi did not get his pall before 1054.—R.P.

[a] D.

this year there was no archbishop in this land ; but bishop
Stigand held the bishopric of Canterbury at Christchurch,
and Kynsige that of York ; and *Leofwine and Wulfwi went * of Lichfield.
over sea, and there caused themselves to be ordained bishops.
Wulfwi succeeded to the *bishopric that Ulf had had, he being * Dorchester.
living, and driven away.

An. M.LIV. In this year *earl Siward went with a great * of Northum-
army into Scotland, and made great slaughter of the Scots, bria.
and put them to flight, and the king escaped. Many also fell
on his side, both Danish and English, and also his own son.
In the same year was hallowed the monastery at Evesham, on
the VIth of the Ides of October (Oct. 10th). In the same
year *bishop Ealdred went south over sea to Saxony, and * of Worcester.
was received there with great veneration. In the same year
Osgod Clapa died suddenly as he lay on his bed. In this year
died *Leo, the holy pope of Rome. And in this year was so * IX.
great a murrain among the cattle, as no man remembered for
many winters before. And Victor was chosen pope.

An. M.LIII. In this year died earl Godwine, on the XVIIth
of the Kal. of May (Apr. 15th), and he is buried at Winchester,
in the Old monastery ; and earl Harold, his son, succeeded to
the earldom, and to all which his father had owned ; and earl
Ælfgar succeeded to the earldom which Harold had before
possessed.*

An. M.LIV. In this year earl Siward went with a large army
to Scotland, both with a naval force and with a land force, and
fought against the Scots, and put to flight the king Macbeth,
and slew all that was best there in the land, and led thence
great booty, such as no man had before obtained. But his son
Osbern, and his sister's son Siward, and some of his 'húscarls,'
and also of the king's, were there slain, on the day of the Seven
Sleepers (July 27th). In the same year bishop Ealdred went
to Cologne over sea, on the king's errand, and was there
received with great worship by the *emperor ; and there he * Henry III.
abode well nigh a year ; and each gave him entertainment,

---

* E. F.

An. M.LV. In this year earl Siward died at York, and his body lies within the monastery of Galmanhô, which he himself had before built, to the glory of God and all his saints. Then, thereafter, within a little space, was a ' witena-gemôt ' at London ; and earl Ælfgar, earl Leofric's son, was outlawed without any guilt ; and he went then to Ireland, and there got him a fleet, that was eighteen ships, besides his own ; and
*of N. Wales. they went thence to Brytland (Wales) to * king Griffith, with that force, and he received him in his friendship. And they gathered then a great force, with the Irishmen and with the Welsh race ; and earl Ralph gathered a great force against them at Hereford town. And they sought them there ; but before there was any spear shot the English folk fled, because they were on horses ;¹ and a great slaughter was made there,

---

324.   both the bishop of Cologne and the emperor. And he allowed
*of Lichfield.   * bishop Leofwine to hallow the monastery at Evesham, on the vᴛth of the Ides of October (Oct. 10th). And in this year Osgod Clapa died suddenly in his bed. And in this year died St. Leo the pope; and Victor was chosen pope in his stead.ª

An. M.LV. In this year earl Siward died at York, and he lies at Galmanhô, in the monastery which he himself had caused to be built and hallowed in the name of God and St. .Olaf ; and Tostig succeeded to the earldom which he had had.
*of York.   And *archbishop Kynsige fetched his pall from pope Victor. And soon thereafter, ²earl Ælfgar, son of earl Leofric, was outlawed, almost without guilt. But he went ɟo Ireland and

---

¹ Florence of Worcester removes all doubt as to which were mounted on horses. " Timidus dux Radulfus " illis occurrens, Anglos contra " morem in equis pugnare jussit: " sed cum prœlium essent commis-" suri, comes cum suis Francis et " Nortmannis fugam primitus capes-

" sit. Quod videntes Angli, ducem " suum fugiendo sequuntur," etc.
² " Algarus comes exul factus " est propterea quod debuit esse " delator patriæ, quod ipse ante " cognovit ita esse, licet verbum " illud improviso exprimerit." F. Lat.

ª D.

about four or five hundred men, and on the other side not one. And they went then to the town and burned it, and the great monastery, which the venerable bishop Æthelstân had before caused to be built, that they plundered, and bereaved of relics and of vestments, and of all things ; and slew the folk, and led some away. Then a force was gathered from very near all England, and they came to Gloucester, and so went out, not far into Wales, and there lay some while. And earl Harold meanwhile caused a ditch to be dug about the * town. Then * Hereford. in the interval peace was spoken for, and Earl Harold and those who were with him came to Bilsley, and there peace 326. and friendship were confirmed between them. And earl Ælf-

---

to Brytland (Wales), and got him there a great band, and so went to Hereford ; but there came against him earl Ralph, with a large army ; and with little trouble he brought them to flight, and slew a great number in the flight ; and went then to Hereford town, and harried it, and burned the great monastery which bishop Æthelstân had built, and slew the priests within the monastery, and many besides, and took all the treasures therein, and led away with them. And when they had done the most evil, the counsel was resolved on that earl Ælfgar should be inlawed, and his earldom restored to him, and all that had been taken from him. This harrying took place on the ixth of the Kal. of November (Oct. 24th). In ˄ the same year died Tremerin, the Welsh bishop, soon after that harrying ; and he was bishop Æthelstân's substitute after he was infirm.ᵃ

An. M.LV. In this year earl Siward died ; and then was summoned a general ‘ witena-gemôt,’ seven nights before 325. Midlent (Mar. 20th) ; ¹ and earl Ælfgar was outlawed, because it was cast upon him that he was a traitor to the king and to all the people of the land. And he confessed it before all the men who were there gathered ; though the word escaped him involuntarily. And the king gave the earldom to gar was then inlawed, and there was restored to him all that had before been taken from him. And the fleet went to

---

¹ See *note* ², p. 156.

ᵃ D.

Chester, and there awaited their pay, which Ælfgar had promised them. The slaughter was on the ixth of the Kal. of
November (Oct. 24th). In the same year died Tremerig, the
* of St. David's. *Welsh bishop, soon after that harrying : he was bishop
Æthelstân's substitute, after he was infirm.

An. M.LVI. In this year bishop Ægelric left his bishopric at
Durham, and went to Peterborough, to St. Peter's monastery;
and his brother Ægelwine succeeded thereto. In this year
died Æthelstân, the venerable bishop, on the ivth of the Ides
of February (Feb. 10th), and his body lies at Hereford town ;
and Leofgar was appointed bishop. He was earl Harold's
* had. D. mass-priest. He *wore his ¹ 'kenepas' in his priesthood, until
he was a bishop : he forsook his chrism and his rood, his
ghostly weapons, and took to his spear and to his sword, after
his bishophood, and so went in the force against Griffith, the
Welsh king, and he was there slain, and his priests with him,
and Ælfnoth the shire-reeve, and many good men with them;
and the others fled away. This was eight nights before Midsummer. It is difficult to tell the misery, and all the marches,
and the encamping, and the labour, and the destruction of
men, and also of horses, which all the English army under-
* of Mercia. went, until *earl Leofric met them, and earl Harold, and
* of Worcester. *bishop Ealdred, and made peace between them ; so that
Griffith swore oaths, that he would be to king Eadward a
faithful and unfailing under-king. And bishop Ealdred succeeded to the bishopric that Leofgar had before had for eleven

---

Tostig, son of earl Godwine, which earl Siward had before
possessed. And earl Ælfgar sought the protection of Griffith,
in North Wales. And in this year Griffith and Ælfgar
burned St. Æthelbryht's monastery, and all the town of
Hereford.ᵃ

---

¹ Qu. *headpiece*, Scot. knapscap?
   " Let ilca ane his *knapscap* lace,
   " Let ilca ane his steil-jack brace."
                          Minstr. of Scot. Border, III. 476, edit. 1821.
   Or *Knapsack*, Fr. canapsa?

ᵃ E.

weeks and four days. In the same year died [1] Cona the emperor. In this year died *earl Odda, and his body lies at *of Devon. Pershore; and he was ordained monk before his end, a good man and pure, and very noble; and he died on the iind of the Kal. of September (Aug. 31st.)

An. M.LVII. In this year came Eadward ætheling to England; he was king Eadward's brother's son, king Eadmund, who was called Ironside for his valour. This ætheling had king Cnut sent away to Hungary to be betrayed; but he there throve into a good man, as him God granted, and him well became; so that he got the emperor's *kinswoman to *niece. wife, and by whom a fair offspring he begot: she was named Agatha. We know not for what cause it was done, that he might not see his kinsman king Eadward. Alas! that was a rueful hap, and a baleful, for all this nation, that he so quickly his life ended, after he came to England, to the unhappiness of this poor nation. In the same year died earl Leofric, on the iind of the Kal. of October (Sept. 30th). He was very wise 'fore God and also 'fore the world, which profited all this nation. He lies at Coventry, and his son Ælfgar succeeded to his government. And in that year earl Ralph died, on the xiith of the Kal. of January (Dec. 21st), and lies at Peterborough. Also died bishop Heca in Sussex, and Ægelric was raised to his *see. And in this year † pope Victor died, *Selsey. †II. and *Stephen was chosen pope.   *IX.

328.

An. M.LVII. In this year Eadward ætheling, king Eadmund's son, came hither to land, and shortly after died; and his body is buried within St. Paul's monastery at London. And pope Victor died, and Stephen was chosen pope: he was abbot of Monte-Cassino. And earl Leofric died, and Ælfgar his son succeeded to the earldom which his father before had.[a]

329.

---

[1] I can account for this extraordinary appellation bestowed on the emperor Henry III. only by supposing it extracted by the simple scribe from the word Franconia, Henry III. being of the Franconian line of emperors.

[a] E.

An. M.LVIII. In this year earl Ælfgar was banished ; but
*k. of N. Wales. he soon came in again with force, through *Griffith's aid.
And this year came a naval force from Norway. It is longsome to tell how it all went. In the same year bishop
Ealdred hallowed the monastery at Gloucester, which he
himself had raised to the glory of God and St. Peter ; and
then went to Jerusalem, with such state as no other did
before him, and there devoted himself to God, and also offered
a worthy gift at our Lord's sepulchre, that was a golden
chalice of five marks, of very wondrous work. In the same
*X. year died pope Stephen, and *Benedict was appointed pope :
he sent a pall to bishop Stigand. Ægelric was ordained
*of Selsey. *bishop in Sussex, and abbot Siward bishop of Rochester.
*II. An. M.LIX. In this year *Nicholas was chosen pope ; he had
before been bishop of the city of Florence ; and Benedict was
driven out, who was pope there before. And in this year the
steeple was hallowed at Peterborough, on the XVIth of the
Kal. of November (Oct. 17th).

An. M.LVIII. In this year pope Stephen died, and Benedict
was hallowed pope : the same sent hither to land the pall to
archbishop Stigand. And in this year died Heca, bishop of
Sussex ; and archbishop Stigand ordained Ægelric, a monk
of Christ-church, bishop of Sussex, and abbot Siward bishop
of Rochester.* .
*Wells. An. M.LXI. In this year died Duduc bishop of *Somerset, and
*of Rochester. Gisa succeeded. And in the same year died *bishop Godwine
at St. Martin's, on the VIIth of the Ides of March (Mar. 9th).
And in the same year died Wulfric, abbot of St. Augustine's,
within the Easter week, on the XIVth of the Kal. of May
(Apr. 18th). When word came to the king that abbot Wulfric was departed, he chose Æthelsige, a monk, in his stead,
*at Winchester. from the *Old monastery : he then followed archbishop
Stigand, and was hallowed abbot at Windsor, on St. Augustine's mass-day (May 26th).b

---

* E. F. Here ends MS. Cott. Domit. A. VIII. b E.

An. M.LX. In this year there was a great earthquake, on the Translation of St. Martin (July 4th); and king [*]Henry died [*]1. in France ; and Kynsige, archbishop of York, departed on the XIth of the Kal. of January (Dec. 22nd), and he lies at Peterborough ; and [*]bishop Ealdred succeeded to the bishopric ; [*]of Worcester. and Walter succeeded to the bishopric of Herefordshire ; and bishop Duduc also died, who was bishop of [*]Somerset; and [*]Wells. Gisa, a priest, was set in his stead.

An. M.LXI. In this year bishop Ealdred went to Rome after his pall, and he received it from pope Nicholas. And earl Tostig and his wife also went to Rome ; and the bishop and the earl suffered great hardship when they came homeward. And in this year died [*]bishop Godwine, at [†]St. Martin's ; [*]of Rochester. [†]at Canterbury. and Wulfric, abbot of St. Augustine's, on the XIVth of the Kal. of [*]April (Mar. 19th). And pope Nicholas died, and [*]May? see p. 160. [*]Alexander was chosen pope ; he had been bishop of Lucca. [*]II.

An. M.LXII.

An. M.LXIII. In this year, after Midwinter, earl Harold 330. went from Gloucester to Rhuddlan, which was Griffith's, and burned the residence, and his ships, and all the equipments which belonged thereto, and put him to flight. And then, at the Rogation days (May 26th), Harold went with ships from Bristol about Brytland (Wales), and the people made peace, and gave hostages. And Tostig went with a land-force against them, and they subdued the land. But in this same year, in autumn, king Griffith was slain, on the Nones of August (Aug. 5th), by his own men, because of the war which he

---

An. M.LXII. In this year Le Maine was subjugated by William, count of Normandy.[a]

An. M.LXIII. In this year earl Harold and his brother, earl 331. Tostig, went both with a land-force and with a naval force into Brytland (Wales), and they subdued the land ; and the people gave them hostages, and submitted; and went after that and slew their king Griffith, and brought his head to Harold ; and he appointed another king thereto.[a]

---

[a] E.

warred against earl Harold.   He was king over all the Welsh
race ; and his head was brought to earl Harold, and Harold
brought it to the king, and his ship's head, and the 'top therewith.   And king Eadward delivered the land over to his
two brothers, Blethgent and *Rigwatla ; and they swore oaths,
and gave hostages to the king and to the earl, that they would
be faithful to him in all things, and ready to [serve] him
everywhere by water and by land, and to pay such requisitions
from the land as had been done before to any other king.

An. M.LXIV.

An. M.LXV. In this year, before Lammas (Aug. 1st), earl
Harold ordered a building to be erected in Brytland (Wales) at
Portskewet, when he had subdued it ; and had thereto gathered
much property, and thought to have king Eadward there for
the sake of hunting.   But when it was all ready, then went
Cradoc, the son of Griffith, with all the gang which he could
get, and slew almost all the people who were there building,
and took the property which was there prepared.   We know
not who first counseled this evil counsel. ² This was done on
St. Bartholomew's mass-day (Aug. 24th).   And shortly after
this, all the thanes in Yorkshire and in Northumberland
gathered together, and outlawed their earl Tostig, and slew all
his household-men that they could come at, both English and
Danish, and took all his weapons at York, and gold and silver,
and all his treasures which they could anywhere hear of, and
sent after Morkere, son of earl Ælfgar, and chose him for their

*Rithwalan,
Fl. Wigorn.

332.

---

²An. M.LXV. —And the slaughter was on St. Bartholomew's
mass-day (Aug. 24th).   And then, after St. Michael's, all the
thanes in Yorkshire went to York, and there slew all earl
Tostig's 'hûscarls' whom they might hear of, and took his
treasures.   And Tostig was then at Brytford with the king.
And then, very shortly after, there was a great 'gemôt'
at Northampton ; and so at Oxford, on the day of St. Simon

---

¹ For 'bone' of the text we
should probably read bune, car-
chesium, so called apparently from
its cup-like form in the ancient vessels. Florence renders 'bone' by
ornatura.

earl : and he went south with all the shire, and with Nottinghamshire, and Derbyshire, and Lincolnshire, until he came to Northampton : and his brother Eadwine came to meet him with the men who were in his earldom, and also many Britons 333. came with him. There came earl Harold to meet them, and they laid an errand on him to king Eadward, and also sent messengers with him, and prayed that they might have Morkere for their earl. And the king granted it, and sent Harold again to them at Northampton, on the eve of St. Simon and St. Jude's mass (Oct. 27th) ; and he made known the same to them, and gave his hand thereto ; and he there renewed Cnut's law. And the 'Rythrenan did great harm about Northampton, while he went on their errand, inasmuch as they slew men, and burned houses and corn, and took all the cattle which they could come at, that was many thousand; and many hundred men they took, and led north with them ; so that the shire, and the other shires which are nigh there, were for many winters the worse. And earl Tostig, and his wife, and all those who would what he would, went south over sea with him to *count Baldwine, and he received them all, and * of Flanders. they were all the winter there. And king Eadward came to Westminster at Midwinter, and there caused the monastery to be hallowed, which he himself had built to the glory of God,

----

and St. Jude (Oct. 28th). And earl Harold was there, and would work their reconciliation, if he could, but he could not ; for all his earldom unanimously renounced and outlawed him (Tostig), and all who raised up lawlessness with him ; because he first robbed God, and bereaved all those of life and of land over whom he had power. And they then took to them Morkere for earl ; and Tostig then went over sea, and his wife with him, to Baldwine's land, and took a winter-residence at St. Omer's, etc.[a]

----

[1] þa Northernan men.—E.

----

[a] C.

and St. Peter, and to all God's saints : and the church-hallow-
ing was on Childermas day (Dec. 28th). And he died on
Twelfth-day eve (Jan. 5th), and was buried on Twelfth-day,
in the same monastery, as it hereafter says :

This year king Eadward,
of Angles lord,
sent his truthful
soul to Christ,
into God's protection,
a holy spirit.
He in the world here
abode a while
in kingly majesty,
334.   of counsels mighty.
Four and twenty
winters number'd
the noble ruler,
wealth dispens'd ;
and he a prosperous time,
ruler of men,
illustrious govern'd
Welsh and Scots,
and Britons eke,
the son of Æthelred,
Angles and Saxons,
champions bold,
whom clasp around
cold ocean-waves,
all that to Eadward,
noble king,
faithfully obey'd,
warrior men.
Was aye blithe of mood
the baleless king,
though he long ere
of land bereft,
in exile dwelt,
widely on earth,

after that Cnut o'ercame
the race of Æthelred,
and Danes rul'd o'er
the dear realm
of England,
eight and twenty
winters number'd,
wealth dispens'd.
After that came forth
in trappings goodly,
a king in virtues good,
chaste and mild :
Eadward the noble,
his country guarded,
his land and people,
until came suddenly
the bitter death,
and so dearly took   335.
the noble [king] from earth.
Angels bore
the truthful soul
into heaven's light :
and the sage nathless
the realm committed
to an illustrious man,
Harold himself,
a noble earl,
He in all time
faithfully obey'd
his lord,
by words and deeds,
nor aught neglected
of what was needful
to his sovereign king.

And in this year also earl Harold was hallowed king ; and he
experienced little quiet therein, the while that he ruled the
realm.

✔ An. M.LXVI. In this year king Harold came from York to Westminster, at the Easter which was after the Midwinter in which the king died ; and Easter was then on the day the XVIth of the Kal. of May (April 16th). Then was seen over all England such a sign in the heavens as no man ever before saw. ✦Some men said that it was the star cometa, which some men call the haired star ; and it first appeared on the eve of Litania major, the VIIIth of the Kal. of May (Apr. 24th), and so shone all the seven nights. And shortly after, earl Tostig came from beyond sea into Wight, with as large a fleet as he could get ; and there he was paid both in money and provisions. [1] And king Harold his brother gathered so great a naval force, and also a land-force as no king here in the land had before done : because it had been made known to him that William the Bastard would come hither and win this land ; all as it afterwards came to pass. And the while came earl Tostig into the Humber with sixty ships ; and earl Eadwine came with a land-force and drove him out. And the *sailor* 'butse-carls' forsook him ; and he went to Scotland with twelve smacks; and there Harald, king of Norway, met him

336.

An. M.LXVI. In this year king Eadward died, and earl Harold succeeded to the kingdom, and held it forty weeks and one day. And in this year William came, and won England. And in this year Christchurch was burnt. And in this year a comet appeared on the XIVth of the Kal. of May (Apr. 18th).[a]

An. M.LXVI. [1]—And he then went thence, and did harm everywhere by the sea-coast where he could approach, until he came to Sandwich. Then it was made known to king Harold, who was in London, that Tostig his brother was come to Sandwich. He then gathered so great a naval force, and also a land-force, as no king here in the land had before gathered ; because it had for truth been said to him, that count William from Normandy, king Eadward's kinsman, would come hither and subdue this land, all as it afterwards came to pass. When Tostig learned that, that king Harold was proceeding towards Sandwich, he went from Sandwich, and took some of the 'butse-carls' with him, some willingly, some unwillingly ;·

[a] A.

with three hundred ships ; and Tostig submitted to him, and became his man ; and then they both went into the Humber, until they came to York ; and there fought against them earl Eadwine and earl Morkere his brother ; but the Normen had the victory. It was then made known to Harold, king of the Angles, that this had thus happened : and this battle was on St. Matthew's eve (Sept. 20th). Then came Harold our king unawares on the Normen, and met with them beyond York, at Stamford-bridge, with a large army of English folk ; and there during the day was a very severe fight on each side. There were slain Harald [1] Hârfagri and earl Tostig ; and the Normen who were there left were put to flight ; and the English hotly slew them from behind, until they came to their ships ; ·some were drowned, and some also burnt, and so diversly perished, that few were left ; and the English had possession of the place of carnage. The king then gave peace to Olaf, the Normen's king's son, and to their bishop, and to the earl

* Pall.

of * Orkney, and to all those who were left in the ships ; and they then went up to our king, and swore oaths, that they would ever observe peace and friendship to this land ; and the king let them go home with twenty-four ships. These

---

and then went north into the Humber, and there harried in Lindsey, and there slew many good men. When earl Eadwine and earl Morkere were apprized of that, they came thither, and drove him from the land ; and he then went to Scotland, and the king of the Scots gave him an asylum, and aided him with provisions, and he there abode all the summer.

338.

Then came king Harold to Sandwich, and there awaited his fleet, because it was long before it could be gathered. And when his fleet was gathered, he went to Wight, and there lay all the summer and the autumn; and a land-force was kept everywhere by the sea, though at the end it availed naught. When it was the Nativity of St. Mary (Sept. 8th) the men's provisions were gone, and no man could longer keep them there. The

---

[1] The English chroniclers give the surname of Hârfagr, *Fair-hair*, *Fairfax*, to this prince, instead of   Hardrâda, *Severe*.   Harald Hârfagri died in 934.

two great battles were fought within five nights. Then came
William count of Normandy to Pevensey, on St. Michael's
mass-eve (Sept. 28th) ; and immediately after they were
ready, they constructed a castle at the town of Hastings. This
was then made known to king Harold, and he gathered a great
army, and came to meet him at the hoar apple-tree. And
William came against him unawares, ere his people were in
battle order. But the king, nevertheless, boldly fought
against him with those men who would follow him ; and there
was a great slaughter made on each side. There were slain
king Harold, and earl Leofwine his brother, and earl Gyrth
his brother, and many good men ; and the French had possession of the place of carnage, as to them God granted for the
people's sins. Archbishop Ealdred then, and the townsmen of
London would have Eadgar child for king, as was indeed his

men were then allowed to go home, and the king rode up, and
the ships were [1] driven to London, and many perished before
they came thither. When the ships were come home, came
king Harald from Norway, north into the Tyne, and unawares
with a very large naval force, and no little . . . . that might
be . . . or more. And earl Tostig came to him with all that
he had got, as they had before settled : and then they both
went, with all the fleet, along the Ouse, up towards York.
When it was announced to king Harold in the south, when he
had come from on ship-board, that king Harald of Norway and
earl Tostig had landed near York, he went northward, by day
and by night, as speedily as he could gather his force. Then,
before that king Harold could come thither, earl Eadwine and
earl Morkere had gathered from their earldom as large a body
as they could get, and fought against the army, and made
great slaughter, and there were many of the English people
slain, and drowned, and driven in fight ; and the Normen had
possession of the place of carnage. And this flight was on the
vigil of Matthew the apostle (Sept. 20th), and it was Wednes-

---

[1] A similar use of drífan, *to drive*, as a nautical term, occurs in Beowulf,
5607.

" þa þe brentingas	*those who their foamy barks*
" ofer flóda genipu	*over the mists of floods*
" feorran drífað."	drive *from afar.*

natural right ; and Eadwine and Morkere promised him that
they would fight with him ; but as it ever should be the forwarder so was it ever, from day to day, slower and worse, as
at the end it all went. ⌈This fight was fought on the day of
Calixtus the pope (Oct. 14th).⌉ And count William went afterwards again to Hastings, and there awaited whether the nation
would submit to him ; but when he perceived that they would
not come to him, he went up with all his army which was left
to him, and what had afterwards come over sea to him, and
harried all that part which he passed over, until he came to
of York.   Berkhampstead.   And there came to meet him * archbishop
Ealdred, and Eadgar child, and earl Eadwine, and earl Morkere, and all the best men of London, and then from necessity

----

day.   And then, after the fight, king Harald of Norway and
earl Tostig went to York, with as many people as to them
339.   seemed good.   And they gave them hostages from the city,
and aided them in procuring food, and so they went thence to
their ships, and agreed to full peace, so that they should all go
with him south and this land subdue.   Then, during this,
came Harold, king of the Angles, with all his force, on the
Sunday, to Tadcaster, and there arrayed his fleet ; and then
on Monday went out through York.   And king Harald of
Norway, and earl Tostig, and their army were gone from their
ships beyond York to Stamford-bridge, because it has been
promised them as certain, that there, from all the shire, hostages would be brought to meet them.   Then came Harold,
king of the Angles, against them, unawares, beyond the bridge,
and they there engaged together, and were fighting very boldly
long in the day ; and there were king Harald of Norway, and
earl Tostig slain, and numberless people with them, both Normen and English ; and the Normen fled from the English.
' Then was there one of the Norwegians who withstood the
English folk, so that they could not pass over the bridge or
gain the victory.   Then an Englishman aimed at him with an
arrow, but it availed naught ; and then came another under
the bridge, and pierced him through under the corselet.   Then
came Harold, king of the Angles, over the bridge, and his force

---

' What follows is in a later hand, and exceedingly corrupt as to language.

submitted when the greatest harm had been done ; and it was
very imprudent that it was not done earlier, as God would
not better it for our sins : and they gave hostages, and swore
oaths to him ; and he promised them that he would be a kind
lord to them ; and yet, during this, they harried all that they
passed over. Then on Midwinter's day, archbishop Ealdred
hallowed him king at Westminster ; and he pledged him on
* Christ's book, and also swore, before he would set the crown   * the Gospels.
on his head, that he would govern this nation as well as any
king before him had best done, if they would be faithful to

---

onward with him, and there made great slaughter of both
Norwegians and Flemings : and the king's son Hetmund
Harold let go home to Norway with all the ships.[1]
   An. M.LXVI. In this year the monastery at Westminister   337.
was hallowed on Childermas day (Dec. 28th). And king
Eadward died on Twelfth-mass eve (Jan. 5th); and he was
buried on Twelfth-mass day, within the newly hallowed
church at Westminster. And earl Harold succeeded to the
kingdom of England, as the king had granted it to him, and
men had also chosen him thereto; and he was blessed as king
on Twelfth-mass day. · And in the same year that he was
king, he went out with a naval force against * William; and   * of Normandy.
the while came earl Tostig into the Humber with sixty ships.
Earl Eadwine came with a land-force and drove him out, and
the ' butse-carls ' forsook him. And he went to Scotland with
twelve smacks and Harald the Norwegian king met him with
three hundred ships, and Tostig submitted to him; and they
both went into the Humber, until they came to York. And
earl Morkere and earl Eadwine fought against them, and the
Norwegian king had the victory. And it was made known to
king Harold how it was there done and had happened ; and
he came with a great army of Englishmen, and met him at
Stamford-bridge, and slew him and the earl Tostig, and bravely
overcame all the army. And the while count William landed
at Hastings, on St. Michael's mass-day; and Harold came
from the north and fought against him before his army had all
come ; and there he fell, and his two brothers, Gyrth and
Leofwine; and William subdued this land, and came to West-

---

[1] Here ends MS. Cott. Tiber. B. I. C .

him. Nevertheless, he laid a very heavy contribution on the people, and then, in Lent, went over sea to Normandy, and took with him archbishop Stigand, and Ægelnoth, abbot of Glastonbury, and Eadgar child, and earl Eadwine, and earl Morkere, and earl Waltheof, and many other good men of England. And [1]bishop Odo, and [2]earl William remained here

minster, and archbishop Ealdred hallowed him king; and men paid him tribute and gave him hostages, and afterwards bought their land. And then was Leofric abbot of Peterborough with that same force, and sickened there, and came home, and died soon after, on All-Hallows mass-night (Nov. 1st): God be merciful to his soul! In his day there was all bliss and all good in Peterborough ; and he was dear to all people, so that the king gave to St. Peter and him the abbacy of Burton and that of Coventry, which earl Leofric, who was his uncle, had before founded, and that of Crowland, and that of Thorney. And he did so much for its good to the monastery of Peterborough, in gold, and in silver, and in clothing, and in land, as never any other did before him, or any after him. Then [3]Golden Borough became Wretched Borough. The monks then chose for abbot the provost Brand, because he was a very good man, and very wise, and sent him to Eadgar ætheling, because the people of the land weened that he should be king; and the ætheling blithely assented thereto. When king William heard that say he was very wroth, and said that the abbot had contemned him. Then went good men between them and reconciled them ; because the abbot was a good man. He then gave the king forty marks of gold for a reconciliation ; and he then lived a little while after, only three years. After that came every tribulation and every evil to the monastery. God be merciful to it! [a]

[1] Odo, bishop of Bayeux, half brother of the Conqueror, being the son of his mother Arlette by her husband Herluin de Conteville.

[2] William Fitz Osbern, created by William earl of Hereford.

[3] See page 153.

[a] E.

behind, and wrought castles widely throughout the nation, and oppressed the poor people ; and ever after that it greatly grew in evil. May the end be good when God will.]

An. M.LXVII. In this year the king came again to England, on St. Nicholas' mass-day (Dec. 6th) ; and on that day Christchurch at Canterbury was burnt, and bishop Wulfwig died, and is buried at his episcopal see in Dorchester. And Eadric child and the Britons were in a state of hostility, and were warring against the castlemen at Hereford, and doing them much harm. And in this year the king set a heavy tax on the poor people ; and, nevertheless, caused to be harried all that they passed over. And then he went to Devonshire, and besieged the town of Exeter for eighteen days, and there many of his army perished ; but he promised them well, and ill performed. And they gave the town up to him, because the thanes had deceived them. And in this summer Eadgar child went out, with his mother Agatha, and his two sisters, Margaret and Christina, and Mærleswegen and many good men with them, and came to Scotland, under the protection of king Malcolm, and he received them all. Then king Malcolm began to yearn after *his sister Margaret to wife ; *Eadgar's. but he and all his men long refused ; and she herself also declined, and said,—

that she nor him nor any one would have, if to her the heavenly Clemency would grant, that she in maidenhood

the mighty Lord, with corporal heart, in this short life, in pure continence, might propitiate.

The king earnestly urged her brother, until he answered

340.

An. M.LXVII. In this year the king went over sea, and had with him hostages and treasures, and came in the next year, on St. Nicholas' mass-day ; and on that day was Christchurch at Canterbury burnt. And when he came back, he gave away every man's land. And this summer, Eadgar child went out, and Mærleswegen, and many men with them, and went to Scotland ; and king Malcolm received them all, and took the child's sister Margaret to wife.ᵃ

341.

ᵃ E.

'yea;' and indeed he durst not otherwise, because they were
come into his power. It then came to pass as God had before
provided, and it might not be otherwise, as he himself in his
gospel saith, that not even a sparrow may fall into a snare
without his providence. The prescient Creator knew beforehand what he would have done by her ; for she was to increase the praise of God in the land and direct the king from
the erroneous path, and incline him, together with his people,
to a better way, and suppress the evil habits which the nation
had previously cultivated : as she afterwards did. The king
then received her, though it was against her will ; and her
manners pleased him, and he thanked God who had mightily
given him such a mate, and wisely bethought him—as he was
a very sagacious man—and turned himself to God, and contemned every impurity ; according to what the apostle Paul,
the teacher of all the gentiles, said : " Salvabitur vir infidelis
" per mulierem fidelem ; sic et mulier infidelis per virum
" fidelem," etc. ; that is in our tongue : *Full oft the unbe-*
lieving man is hallowed and healed through the righteous
(believing) woman; and, in like manner, the woman through
the believing man. This aforesaid queen afterwards performed many useful deeds in the land, to the glory of God
and also in royal qualities bore herself well, as to her was
natural. Of a believing and noble race she sprang : her
father was Eadward ætheling, son of king Eadmund, Eadmund was son of Æthelred, Æthelred of Eadgar, Eadgar of
*Eadred, and so on in that royal kin: and her mother's kin
goes to the emperor Henry, who had dominion over Rome.
And in this year Gytha, Harold's mother, went out, and
many good men's wives with her, to Flatholm, and there
abode some while ; and so went thence over sea to St. Omer's.
At this Easter the king came to Winchester ; and Easter was
then on the xth of the Kal. of April (Mar. 23rd). And soon
after that came Matilda the lady hither to land : and archbishop Ealdred hallowed her queen at Westminster, on Whit-
sunday (May 11th). It was then announced to the king that
the people in the north had gathered themselves together,
and would stand against him if he came. He then went to
Nottingham, and there wrought a castle ; and so went to
York, and there wrought two castles, and in Lincoln, and
everywhere in that part. And earl Gospatric and the best

* Sic MS. for
Eadmund.

342.

men went to Scotland. And in the same time came one of Harold's sons from Ireland, with a naval force, into the mouth of the Avon unawares, and immediately harried over all that part ; they then went to Bristol, and would storm the town, but the townsmen fought stoutly against them; and when they could gain nothing from the town, they went to the ships with the plunder they had taken ; and so they went to Somerset-shire, and there landed. And Eadnoth the *constable fought *stallere. against them, and was there slain, and many good men on each side ; and those who were left went away thence.

An. M.LXVIII. In this year king William gave to *earl Robert *de Comines. the government over Northumberland ; but the men of the country surrounded him in the burgh at Durham, and slew him and nine hundred men with him. And immediately after Eadgar ætheling came with all the Northumbrians to York, and the townsmen made peace with them : and king William came unawares on them from the south, with an overwhelming army, and put them to flight, and slew those who could not flee, which were many hundred men, and plundered the town, and defiled St. Peter's monastery, and also plundered and oppressed all the others. And the ætheling went back again to Scotland. After this came the sons of Harold from Ireland, at Midsummer, with sixty-four ships, into the mouth of the Taw, and there heedlessly landed ; and ¹earl Brian came against them unawares, with no small force, and fought against them, and there slew all the best men that were in the

---

An. M.LXVIII. In this year king William gave to earl Robert the earldom of Northumberland. Then came the men of the country against him, and slew him, and nine hundred men with him. And Eadgar ætheling came then with all the Northumbrians to York, and the townsmen made peace with him. And king William came from the south with all his force, and ravaged the town, and slew many hundred men. And the ætheling went back again to Scotland.ᵃ

343.

---

¹ Brian was a son of Eudes, count of Brittany. See his pedigree in | Maseres, Selecta Monumenta, p. 219, note.

ᵃ E.

fleet ; and the others in a small body fled to the ships.   And
the sons of Harold went back again to Ireland.

An. M.LXIX. In this year died archbishop Ealdred in York,
and is there buried at his episcopal see : and he departed on
the day of Prothus and Hyacynthus (Sept. 11th) ; and he held
the archiepiscopal chair with great dignity ten years, wanting
fifteen weeks.   Soon after this came from Denmark three
sons of king Svein, and Asbiörn jarl and Thorkell jarl, with
two hundred and forty ships, into the Humber ; and there
came to meet them Eadgar child, and earl Waltheof, and
Mærleswegen, and earl Gospatric, with the Northumbrians
and all the country people, riding and walking, with a countless army, greatly rejoicing, and so all unanimously went to
York, and stormed and demolished the castle, and gained
innumerable treasures therein, and slew there many hundred
Frenchmen, and led many with them to the ships ; but before
the shipmen came thither, the French had burnt the town,
and also plundered and burnt the holy monastery of St. Peter.
When the king learned this, he went northward with all his

---

* of Durham.   An. M.LXIX. In this year * bishop Ægelric was accused at
Peterborough, and sent to Westminster ; and his brother,
* of Durham. * bishop Ægelwine, was outlawed.   Then betwixt the ¹ two
St. Mary's masses, came from the east, from Denmark, with
three hundred ships, the sons of king Svein and his brother,
Asbiörn jarl.   And then earl Waltheof went out ; and he,
and Eadgar ætheling, and many hundred men with them,
came and met the fleet in the Humber, and went to York, and
landed, and won the castles, and slew many hundred men, and
led to the ships much treasure, and had the chief men in captivity ; and they lay between the Ouse and the Trent all the
winter.   And king William went into the shire and ravaged
it all.   And in this same year died Brand, abbot of Peterborough, on the vth of the Kal. of December (Nov. 27th).*

---

¹ The Assumption (Aug. 15th) and | of Worcester has : " Ante Nativita-
the Nativity (Sept. 8th).   Florence | " tem S. Mariæ."

---

* E.

force that he could gather, and completely harried and laid waste the shire. And the fleet lay all the winter in the Humber, where the king could not come at them. And the king was on the day of Midwinter at York ; and so all the winter in the land ; and came to Winchester at the 'same Easter. And * bishop Ægelric was accused, who was in Pe- * of Durham. terborough, and he was led to Westminster ; and his brother, * bishop Ægelwine, was outlawed. * of Durham.

An. M.LXX.

M.LXX. In this year Lanfranc, who was abbot of Caen, came to England, who, after a few days became archbishop of Canterbury. He was ordained on the ivth of the Kal. of September (Aug. 29th) in his own episcopal see, by eight bishops, his suffragans. The others who were not there showed by messengers and by letters why they could not be there. In that year Thomas, who was chosen bishop of York, came to Canterbury that he might be there ordained according to the old custom. When Lanfranc craved confirmation of his obedience by oath-swearing, he refused, and said that he ought not to do it; the archbishop became wroth, and ordered the bishops who were come thither, by the archbishop Lanfranc's command, to do the service, and all the monks to unrobe themselves ; and, by his command, they so did. So Thomas for that time went back without the blessings. Then soon after this it befel that the archbishop Lanfranc went to Rome, and Thomas along with him. When they came thither, and had spoken about other things, about which they would speak, Thomas began his speech, how he came to Canterbury, and how the archbishop asked obedience, with oath-swearing, from him, and he refused it. Then the archbishop Lanfranc began to show openly and distinctly that he with right craved that which he craved, and with strong discourses confirmed the same before the pope *Alexander, and before all the council * II. that was there gathered ; and so they went home. After this, Thomas came to Canterbury, and all that the archbishop craved of him humbly fulfilled, and then received the blessings.[1]

Here ends MS. C.C.C.C. C.LXXIII. A

344.   An. M.LXXI. In this year earl Waltheof made his peace with the king ; and in the following Lent (Feb. 17th) the king caused all the monasteries that were in England to be ¹ plundered. And in this year there was a great famine, and the monastery at Peterborough was plundered. It was by the men whom bishop Ægelric had before excommunicated, because

345.   An. M.LXX. In this year earl Waltheof made his peace with the king ; and in the following Lent the king caused all the monasteries that were in England to be plundered. Then, in the same year came ²Svein king of Denmark into the Humber; and the country people came to meet him, and made peace with him, weening that he would overrun the land, Then *of Aarhus. came to Ely Christian, the *Danish bishop, and Asbiörn jarl, and the Danish 'húscarls' with them ; and the English folk from all the fen-lands came to them, weening that they would win all the land. Then the monks of Peterborough heard say that their own men would plunder the monastery, that was Hereward and his company. That was because they had heard say that the king had given the abbacy to a French abbot named Turold, and that he was a very stern man, and was then come to Stamford with all his Frenchmen. There was then a church-ward there named Yware, who took by night all that he could ; that was, gospels, mass-mantles, cantor-copes, and robes, and such little things, whatever he could; and went forthwith, ere day, to the abbot Turold, and told him that he sought his protection, and informed him how the outlaws were to come to Peterborough, and that he did all by the advice of the monks. Then soon on the morrow came all the outlaws with many ships, and would enter the monastery, and the monks withstood so that they could not come

---

¹ The monasteries were the depositories of treasure belonging to rich individuals ; of this William despoiled them : " rex Willelmus " monasteria totius Angliæ per- " scrutari, et pecuniam quam ditiores " Angli, propter illius austeritatem " et depopulationem, in eis depo-

" suerant, auferri et in ærarium " suum jussit deferri." Flor. Wigorn, a. 1070.
² Svein did not come, but sent his two sons, Harald and Cnut, with their uncle Asbiörn jarl. See Dahlmann, Gesch. v. Dannem. I. p. 176.

they had there taken all that he owned. And in the same
summer the fleet came into the Thames, and lay there two
nights, and then held on their course to Denmark. And °earl • of Flanders.
Baldwine died, and Arnulf his son succeeded to the government ; and the °king of the Franks and ¹ earl William were to • Philip I.
be his guardians. But there came • Robert, and slew Arnulf • surnamed the
his kinsman, and the earl William, and many thousands of his   Frisian.
men.

---

in. They then set it on fire and burned all the monks' houses,
and all the town, save one house. They then came in through
fire, in at ² Bolhithe gate, and the monks came to meet them,
praying for peace. But they recked of nothing, went into the
monastery, clomb up to the holy rood, then took the crown from
our Lord's head, all of beaten gold ; then took the ' foot-spur '
that was underneath his foot, which was all of red gold. They
clomb up to the steeple, brought down the crosier that was
there hidden; it was of gold and of silver. They took there two
golden shrines, and nine of silver ; and they took fifteen great
roods, both of gold and of silver. They took there so much gold
and silver, and so many treasures in money, and in raiment,
and in books, as no man may tell to another, saying that they
did it from affection to the monastery. They then betook themselves to the ships, proceeded to Ely, and there deposited all the
treasures. The Danish men weened that they should overcome
the Frenchmen ; they then dispersed all the monks, none remaining there save one monk named Leofwine Lange; he lay
sick in the sick man's ward. Then came abbot Turold, and
eight times twenty Frenchmen with him, and all fully armed.
When he came thither, he found within and without all burnt,
save only the church. The outlaws were then all afloat, knowing
that he would come thither. This was done on the day the ivth
of the Nones of June (Jun. 2nd). The two kings, William and

---

¹ William Fitz Osbern, created by
the Conqueror earl of Hereford. See
for an account of him, Will. Gem-
met. cc. vii. viii. Ord. Vital. pp.
526, sq. (edit. Maseres, pp. 270, 271).
Roman de Rou, ii. pp. 122–126.

W. Malmesb. pp. 431, 432, edit.
E. H. S.
    ² " Janua ab australi parte monas-
" terii Petroburgensis, vulgo hodie
" Bulldykegate dicta." Hugo Can-
didus ap. Sparke, p. 49.

346.   An. M.LXXII. (M.LXXI.) In this year earl Eadwine and earl
Morkere fled away, and went diversly in woods and in fields,
until Eadwine was basely slain by his own men, and Morkere by
ship went to Ely : and there came bishop Ægelwine, and Sige-
ward Barn, and many hundred men with them.   But when king
William was informed of that, he ordered out a naval force and
a land-force, and beset the land all about, and wrought a bridge
and went in, and the naval force on the water-side.   And then
all the outlaws went and surrendered to the king : these
were bishop Ægelwine, and earl Morkere, and all who were
with them, except Hereward only, and all who could flee away
with him.   And he boldly led them out, and the king took

Svein, became reconciled, when the Danish men went out
from Ely with all the aforesaid treasure, and conveyed it with
them.   When they came in the middle of the sea, a great storm
came and scattered all the ships in which the treasures were :
some went to Norway, some to Ireland, some to Denmark; and
all that thither came were the crosier, and some shrines, and
some roods, and many of the other treasures; and they brought
them to a king's town called . . . . , and placed them all in
the church.   Then afterwards, through their heedlessness, and
through their drunkenness, on one night the church was burnt,
and all that was therein.   Thus was the monastery of Peterborough burnt and plundered.   May Almighty God have com-
347.   passion on it through his great mercy.   And thus the abbot
Turold came to Peterborough, and the monks then came again,
and did Christ's service in the church, which had a full sennight
before stood without any kind of rite.   When bishop Ægelric
heard that say, he excommunicated all the men who had done
the evil.   Then there was a great famine this year ; and in
the summer came the fleet from the north out of the Humber
into the Thames, and lay there two nights, and afterwards
proceeded to Denmark.   And count Baldwine died, and his son
Arnulf succeeded to the government ; and earl William was
to be his guardian, and the king of the Franks also ; but then
came count Robert and slew his kinsman Arnulf and the earl,
and put the king to flight, and slew many thousands of his
men.[a]

E.

their ships and weapons and many treasures; and all the men he took, and did with them what he would. And bishop Ægelwine he sent to Abingdon, and he there died, in the winter, shortly after.

An. M.LXXIII. (M.LXXII.) In this year king William led a naval force and a land-force to Scotland, and lay about that land with ships on the sea-side; and himself with his land-force went in over the 'ford, [2]and he there found naught for which they were the better.' And king Måcolm came and made peace with king William, and gave hostages, and was his man; and the king went home with all his force. And bishop Ægelric died: he was ordained bishop at York, but it was unjustly taken from him, and the bishopric of Durham given to him, and he had it while he would, and afterwards left it and went to Peterborough, to St. Peter's monastery, and there lived twelve years. Then after that king William had won England, he had him taken from Peterborough and sent him to Westminster. And he there died on the Ides of October (Oct. 15th), and is there buried within the monastery, in the porch of St. Nicholas.

An. M.LXXIV. (M.LXXIII.) In this year king William led an English and French force over sea, and won the land of Le Maine. And the Englishmen greatly wasted the land; vineyards they ruined, and towns burned, and greatly wasted the land, and reduced it all into the hand of king William; and they afterwards went home to England.

An. M.LXXV. In this year king William went over sea to Normandy; and Eadgar child came from the Flemings' land to Scotland, on St. Grimbald's mass-day (July 8th); and king Malcolm and his sister Margaret received him with

---

An. M.LXXIV. In this year king William went over sea to Normandy, and Eadgar child came from Scotland to Normandy; and the king inlawed him and all his men; and he

---

[1] " His land-fyrde æt þam gewæde " in lædde."—*led his land-force in* *at the ford,* probably at the Forth.—E. " in loco qui dicitur Abernithici." Flor. Wigorn. Whence it would seem that he reached the Tay.

[2] I cannot satisfactorily interpre this passage. Lingard renders it : " He there found naught that him " better was," which is not very intelligible. See his note.

* I.

* minever?

348, 349.

great worship. At that same time *Philip king of France wrote to him, and bade him come to him, and he would give him the castle of Montreuil, that he might then daily do harm to his enemies. Moreover, king Malcolm and his sister Margaret gave him and all his men great gifts and many treasures, in skins decked with purple, and in pelisses of marten skin, and *weasel skin, and ermine skin ; and in palls, and in golden and silver vessels ; and led him and all his shipmen with great worship from his dominion. But on the voyage evil befel them, when they were out at sea ; so that there came on them very rough weather, and the raging sea and the strong wind cast them on the land so that all their ships burst asunder, and they themselves with difficulty came to land, and almost all their treasures were lost. And some of his men also were seized by the Frenchmen ; but he himself and his best men went back again to Scotland : some ruefully going on foot, and some miserably riding. Then king Malcolm advised him that he should send to king William over sea, and pray his peace ; and he also did so, and the king granted it to him, and sent after him. And king Malcolm and his sister again gave him and all his men innumerable treasures, and very worthily again sent him from their jurisdiction. And the shire-reeve of York came to meet him at Durham, and went all the way with him, and enabled him to find food and fodder at every castle which they came to, until they came over sea to the king. And king William then received him with great worship, and he was there in his court, and took such rights, as he allowed him.

An. M.LXXVI. (M.LXXV.) In this year king William gave to earl Ralph the daughter of William Fitz Osbern. And the same Ralph was a Breton on his mother's side, and Ralph his father was [1] English, named Ralph, and was born in Norfolk.

was in the king's court, and received such privileges as the king granted him.*

---

[1] Probably Radulf the ' stallere ' (constable), who had large possessions in Norfolk and Suffolk, ' Tem-

' pore Regis Edwardi.' Engl. under the Norman Kings, p. 167.

* E.

And on that account the king gave his son the earldom of
Norfolk, and also of Suffolk. He then conducted his wife to
Norwich.
There was that bride-ale,
that was many men's bale.
[1] There were *earl Roger, and earl Waltheof, and bishops and *of Hereford.
abbots ; and they there resolved that they would drive their
royal lord from his kingdom ; and this was forthwith made
known to the king in Normandy. Earl Ralph and earl Roger
were the chiefs in this evil design ; and they enticed the
Bretons to them, and sent also to Denmark for a naval force.
And Roger went west to his earldom, and gathered his people
for the king's detriment, as he thought, but it was to their own
great harm. Ralph would also go forth with his earldom ;
but the castlemen who were in England, and also the country
folk, came against them, and prevented them all, so that they
did nothing ; but he was fain to flee to the ships : and his wife
remained behind in the castle, and held it so long until peace
was granted her ; and she then went out from England, and
all her men that would go with her. And the king afterwards
came to England, and took earl Roger, his kinsman, and set
him in prison. And earl Waltheof went over sea, and accused

An. M.LXXV. —[1] There were earl Roger, and earl Waltheof,
and bishops, and abbots ; and they there so resolved that
they would displace the king from the kingdom of England. And it was forthwith made known to the king in
Normandy how it was resolved. It was earl Roger and earl
Ralph who were the chiefs in that evil design ; and they
enticed the Bretons to them, and sent east to Denmark, for a
naval force to their support. And Roger went west to his
earldom, and gathered his people for the king's detriment ; but
he was prevented. And Ralph, in his earldom, would go forth
with his people ; but the castlemen who were in England, and
also the country folk, came against him, and acted so that he
did nothing, but went on shipboard at Norwich. And his
wife was within the castle, and held it so long until peace was
granted her. And she then went out from England, and all
her men who would go with her. And the king afterwards
came to England, and took earl Roger, his kinsman, and imprisoned him ; and earl Waltheof he also took. And soon

himself, and implored forgiveness, and offered treasures. But
the king treated it lightly until he came to England, and then
caused him to be taken. And soon after this came two hundred ships from Denmark, wherein the chiefs were Cnut, son
of king Svein, and Hakon jarl; but they durst not maintain a
battle against king William; but went to York, and brake
into St. Peter's monastery, and therein took much property,
and so went away; but all perished who were of that counsel;
that was the son of Hakon jarl, and many others with him.
And Eadgyth the lady died seven nights before Christmas,
at Winchester: she was the relict of king Eadward, and
350, 351.   the king had her brought to Westminster with great worship,
and laid her by king Eadward her lord. The king was that
Midwinter at Westminster : there were all the Bretons con-
demned who were at the marriage at Norwich : some were
blinded, and some banished from the land, and some punished
ignominiously. Thus were the king's traitors crushed.

An. M.LXXVII. (M.LXXVI.) In this year died Svein, king of
Denmark, and Harald his son succeeded to his kingdom. In
this year king William gave the abbacy of Westminster to
* abbot super-
scribed.   abbot ¹Vitalis, who had before been a *monk at Bernay. And
in this year earl Waltheof was beheaded at Winchester, on
St. Petronilla's mass-day (May 31st) ; and his body was con-

---

after that there came from the east two hundred ships from
Denmark, and therein were two chieftains, Cnut son of Svein,
and Hakon jarl ; but they durst not maintain a battle against
king William, but proceeded over sea to Flanders. And Eadgyth the lady died at Winchester, seven nights before Christmas. And the king had her brought to Westminster, with
great worship, and laid her by king Eadward her lord. And
he was at Westminster that Midwinter. And all the Bretons
were fordone who were at the bride-ale at Norwich : some
were blinded, and some driven from the land. So were
William's traitors crushed.ᵃ

---

¹ A large slab covers his remains in the cloister at Westminster.

ᵃ E.

veyed to Crowland, and ho is there buried. And king William went over sea, and led a force to Brittany, and besieged the castle of Dôle ; but the Bretons held it until the king came from France, and king William then went thence, and there lost both men and horses, and innumerable treasures.

An. M.LXXVIII. In this year the moon was eclipsed three nights before Candlemas (Feb. 2nd). And Ægelwig, the 'world-wise' abbot of Evesham, died on St. Juliana's mass-day (Feb. 16th) ; and Walter was set as abbot in his stead. And bishop Hereman died, who was bishop of Berkshire, and of Wiltshire, and of Dorsetshire. And in this year king Malcolm won the mother of Mælslæht . . . . . . and all his best men, and all his treasure, and his cattle, and he himself escaped with difficulty. And in this year was the dry summer, and wildfire came in many shires, and burned many towns ; and also many burghs were burnt.

An. M.LXXIX. In this year Robert, the son of king William, fled from his father to his uncle Robert in Flanders ; because his father would not let him rule over his county of Normandy, which he himself, and also king Philip, with his consent, had given him ; and those who were best in the land had sworn oaths to him, and taken him for lord. In this year Robert fought against his father, and wounded him in the hand, and

---

An. M.LXXVII. In this year the king of the Franks and king William of England were reconciled ; though it lasted but a little while. And in this year London was burnt, one night before the Assumption of St. Mary (Aug. 15th) so extensively as it never was before since it was founded. And in this year died Ægelwig, abbot of Evesham, on the day the XIVth of the Kal. of March (Feb. 16th). And bishop Hereman also died, on the day the Kal. of March (Mar. 1st).[a]

An. M.LXXIX. In this year Malcolm, king of Scotland, came into England, betwixt the two St. Mary's masses,[1] with a large force, and harried Northumberland, until he came to the Tyne, and slew many hundred men ; and led home many treasures

---

[1] " post Assumptionem S. Mariæ." Flor. Wigorn. See p. 174, *note*.

[a] E.

his (father's) horse was shot under him, and he who brought another to him was straightways shot with a cross-bow : that was Toki, son of Wiggod. And many were there slain, and also taken ; and Robert went again to Flanders. We will, however, write down no more injury which he . . his father
. . . . . .[1]

An. M.LXXX. In this year bishop Walchere was slain in Durham, at a meeting, and a hundred men with him, French and Flemish ; but he was himself born in Lorraine. This the Northumbrians did in the month of May.

An. M.LXXXI. In this year the king led a force into Wales, and there freed many hundred men.

An. M.LXXXII. In this year the king took bishop Odo ; and in this year there was a great famine.

An. M.LXXXIII. In this year arose the discord at Glastonbury, betwixt the abbot Thurstân and his monks. It came first from the abbot's lack of wisdom, so that he misruled his monks in many things, and the monks meant it kindly to him, and prayed him that he would entreat them rightly, and love them, and they would be faithful to him, and obedient. But the abbot would naught of this, but did them evil, and threatened them worse. One day the abbot went into the chapterhouse, and spake against the monks, and would misuse them, and sent after laymen, and they came into the chapter-house upon the monks full armed. And then the monks were greatly afraid of them, knew not what they were to do, but fled in all directions : some ran into the church, and locked the doors after them ; and they went after them into the

_____

and precious things, and men in captivity. And in the same year king William fought against his son Robert without Normandy, near a castle called Gerberoi ; and king William was there wounded, and his horse slain, on which he sat. And his son William was also there wounded, and many men were slain.[a]

_____

[1] Here ends MS. Cott. Tiber. B. iv.   All that follows is from E.

_____

[a] E.

monastery, and would drag them out, as they durst not go out. But a rueful thing happened there on that day. The Frenchmen broke into the quire, and hurled towards the altar where the monks were ; and some of the young ones went up on the upper floor, and kept shooting downward with arrows towards the sanctuary, so that in the rood that stood above the altar there stuck many arrows. And the wretched monks lay about the altar, and some crept under, and earnestly cried to God, imploring his mercy, seeing that they might not obtain any mercy from men. What can we say, but that they shot cruelly, and the others brake down the doors there, and went in, and slew some of the monks to death, and wounded many therein, so that the blood came from the altar upon the steps, and from the steps on the floor. Three were there slain to death, and eighteen wounded. And in the same year died Matilda, king William's queen, on the day after All-Hallows mass-day (Nov. 2nd). And in the same year, after Midwinter, the king caused a great and heavy tax to be exacted over all England; that was for every hide, two and seventy pence.

An. M.LXXXIV. In this year died Wulfwold, abbot of Chertsey, on the XIIIth day of the Kal. of May (Apr. 19th).

An. M.LXXXV. In this year men declared, and for sooth said, that Cnut king of Denmark, son of king Svein, was bound hitherward, and would win this land with the aid of Robert count of Flanders ; because Cnut had Robert's daughter to wife. When William king of England, who was then residing in Normandy,—because he owned both England and Normandy,—was apprized of this, he went into England with so large an army of horsemen and foot, from France and from Brittany, as never before had sought this land, so that men wondered how this land could feed all that army. But the king caused the army to be distributed through all this land among his vassals ; and they fed the army, each according to the measure of his land. And men had great affliction this year ; and the king caused the land about the sea to be laid waste, so that if his foes should land, they might not have whereon they might so readily seize. But when the king was informed in sooth that his foes were hindered, and could not further their expedition, he let some of the army go to their own land ; and some he held in this land over the winter.

√ [Then at Midwinter tho king was at Gloucester with his 'witan,' and there held his court five days ;[and afterwards the archbishop and clergy had a synod three days. There were Maurice chosen bishop of London, and William to Norfolk, and Robert to Cheshire. They were all the king's clerks] ‾After this the king had a great council, and very deep speech with his 'witan' about this land, how it was peopled, or by what men ; then sent his men over all England, into every shire, and caused to be ascertained how many hundred hides were in the shire, or what land the king himself had, and cattle within the land, or what dues he ought to have, in twelve months, from the shire. Also he caused to be written how much land his archbishops had, and his suffragan bishops, and his abbots, and his earls ; and—though I may narrate somewhat prolixly—what or how much each man had who was a holder of land in England, in land, or in cattle, and how much money it might be worth. So very narrowly he caused it to be traced out, that there was not one single hide, nor one ²yard of land, nor even—it is shame to tell, though it seemed to him no shame to do—an ox, nor a cow, nor a swine, was left, that was not set down in his writ. And all the writings were brought to him afterwards.]

MS. M.LXXXV.   An. ⁰M.LXXXVI. In this year the king bare his crown, and held his court in Winchester, at Easter ; and so he went that he was by Pentecost at Westminster, and dubbed his son Henry a knight there. After that he went about, so that he came by Lammas to Salisbury, and there his 'witan' came to him, and all the landholders that were of account over all England, ³be they the men of what man they might ; and they all submitted to him, and were his men, and swore to him oaths of fealty, that they would be faithful to him against all other men. Thence he went to Wight, because he would go to Normandy, and afterwards did so ; and yet he first did after his wont, obtained a very great treasure from his subjects, where he could have any accusation, either with justice or otherwise. He then went afterwards to Normandy ; and Eadgar ætheling, the kinsman of king Eadward, revolted from

---

¹ Here is the beginning of the great Domesday survey.

² For the virgate, or yard, of land,

see Ellis. Introd. to Domesday, i p. 155.

³ i.e. the vassals of what lord soever.

him, because he had no great honour from him ; but may the
Almighty God give him honour in the life to come. And
Christina, the ætheling's sister, retired to the monastery at
Rumsey, and received the holy veil. And the same year was
a very heavy, and toilsome, and sorrowful year in England,
through murrain of cattle, and corn and fruits were at a stand,
and so great unpropitiousness in weather, as no one can easily
think : so great was the thunder and lightning, that it killed
many men ; and ever it grew worse with men more and more.
May God Almighty better it, when it shall be his will.

An. *M.LXXXVII. After the birth-tide of our Lord Jesus Christ • MS. M.LXXXVI.
one thousand and seven and eighty winters, in the one and
twentieth year after William ruled and held despotic sway over
England, as God had granted him, there was a very heavy
and very pestilent year in this land. Such a malady came on
men that almost every other man was in the worst evil, that is
with fever, and that so strongly that many men died of the evil.
Afterwards there came, through the great tempests which came
as we have before told, a very great famine over all England, so
that many hundred men perished by death through that famine.
Alas ! how miserable and how rueful a time was then ! when
the wretched men lay driven almost to death, and afterwards   354.
came the sharp famine and quite destroyed them. Who cannot feel pity for such a time ? or who is so hard-hearted that
cannot bewail such misfortune ? But such things befal for a
folk's sins, because they will not love God and righteousness :
so as it was in those days, that little righteousness was in this
land with any man, save with the monks alone, wherever they
fared well. The king and the head men loved much, and over
much, covetousness in gold and in silver, and recked not how
sinfully it might be got, provided it came to them. The king
gave his land as dearly for rent as he possibly could ; then
came some other and bade more than the other had before
given, and the king let it to the man who had bidden him
more ; then came a third and bade yet more, and the king
gave it up to the man who had bidden most of all. And he
recked not how very sinfully the reeves got it from poor men,
nor how many illegalities they did; but the more that was said
about right law, the more illegalities were done. They levied
unjust tolls, and many other unjust things they did, which are
difficult to reckon. Also, in the same year, before autumn, the

holy monastery of St. Paul, the episcopal see of London, was
burnt, and many other monasteries, and the greatest and fairest
part of the whole city.   So also, at the same time, almost every
chief town in all England was burnt.   Alas! a rueful and de-
plorable time was it in that year, which brought forth so many
misfortunes!   Also in the same year, before the Assumption
of St. Mary (Aug. 15th), king William went from Normandy
into France with a force, and made war upon his own lord,
Philip the king, and slew a great part of his men, and burned
the town of Mantes, and all the holy monasteries that were
within the town; and two holy men, who obeyed God and dwelt
in a hermitage, were there burnt.   This being thus done, king
William turned again to Normandy.   A rueful thing he did,
and a more rueful befel him.   How more rueful?   He fell
sick, and was severely afflicted.   What can I tell?   Sharp
death, that leaves neither powerful men nor humble, took him.
He died in Normandy, on the next day after the Nativity of
St. Mary (Sept. 9th), and he was buried at Caen, in the monastery of St. Stephen, which he had formerly erected, and
afterwards manifoldly endowed.   Alas! how false and how un-
stable is this world's wealth!   He who was before a powerful
king, and lord of many a land, had then of all his land only a
portion of seven feet; and he who was whilom decked with gold
and with gems, lay then covered over with mould!   He left after
him three sons; Robert was the eldest named, who was count of
Normandy after him; the second was called William, who bare
after him the royal crown in England; the third was called
Henry, to whom his father bequeathed treasures innumerable.
If any one desires to know what kind of man he was, or what
worship he had, or of how many lands he was lord, then we will
write of him so as we understood him who have looked on him,
and, at another time, sojourned in his court.   The king William, about whom we speak, was a very wise man, and very
powerful, more dignified and strong than any of his predecessors
were.   He was mild to the good men who loved God ; and
over all measure severe to the men who gainsayed his will.
On that same stead, on which God granted him that he might
subdue England, he reared a noble monastery, and there placed
355.   monks, and well endowed it.   In his days was the noble monastery at Canterbury built, and also very many others over all
England.   This land was also plentifully supplied with monks,

and they lived their lives after the rule of St. Benedict. And
in his day Christianity was such that every man who would
followed what belonged to his condition. He was also very
dignified ; thrice every year he bare his crown, as oft as he
was in England. At Easter he bare it in Winchester ; at
Pentecost in Westminster; at Midwinter in Gloucester. And
then were with him all the great men over all England, archbishops and suffragan bishops, abbots and earls, thanes and
knights. So also was he a very rigid and cruel man, so that no
one durst do anything against his will. He had earls in his
bonds, who had acted against his will ; bishops he cast from
their bishoprics, and abbots from their abbacies, and thanes into
prison; and at last he spared not his own brother named Odo :
he was a very rich bishop in Normandy, at Bayeux was his
episcopal see; and he was the foremost man besides the king ;
and he had an *earldom in England, and when the king was • Kent.
in Normandy, then was he the most powerful in this land: and
him he set in prison. Among other things is not to be for-
gotten the good peace that he made in this land ; so that a
man ¹who had any confidence in himself might go over his
realm, with his bosom full of gold, unhurt. Nor durst any
manslay another man had he done ever so great evil to the
other. And if any common man lay with a woman against
her will, he forthwith lost the members that he had sinned
with. He reigned over England, and by his sagacity so tho-
roughly surveyed it, that there was not a hide of land within
England that he knew not who had it, or what it was worth,
and afterwards set it in his writ. Brytland (Wales) was in his
power, and he therein wrought castles, and completely ruled
over that race of men. In like manner he also subjected Scotland to him by his great strength. The land of Normandy was
naturally his, and over the county which is called Le Maine he
reigned ; and if he might yet have lived two years he would,
by his valour, have won Ireland, and without any weapons.
Certainly in his time men had great hardship and very many
injuries. Castles he caused to be made, and poor men to be
greatly oppressed. The king was so very rigid, and took from
his subjects many a mark of gold, and more hundred pounds

---

¹ 'þe himsylf aht wære,' *who in*   correctly expressed the sense of the
himself was aught? I believe I have   words.

* MS. be wihte,
by weight?
of silver, which he took, by *right and with great unright, from his people, for little need. He had fallen into covetousness, and altogether loved greediness. He planted a great 'preserve for deer, and he laid down laws therewith, that whosoever should slay hart or hind should be blinded. He forbade the harts and also the boars to be killed. As greatly did he love the tall deer as if he were their father. He also ordained concerning the hares, that they should go free. His great men bewailed it, and the poor men murmured thereat ; but he was so obdurate, that he recked not of the hatred of them all; but they must wholly follow the king's will, if they would live, or have land, or property, or even his peace. Alas! that any man should be so proud, so raise himself up, and account himself above all men ! May the Almighty God show mercy to his soul, and grant him forgiveness of his sins ! These things we have written concerning him, both good and evil, that good men may imitate their goodness, and wholly flee from the evil, and go in the way that leads us to the kingdom of heaven. Many things we may write which happened in the same year. So it was in Denmark, that the Danish, that earlier was accounted the most faithful of all folks, were turned to the greatest faithlessness, and to the greatest treachery that ever could be. They chose and submitted to king Cnut, and swore to him oaths, and afterwards ²basely slew him in a church. In Spain also it befel, that the heathen men went and committed ravages on the Christian men, and reduced much under their sway. But the Christian king, Alfonso by name, sent everywhere into every land, and desired aid ; and aid came to him from every land that was Christian ; and they went and slew and drove away all the heathen folk, and won their land again, through God's support. Also in this same land, in the

356.

---

¹ The word deor (like the Ger. Thier, Dan. Dyr) signifies *beast* in general ; here it is applied to beasts of venery only. The allusion is evidently to the New Forest. If the manuscript is correct, fri∂ in the sense of *enclosure* is neuter, while fri∂, *peace*, is masculine.

² He was afterwards canonized and became the patron saint of Denmark. Cnut the saint perished in an insurrection caused by his exactions ; he was assassinated in the church of St. Alban (afterwards St. Cnut's) at Odense, in the island of Fyen, in which he had taken refuge.

same year, died many great men : Stigand bishop of Chichester, and the abbot of St. Augustine's, and the abbot of Bath, and the *(abbot) of Pershore, and then the lord of them all, William king of England, of whom we before spake. After his death, his son, called also William, like his father, succeeded to the kingdom, and was blessed for king by archbishop Lanfranc at Westminster, three days before Michaelmas day. And all the men in England submitted to him, and swore oaths to him. This being thus done, the king went to Winchester and inspected the treasury and the riches which his father had before gathered ; it was not to be expressed by any man how much was there gathered in gold, and in silver, and in vessels, and in robes, and in gems, and in many other precious things, which are difficult to recount. The king then did as his father had commanded him ere he died, distributed the treasures, for his father's soul, to every monastery that was in England : to one monastery ten marks of gold ; to one, six ; to every country church, sixty pence ; and into every shire were sent a hundred pounds in money, to distribute to poor men for his soul. And before he departed, he commanded that all the men should be released, who were in durance under his power. And the king was that Midwinter in London.

An. M.LXXXVIII. In this year this land was much disturbed, and filled with great treason ; so that the most powerful Frenchmen that were in this land would betray their lord the king, and would have for king his brother Robert, who was count of Normandy. In this plot the first was bishop Odo, and *bishop Geoffrey, and William bishop of Durham. So well had the king done by the *bishop, that all England went after his counsel, and so as he would : and he thought to do by him as Judas Iscariot did by our Lord. And *earl Roger was also at that plotting, and very many people with them, all Frenchmen. And this plot was formed in Lent (Mar. 1st). As soon as Easter came, they went and ravaged, and burned, and laid waste the king's farm-vills, and laid waste the lands of all the men who remained faithful to the king. And each of them went to his castle, and manned it, and provisioned it as he best could ; and bishop Geoffrey and Robert of *Monbrni went to Bristol, and harried, and brought the booty to the castle. And afterwards they went out from the castle and

Thurstan.
lor. Wigorn

* of Coutances.

* of Durham.

* of Shrewsbury.

* Also Molbray, Moubray.

357.

ravaged Bath and all the land thereabout, and all the district of Berkeley they laid waste. And the chief men of Hereford and all that shire forthwith, and the men of Shropshire with many people from Brytland (Wales), came and harried and burned in Worcestershire, on till they came to the city itself; and would then burn the city, and plunder the monastery, and win the king's castle into their hands. Seeing these things, the venerable bishop Wulfstân was sorely troubled in his mind; because the castle had been committed to his keeping. Never-theless, the men of his household went out with a few men from the castle, and, through God's mercy and through the bishop's deserts, slew and captured five hundred men, and put all the others to flight. The bishop of Durham did all the harm he could everywhere in the north. One of them was called *Roger, who ¹ seized by surprise' the castle at Norwich, and did yet the worst of all over all that land. *Hugo was also one who did nothing better, either in Leicestershire or in Northamptonshire. The bishop Odo, ²who by his mother was related to the king,' went into Kent to his earldom, and sorely ruined it, and laid completely waste the lands of the king and the archbishop, and brought all the spoil into his castle of Rochester. When the king was apprized of all these things, and what treason they were practising against him, he was greatly troubled in mind. He then sent after English-men, and told to them his need, and desired their support, and promised them the best laws that ever were before in this land; and every unjust impost he forbade, and granted to men their woods and liberty of the chase; but it stood no while. But the Englishmen, nevertheless, betook them to the aid of the king their lord. They then went towards Rochester, and wished to get bishop Odo, thinking that if they had him who was erewhile the head of the evil counsel, they might the better get all the others. They came then to the castle at Tonbridge: in the castle then were bishop Odo's knights, and many others, who wished to hold it against the king. But the Englishmen went and brake into the castle, and the men who were therein made peace with the king. The king with his

---

¹ hleop into þam castele, literally *ran or leaped into.*

²' Here the original text is either defective or corrupt.

army went towards Rochester, and they weened that the
bishop was therein ; but it became known to the king that the
bishop was gone to the castle at Pevensey ; and the king with
his army went after, and beset the castle about, with a very
large army, full six weeks. In the meanwhile, Robert the
count of Normandy, the king's brother, gathered a very large
force, and thought to win England, with the aid of the men
who were in this land against the king : and he sent some of
his men to this land, and would come himself after. But the
Englishmen who guarded the sea seized some of the men, and
slew and drowned more than any man could tell. After that,
food failed those within the castle ; they then desired peace,
and gave it up to the king ; and the bishop swore that
he would depart from England, and come no more into this
land, unless the king sent after him ; and that he would give
up the castle of Rochester. Just as the bishop was gone,
and was to give up the castle, and the king had sent his men
with him, the men who were within the castle rose, and took
the bishop and the king's men, and put them in durance.
Within the castle were some very good knights : * Eustace the * of Boulogne.
young, and three sons of earl Roger, and all the best born men
that were in this land or in Normandy. When the king was
apprized of these things, he went after with the army that he
had there, and sent over all England, and bade that every man   358.
that was ' unniðing' should come to him, French and English,
from town and from country. Then much folk came to him,
and he went to Rochester, and beset the castle, until they who
were therein made peace and gave up the castle. Bishop Odo,
with the men who were within the castle, went over sea ; and
so the bishop left the dignity that the had in this land. The
king afterwards sent an army to Durham, and caused the
castle to be beset ; and the bishop made peace, and gave up
the castle, and left his bishopric, and went to Normandy.
Many Frenchmen also left their lands, and went over sea : and
the king gave their lands to the men who had been faithful to
him.

An. M.LXXXIX. In this year the venerable father and com-
fort of monks, archbishop Lanfranc, departed from this life ;
but we hope that he went to the heavenly kingdom. Likewise
there happened over all England a great earthquake, on the
day the iiird of the Ides of August (Aug. 11th). And it was

a very backward year in corn and in fruits of every kind ; so that many men reaped their corn about Martinmas (Nov. 11th), and yet later.

An. M.XC. Indiction XIII. This being thus done, as we have before above said, relative to the king and to his brother, and to his men, the king was considering how he might take vengeance on his brother Robert, most annoy him, and win Normandy from him. Thus through his cunning, or through treasures, he obtained the castle of St. Valery and the haven ; and so he got that at Albemarle ; and therein he set his foot-soldiers ; and they did harm upon the land in harrying and in burning. After this he got more castles in the land, and therein placed his knights. When the count of Normandy, Robert, found that his sworn men deserted him, and gave up their castles to his harm, he sent to his lord Philip, king of the Franks, and he came to Normandy with a large army ; and the king and the count, with an immense force, beset the castle about wherein were the men of the king of England. King William of England then sent to Philip, king of the Franks, and he, for his love, or for his great treasures, deserted his vassal, the count Robert, and his land, and went again to France, and left them as they were. And amid these things this land was sorely fordone by unlawful imposts and many other calamities.

An. M.XCI. In this year king William held his court at Christmas in Westminster ; and thereafter at Candlemas (Feb. 2nd) he went, to the detriment of his brother, out of England into Normandy. While he was there, their reconciliation took place, on the condition, that the count should cede to him Fécamp, and the county of Eu, and Cherbourg, and, in addition thereto, that the king's men should be sackless in the castles that they had gotten against the will of the count. And the many which their father had won, and those which had revolted from the count, the king in return promised to reduce to obedience ; and all that his father had there beyond, except those which he then ceded to the king ; and that all those who in England had before lost their land for the count, should by this agreement have it back ; and that the count should have in England as much as was in their treaty. And if the count died without a son by lawful wedlock, the king should be heir of all Normandy: by this same treaty, if the king died, the count should be heir of all England. To this treaty swore twelve

359.

of the °best on the king's side, and twelve on the count's; yet it °barones. *Fl. Wigorn.*
stood but a little while afterwards.   While this reconciliation
was pending, Eadgar ætheling was deprived of the land which
the count had previously ceded to him; and went out of
Normandy to the king, his [1]brother-in-law, in Scotland,
and to his sister.   While king William was out of England,
king Malcolm of Scotland came hither into England, and
harried a great deal of it, until the good men who had charge
of this land sent a force against him, and turned him back.
When king William in Normandy heard of this, he made ready
for his departure, and came to England, and his brother the
count Robert with him, and forthwith ordered a force to be
called out, both a ship-force and a land-force; but the ship-
force, ere he could come to Scotland, almost all perished miserably, a few days before St. Michael's mass: and the king and
his brother went with the land-force.   But when king Mal-
cholm heard that they would seek him with a force, he went
with his force out of Scotland into the °district of Leeds, in °provincia Loidis.
England, and there awaited.   When king William with his *Fl. Wigorn.*
force approached, then intervened count Robert and Eadgar
ætheling, and so made a reconciliation between the kings;
so that king Malcolm came to our king, and became his man,
with all such obedience as he had before paid to his father, and
that with oath confirmed.   And king William promised him in
land and in all things that which he had had before under his
father.   In this reconciliation Eadgar ætheling was also reconciled with the king; and the kings then, with great good
feeling, separated; but that stood only a little while.   And count
Robert continued here with the king almost to Christmas, and
during that time found little of the truth of their compact;
and two days before that tide, took ship in Wight, and went to
Normandy, and Eadgar ætheling with him.

    An. M.XCII.   In this year king William, with a large force,
went north to Carlisle, and [2]restored the town, and raised the
castle; and drove out Dolphin, who previously had ruled the
land there; and garrisoned the castle with his own men, and

---

[1] The word 'aðum' usually signifies *son-in-law*.
[2] " a Danis paganis ante CC. an-

" nos diruta, et usque ad id tempus
" mansit deserta."   Flor. Wigorn.

then returned south hither. And very many country folk
with wives and with cattle, he sent thither, there to dwell and
to till the land.

An. M.XCIII. In this year, in Lent, the king William was
taken so sick at Gloucester, that he was everywhere reported
dead. And in his illness he promised many promises to God :
to lead his own life righteously, and to grant peace and protection to God's churches, and never more again for money to
sell them, and to have all just laws among his people. And
the archbishopric of Canterbury, that had before remained in
his own hand, he delivered to Anselm, who had before been
abbot of Bec ; and to Robert his chancellor, the bishopric of
Lincoln ; and to many monasteries he granted land ; but which
he afterwards withdrew, when he became well ; and abandoned
all the good laws that he had before promised us. Then after
this, the king of Scotland sent, and demanded the fulfilment of
the treaty that had been promised him. And king William
summoned him to Gloucester, and sent him hostages to Scotland,
and Eadgar ætheling afterwards, and the men back again,
who brought him with great worship to the king. But when
he came to the king, he could not be held worthy either the
speech of our king, or the conditions that had previously been
promised him ; and therefore in great hostility they parted, and
king Malcolm returned home to Scotland. But as soon as he
came home, he gathered his army, and marched into England,
harrying with more animosity than ever behoved him. And
then Robert the earl of Northumberland ensnared him with his·
men unawares, and slew him. Morel of Bamborough slew him,
who was the earl's steward and king Malcolm's gossip. With
him was also slain his son Edward, who should, if he had lived,
have been king after him. When the good queen Margaret
heard this—her dearest lord and son thus deceived—she was in
mind afflicted to death ; and with her priests went to church,
and received her rites, and obtained by prayer to God that she
might give up her spirit. And the Scots then chose Donald,
Malcolm's brother, for king, and drove out all the English,
who were before with king Malcolm. When Duncan, king
Malcolm's son, who was in king William's court,—his father
having before given him as a hostage to our king's father, and
had so remained afterwards,—heard all that had thus taken
place, he came to the king, and performed such fealty, as the

360.

king would have of him, and so, with his permission, went to Scotland, with the support that he could get of English and French, and deprived his kinsman Donald of the kingdom, and was received for king. But some of the Scots afterwards gathered together, and slew almost all his followers, and he himself with a few escaped. Afterwards they were reconciled, on the condition that he never again should harbour in the land either English or French.

An. M.XCIV. In this year king William had his court at Christmas in Gloucester, and messengers came to him thither from his brother Robert of Normandy, who declared that his brother renounced all peace and agreement, unless the king would perform all that they had before settled in the agreement; and besides that he called him forsworn and faithless, unless he held to the agreement, or went thither and there exculpated himself where the agreement had before been made and also sworn to. Then went the king to Hastings, at Candlemas (Feb. 2nd); and while he was there waiting for weather, he caused the monastery at Battle to be hallowed, and took his staff from Herbert *Losang, bishop of Thetford; and thereafter at * de Losinga. Mid-Lent went over sea to Normandy. After he came thither he and the count Robert, his brother, said that they should come together in peace, and they did so, yet might not be reconciled. After that they came together again with the same men who had before made the compact and also sworn the oaths, and they charged the whole breach upon the king : but he would neither allow this nor also hold to the agreement ; and there· fore they separated with great animosity. And the king afterwards won the castle at Bures, and took the count's men therein, some of whom he sent hither to this land. Against this, the count, with the support of the king of France, won the castle of Argences, and therein took Roger Poitevin, and seven hundred of the king's knights with him; and afterwards that at Houlme : and repeatedly each of them against the other burned the towns and took the men. Then the king sent hither to this land, and commanded twenty thousand Englishmen to be called out to his support in Normandy ; but when they came to the sea, they were ordered to return, and to give, for the king's behoof, the money that they had received; that was   361. half a pound each man : and they did so. And after this, the count, within Normandy, with the king of France, and with all those that they could gather, went towards Eu, wherein was the king William, and thought to besiege him therein; and so proceeded until they came to Longueville. There was the king of France turned back by craft, and all the expedition was afterwards dispersed. In the meanwhile king William sent after his brother Henry, who was in the castle of Dom-front; but because he could not pass through Normandy in peace, he sent ships after him and Hugh earl of Chester. But when they should have gone towards Eu, where the king was, they went to England, and arrived at Southampton on All-Hallows eve (Oct. 31st), and there afterwards continued, and at Christmas were in London. Also in this same year the Welshmen assembled and raised a war against the French who were in Wales, or in the neighbourhood, and had previously deprived them of their lands, and demolished many fastnesses and castles, and slew many men; and after their multitude had increased they divided themselves into more. Against one of those parties Hugh earl of Shropshire fought and put them to flight. But, nevertheless, the others all this year ceased from no evil which they could perpetrate. In this year also the Scots ensnared and slew their king Duncan, and after took to them again, a second time, his paternal uncle Donald for king, through whose machination and incitement he was betrayed to death.

An. M.XCV. In this year was king William the first four days of Christmas at Wissant, and after the fourth day came hither to land, and arrived at Dover. And Henry, the king's brother, dwelt in this land till Lent, and then went over sea to Normandy, with great treasure, on the king's behalf, against their brother, count Robert, and frequently warred upon the count, and did him great harm both in land and in men. And then at Easter the king held his court at Winchester, and the earl Robert of Northumberland would not come to court, and the king on that account was sorely excited against him, and sent to him, and harshly commanded, if he would be worthy of protection, that he should come to court at Pentecost. In this year Easter was on the VIIIth day of the Kal. of April (March 25th) [1]; and then at Easter, on the mass-night of St.

---

[1] The dates here appear to be inaccurate.

Ambrose, that is the IInd of the Nones of April (April 4th), there were seen, nearly over all this land, and nearly all the night, very many stars, as it were, to fall from heaven, not by one or two, but so thickly that no man could count them. Hereafter at Pentecost the king was at Windsor, and all his 'witan' with him, except the earl of Northumberland; because the king would neither give him hostages, nor grant upon pledged faith that he might come and go with peace. And the king therefore ordered his army, and went against the earl to Northumberland. And soon after he came thither, he won many and almost all of the best of the earl's retainers in a fastness, and placed them in durance. And the castle at Tynemouth he besieged until he won it, and the earl's brother therein, and all those who were with him; and afterwards went to Bamborough, and besieged the earl therein. But when the king saw that he could not win it, he ordered a castle to be made before Bamborough, and called it in his speech 'Malveisin,' that is in English, 'Evil neighbour,' and garrisoned it strongly with his men, and afterwards went southward. Then immediately after that the king was gone south, the earl one night went out from Bamborough towards Tynemouth; but those who were in the new castle were aware of him, and went after him, and attacked and wounded, and afterwards captured him; and of those who were with him some were slain, some taken alive. In the meanwhile it became known to the king that the Welshmen in Wales had demolished a castle called Montgomery, and slain earl Hugh's men who had to hold it; and he therefore commanded a second army to be suddenly levied, and after St. Michael's mass went into Wales, and distributed his force, and penetrated all the land, so that the force all came together on All-Hallows (Nov. 1st) at Snowdon. But the Welsh went constantly before into mountains and moors, so that it was impossible to come at them. And the king then turned homewards, because he saw that he could not do more there that winter. When the king came back, he commanded earl Robert of Northumberland to be taken and led to Bamborough, and both his eyes to be put out, unless those who were therein would give up the castle. His wife and Morel, who was his steward, and also his kinsman, held it. Through this the castle was then given up; and Morel was then in the king's court, and through him were many, both

362.

ordained and also lay, discovered, who with their counsel had been among the adversaries of the king. The king had then before this time commanded some to be brought into durance, and it afterwards to be very rigorously announced over all this land, that all who held land of the king, as they would be worthy of protection, should be at court in time. And the king commanded the earl Robert to be led to Windsor, and to be there held within the castle. Also in this same year, towards Easter, the pope's legate came hither to this land. This was Walter, a man of very good life, bishop of the city of Albano; and at Pentecost, on behalf of pope Urban, gave to archbishop Anselm his pall ; and he received him at his archiepiscopal see of Canterbury. And the bishop Walter continued this year long afterwards in the country ; and afterwards the Rome-scot was sent by him, which had not been done for many years before. In this year also were very unseasonable tempests, and therefore, through all this land, the earth-fruits were all turned to mediocrity.

An. M.XCVI. In this year king William held his court at Christmas in Windsor ; and William, bishop of Durham, died there on New year's day. And in the Octaves of the Epiphany (Jan. 13th) the king and all his council were at Salisbury. There Geoffrey Bainard accused William of Eu, the king's kinsman, that he had been in the treason against the king, and maintained it against him by fight, and overcame him in single combat, and after he was overcome, the king commanded his eyes to be put out, and afterwards to emasculate him; and his

* amitæ.
Fl. Wigorn.

steward named William, who was the son of his *maternal aunt, the king commanded to be hanged on a rood. Then also were Eudes, count of Champagne, the king's 'cousin, and many others, deprived of their lands, and some led to London, and there ² deprived (of sight). In this year also, at Easter, there was a great excitement through all this nation and many other nations, through Urban, who was called pope, though he

---

¹ In the text he is called 'aðum,' which usually signifies son-in-law ; but see his relationship in Orderic. Vitalis, p. 254, edit. Maseres.

² This rendering of ' spilde ' is conjectural, but is supported by the passage (a. 1124), 'spilde of here ' ægon.' The punishment being common, the word ' spillan ' might have sufficiently designated it, without further specification. Or it may, perhaps, simply mean destroyed.

had nothing of the see at Rome. And numberless people, with wives and children, went in order that they might fight against the heathen nations. Through this expedition, the king and his brother, count Robert, became reconciled, so that the king went over sea, and for money received from him all Normandy in pledge, so that they then were reconciled. And the count afterwards went, and with him the counts of Flanders and of Boulogne, and also many other chief men. And count Robert and those who went with him continued during the winter in Apulia. But of the people that went by Hungary, many thousands there and by the way miserably perished; and many sad and 'hunger-bitten,' towards winter, journeyed home. This was a very dismal year over all England, both through manifold imposts and also through a very sad famine that this year afflicted this country. Also in this year the chief men who held this land frequently sent a force into Wales, and many a man thereby sorely afflicted; but there naught was gained but loss of men and waste of money.

363.

An. M.XCVII. In this year was king William at Christmas in Normandy, and then towards Easter was coming hither to this land, because he thought to hold his court at Winchester ; but he was detained by bad weather until Easter-eve, so that he first arrived at Arundel, and therefore held his court at Windsor. And thereafter, with a great army, went into Wales, and penetrated the land in all directions with his force, through some of the Welshmen who came to him, and were his guides ; and he continued therein from Midsummer almost till August, and lost much therein, in men and in horses, and also in many other things. The Welshmen, after they had revolted from the king, chose them many chieftains from themselves ; one of these was called Cadogan, who was the worthiest of them, he was brother's son of king Griffith. And when the king saw that he could there further nothing according to his will, he returned to this land, and shortly after that he caused castles to be made on the borders. Then at St. Michael's mass,[1] the ivth of the Nones of October (Oct. 4th) there appeared an

---

[1] This is an error, Michaelmas being on the 3rd of the Kal. of Oct., as Florence has it.

extraordinary star, shining in the evening, and soon going to
its setting. It was seen in the south-west, and the ray that
stood from it seemed very long, shining south-east ; and almost
all the week it appeared in this wise. Many men supposed
that it was [1] comet. Immediately after this the archbishop
Anselm of Canterbury took leave of the king, though it was
against the king's will, as men supposed, and went over sea ;
because it seemed to him that in this nation little was done
according to right, and according to his instruction. And the
king thereafter, on St. Martin's mass-day (Nov. 11th) went to
Normandy ; but while he was waiting for weather, his court,
in the shires where they lay, did the greatest harm that ever
court or army could do in a peaceable land. This was in all
things a very sad year, and over grievous, from the tempests,
when the land should be tilled, or after, when the produce
should be gathered ; and in unjust imposts which never ceased.
[2] Many ships also, which with their work belonged to London,
suffered great detriment by reason of the wall which they
wrought about the Tower, and of the bridge, which was almost
dispersed by the flood ; and of the king's hall-work, which was
being wrought at Westminster, and many men thereby injured.
Also in the same year, soon after St. Michael's mass, Eadgar
ætheling, with the king's support, went with a force into Scotland, and in a hard-fought battle won that land, and drove out
the king Donald, and in king William's vassalage, set as king
his kinsman Eadgar, who was the son of king Malcolm and
of queen Margaret ; and afterwards returned to England.

364.   An. M.XCVIII. In this year at Christmas king William was
in Normandy ; and Walkelin, bishop of Winchester, and Baldwine, abbot of St. Edmunds, within that tide both died. And
in this year also Turold, abbot of Peterborough, died. In this
year also, in the summer, at Finchamstead in Berkshire, a pool
welled out blood, so as many trustworthy men said who should
* of Shrewsbury. have seen it. And * earl Hugh was slain in Anglesey by

---

[1] That is, the star so called;
our forefathers apparently regarding
comet as a proper name.

[2] This passage, as far as the word
injured, is not very intelligible,

though I believe it to be nearer to
the true meaning of the original
than what is given in former edi-
tions.

[1] vikings, and his brother Robert was his heir, as he had obtained from the king. Before St. Michael's mass, the heaven appeared almost all the night as if it were burning. This was a very sad year, through manifold unjust imposts, and through the great rains, which ceased not all the year : nearly all the tilth in the marsh-land perished.

An. M.XCIX. In this year king William was at Midwinter in Normandy ; and at Easter came hither to this land ; and at Pentecost held his court, for the first time, in his new building at Westminster ; and there gave to * Ranulf his chaplain the * Flambard. bishopric of Durham, who had before [2] held and supervised all his 'motes' over all England. And immediately after, he went over sea, and drove the count * Hélie out of Le Maine, * de la Flèche. and afterwards reduced it under his power ; and so on St. Michael's mass came again hither to land. In this year also, on St. Martin's mass-day (Nov. 11th), the sea-flood sprang up to that degree, and did so much harm, as no man remembered that it ever before did ; and it was on the same day a new moon. And Osmund, bishop of Salisbury, died during Advent.

An. M.C. In this year king William held his court at Christmas in Gloucester, and at Easter in Winchester, and at Pentecost in Westminster. And at Pentecost, at a town in Berkshire, blood was seen to well from the earth, as many said who should have seen it. And thereafter, on the morning after Lammas day (Aug. 1st), king William was shot with an arrow in hunting, by one of his men, and afterwards brought to Winchester, and buried in the bishopric. That was in the thirteenth year after he had succeeded to the realm. He was very rigorous and stern over his land and his men, and towards all his neighbours, and very formidable ; and through the counsels of evil men, that were always grateful to him, and through his own covetousness, he was ever tormenting this nation with an army and with unjust exactions ; because in his days every right fell, and every wrong in the sight of God and of the world rose up. God's churches he depressed, and

---

[1] The viking (útviking of the original) who shot him was Magnus Barfod, king of Norway. See Flor. Wigorn. II. p. 42, ed. E. H. S.; also his Saga in Snorri, and Orderic.

Vitalis, p. 767.
[2] " qui prius tenuerat placita sua " per totam Angliam." Ann. Wav. p. 141. See " England under the Norman Kings," p. 226.

all the bishoprics and abbacies, whose heads died in his days, he either sold for money, or held in his own hand, and let for rent ; because he would be the heir of every man, ordained and lay ; and so that on the day he fell, he had in his own hand the archbishopric of Canterbury, and the bishopric of Winchester, and that of Salisbury, and eleven abbacies, all let to rent. And, though I may longer delay it, all that was hateful to God and oppressive to men, all that was customary in this land in his time ; and therefore he was hateful to almost all his people, and odious to God, as his end made manifest ; for he departed in the midst of his unrighteousness, without repentance and any atonement.   On the Thursday he was slain, and on the morning after buried ; and after he was buried, those of the council who were nigh at hand, chose his brother Henry for king ; and he straightways gave the bishopric of Winchester to William Giffard, and then went to London ; and on the Sunday after, before the altar at Westminster, promised to God and all the people to put down all the injustices that were in his brother's time ; and to maintain the best laws that stood in any king's day before him.   And then, after that, the bishop of London, Maurice, hallowed him king ; and all in this land submitted to him, and swore oaths, and became his men.   And the king soon after this, by the counsel of those who were about him, caused bishop Ranulf of Durham to be taken, and caused him to be brought into the Tower of London, and be there held.   Then, before St. Michael's mass (Sept. 29th), the archbishop of Canterbury, Anselm, came hither to land, as king Henry, by the advice of his council, had sent after him, because he had gone out of this land for the great wrong that king William had done him.   And then soon hereafter the king took to wife Matilda, daughter of king Malcolm of Scotland and the good queen Margaret, king Edward's kinswoman, of the right royal race of England.   And on St. Martin's mass-day (Nov. 11th), she was given to him, with great worship, at Westminster ; and the archbishop Anselm wedded her to him, and afterwards hallowed her queen.   And the archbishop Thomas of York died soon after.   In this same year also, in autumn, count Robert came home to Normandy, and count Robert of Flanders, and Eustace count of Boulogne, from Jerusalem.   And as soon as count Robert came into Normandy, he was joyfully received by all the people, except

365.

the castles, which were occupied by king Henry's men; against which he had many onsets and contests.

An. MC.I. In this year, at Christmas, king Henry held his court in Westminster, and at Easter in Winchester. And then, soon after, the chief men here in the land became hostile against the king, both from their own great faithlessness, and also through count Robert of Normandy, who was meditating a hostile invasion of this land. And the king then sent ships out to sea, to the detriment and hindrance of his brother; but afterwards some of them failed at need, and turned from the king, and submitted to count Robert. Then, at Midsummer, the king went out to Pevensey with all his force against his brother, and there awaited him. But, in the meanwhile, count Robert landed at Portsmouth, twelve nights before Lammas (Aug. 1st), and the king with all his force came against him. But the chief men went between them, and reconciled the brothers, on the condition, that the king should relinquish all that he held by force in Normandy against the count; and that all those in England should have their land again, who had before lost it through the count; and *count [* of Boulogne.] Eustace also all his paternal land here in the country; and that count Robert every year should have three thousand marks of silver from England; and that whichever of the brothers survived the other, should be heir of all England, and also of Normandy, except that the deceased had an heir in lawful wedlock. And this then twelve of the highest on each side confirmed by oath : and the count afterwards continued here in the land until after St.Michael's mass; and his men incessantly did much harm as they went, the while that the count continued here in the country. In this year also bishop Ranulf at Candlemas escaped by night out of the Tower of London, [366.] where he had been in durance, and went to Normandy; through whose machination and instigation chiefly count Robert had this year sought this land with hostility.

An. MC.II. In this year, at the Nativity, king Henry was in Westminster; and at Easter in Winchester. And soon after became inimical to each other the king and the earl Robert of Belesme, who had the earldom of Shrewsbury here in the country, which his father Roger had previously held, and a great territory thereto, both on this side of the sea, and beyond. And the king went and besieged the castle at Arundel; but when he

could not so speedily win it, he caused castles to be built before it, and garrisoned them with his men ; and then with all
his force went to Bridgenorth, and there continued until he
had the castle and deprived earl Robert of his land, and taken
away all that he had in England.   And the earl so retired over
sea, and the army then returned home.   Then after that, at
St. Michael's mass, the king was at Westminster, and all the
chief men in this land, both ordained and lay ; and the [1] archbishop Anselm held a synod of the clergy, and they there set
forth many canons that appertain to Christianity.   And many
there, both French and English, lost their staves and authority
which they had unjustly acquired, or lived on with iniquity.
And in this same year, in Pentecost mass-week, there came
thieves, some from [1]Auvergne, some from France, and some
from Flanders, and broke into the monastery of Peterborough,
and therein took much of value, in gold, and in silver, which
were roods, and chalices, and candlesticks.

An. MC.III.   In this year, at Midwinter, king Henry was at
Westminster.   And soon after the [*]bishop William Giffard
went out of this land, because, against right, he would not
receive his ordination from the archbishop Gerard of York.
And then at Easter the king held his court in Winchester ;
and thereafter the archbishop Anselm of Canterbury went to
Rome, as was agreed by him and the king.   In this year also
count Robert of Normandy came to the country to speak with
the king ; and before he went hence he forgave the three
thousand marks that king Henry, according to agreement, was
to give him every year.   In this year also, at Hampstead in
Berkshire, blood was seen [to well] from the earth.   This was
a very calamitous year in the land, through manifold imposts,
and through murrain of cattle, and perishing of fruits, both
in corn and also in all tree-fruits.   Also in the morning, on
the mass-day of St. Laurence (Aug. 10th), the wind did so
great harm here in the country to all fruits, as no man remembered that it ever did before.   In this same year died Mat-
thias, abbot of Peterborough, who lived not longer than one

[*] of Winton.

---

[1] For the particulars of this
synod, see Eadmer, Hist. Novorum,
p. 67, or Johnson, Eccles. Laws

and Canons, edit. Baron, II. p.
22.

[*] At that time a separate state.

year after he was abbot. After St. Michael's mass, on the xIIth of the Kal. of November (Oct. 21st), he was with procession received as abbot, and on the same day of the second year he was dead in Gloucester, and there buried.

An. MC.IV. In this year king Henry held his court at Christmas in Westminster, and at Easter in Winchester, and at Pentecost again in Westminster. In this year, the first day of Pentecost was on the Nones of June (June 5th); and on the Tuesday after there appeared four circles at mid-day about the sun, of a white hue, each twined under the other as if they were painted. All who saw it wondered, because they never remembered such before. Hereafter were conciliated count Robert of Normandy and Robert de Belesme, whom king Henry had before deprived of his lands and driven from England; and through their conciliation the king of England and the count of Normandy became adversaries. And the king sent his folk over sea to Normandy; and the chief men there in the land received them, and with treason to their lord the count, admitted them into their castles, whence they did the count many injuries by harryings and burning. In this year also William count of Mortain went from this land to Normandy; but after he was gone he wrought against the king, for which the king deprived him of the land and all he had in this country. It is not easy to recount the miseries of this land which it was at this time suffering, through various and manifold illegalities and imposts, which never ceased nor failed. And ever as the king went there was plundering by his followers upon his wretched people, and at the same time very often burnings and murders. All this was to the anger of God, and the torment of the miserable people.

An. MC.V. In this year at the Nativity, king Henry held his court at Windsor; and thereafter, in Lent, he went over sea to Normandy, against his brother count Robert. And while he there abode he won from his brother Caen and Bayeux; and almost all the castles and the chief men there in the land became subjected to him; and he afterwards, at autumn, returned to this land; and what he had won in Normandy continued afterwards in peace, and obedient to him, except those who dwelt anywhere near to the count William of Mortain, whom he repeatedly oppressed to the utmost of his power, for the loss of his land here in this country. And then before

367.

Christmas came Robert de Belesme to this land to the king. This was a very calamitous year in the land, through the perishing of the fruits, and the manifold exactions, which never ceased before the king passed over, and while he was there, and then again after he came back.

An. MC.VI. In this year king Henry was at the Nativity in Westminster, and there held his court ; and at that tide Robert de Belesme went from the king unreconciled, from this land to Normandy. Then afterwards, before Lent, the king was at Northampton, and count Robert his brother came thither to him from Normandy ; and because the king would not give up to him what he had taken from him in Normandy, they parted in enmity ; and the count went immediately back over sea. In the first week of Lent, on the Friday, the XIVth of the Kal. of March (Feb. 16th), there appeared in the evening an uncommon star, and for a long time after was seen shining a while every evening. The star appeared in the south-west ; it seemed little and dark, but the ray that stood from it was very bright, and appeared [1] like an immense beam shining north-east ; and one evening it appeared as if the beam were entering the star from an opposite direction. Some said that they saw more unknown stars at this time, but we do not write it more openly, because we did not ourselves see them. On the night, the morrow of which was Cœna Domini, that is the [2] Thursday before Easter, were seen two moons in the heaven, before day ; one in the east and the other in the west, both full ; and the same day was the XIVth of the moon. At Easter the king was at Bath, and at Pentecost at Salisbury; because he would not hold a court on his departure over sea. Thereafter, before August, the king went over sea to Normandy; and almost all who were there in the land submitted to his will, except Robert de Belesme and the count of Mortain, and a few others of the chief men who yet held with the count of Normandy; and therefore the king afterwards went with an army and besieged a castle of the count of Mortain, called Tinchebray. While the king was besieging the castle, came count Robert of Normandy, on the eve of St. Michael's mass,

366.

---

[1] " quasi ingens trabes." Flor. Wigorn.

[2] Called also Maundy Thursday and Shere Thursday.

against the king with his force, and with him Robert de
Belesme and William count of Mortain, and all who would be
with them; but the strength and the victory were the king's.
There were the count of Normandy taken, and the [1] count of
Mortain, and Robert de Stuttevile, and afterwards sent to
England, and placed in durance. Robert de Belesme was
there put to flight, and William Crespin taken, and many with
him. Eadgar ætheling, who a little before had gone from the
king to the count, was also there taken, whom the king afterwards let go sackless. Afterwards the king subdued all that
was in Normandy, and established it all according to his will
and power. In this year also were very heavy and sinful
contests between the emperor of Saxony and his son ; and
during these contests the father died, and the son succeeded to
the empire.

An. MC.VII. In this year, at Christmas, king Henry was
in Normandy, and ordered and established that land under his
power ; and then afterwards came hither to this land in Lent,
and at Easter held his court in Windsor ; and at Pentecost, in
Westminster. And afterwards, in the beginning of August,
he was again in Westminster, and there gave and appointed to
the bishoprics and abbacies, which in England or Normandy
were without head and shepherd. Of these there were so
many that there was no man that remembered that ever before
so many together were given. And at this same time, among
the others who received abbacies, Ernulf, who before was prior
in Canterbury, succeeded to the abbacy of Peterborough.
This was just about seven years after king Henry succeeded
to the kingdom, and that was the one and fortieth year since
the Franks ruled this land. Many said that they had seen
various tokens in the moon this year, and its light waxing
and waning contrary to nature. In this year died Maurice,

---

[1] "Le vainqueur ne se contenta
" pas de le dépouiller de toutes ses
·" propriétés (et en particulier du
" comté de Mortain, qu'il donna à
" Etienne de Blois) mais encore il le
" renferma dans une étroite capti-
" vité, et poussa la barbarie, dit on,
" jusqu'à lui faire crever les yeux

" de sang-froid ·dans sa prison.
" Cette circonstance ne fut connue
" qu' après la mort de Henri. Voyez
" l'Histoire de Geoffroi Plantagenet,
" par Jean de Marmoutier," cited
by M. A. Le Prevost, Roman de Rou,
II. p. 360, note.

bishop of London, and Robert, abbot of St. Edmundsbury, and Richard, abbot of Ely. In this year also died king Eadgar of Scotland, on the Ides of January (Jan. 13th), and Alexander his brother succeeded to the kingdom, as king Henry granted him.

An. MC.VIII. In this year king Henry was at the Nativity in Westminster, and at Easter in Winchester, and at Pentecost again in Westminster. And, thereafter, before August he went to Normandy. And Philip, king of France, died on the Nones of August (Aug. 5th), and his son *Lewis succeeded to the kingdom; and there were afterwards many strifes betwixt the king of France and him of England, while he abode in Normandy. In this year also died the archbishop Gerard of York, before Pentecost; and Thomas was afterwards thereto appointed.

*VI.

An. MC.IX. In this year king Henry was at Christmas and at Easter in Normandy; and before Pentecost he came to this land, and held his court in Westminster. There were the contracts completed and the oaths sworn for the marriage of his daughter with the *emperor. In this year were very many thunderstorms, and those very awful. And the archbishop Anselm of Canterbury died on the day the XIth of the Kal. of April (March 22nd); and the first day of Easter was on Litania major (April 25th).

369.

* Henry V.

An. MC.X. In this year king Henry held his court at Christmas in Westminster; and at Easter he was at Marlborough; and at Pentecost, for the first time, he held his court in the New Windsor. In this year, before Lent, the king sent his daughter, with manifold treasures, over sea, and gave her to the emperor. On the fifth night of the month of May, the moon appeared in the evening brightly shining, and afterwards, by little and little, its light waned, so that as soon as it was night, it was so completely quenched that neither light nor orb, nor anything at all of it, was seen. And so it continued very near until day, and then appeared full and brightly shining. It was on this same day a fortnight old. All the night the air was very clear, and the stars over all the heaven were brightly shining. And the tree-fruits on that night were sorely nipt. After that, in the month of June, a star appeared in the north-east, and its beams stood before it in the south-west; and thus it was seen for many nights; and further in the night, when

it rose higher, it was seen going back to the north-west. In
this year were Philip de Braiose, and William Malet, and
William Bainard, deprived of their lands. In this year also
died count Hélie, who held Le Maine of king Henry and
'Anjou; and after his decease the count of Anjou assumed
and held it against the king. This was a very calamitous
year in this land, through the taxes which the king levied for
his daughter's marriage, and through tempests, by which the
earth-fruits were greatly injured, and the tree-fruits over all
this land almost all perished. In this year it was first begun
to work on the new monastery at Chertsey.

An. MC.XI. In this year king Henry did not bear his crown
at Christmas, nor at Easter, nor at Pentecost; and in August
he went over sea to Normandy, on account of the hostility
that some had against him on the frontiers of France, and,
above all, on account of the count of Anjou, who held Le
Maine against him. And after he came over thither, many
hostile inroads, and burnings, and harryings they did between
them. In this year died count Robert of Flanders; and his son
Baldwine succeeded thereto. In this year was a very long, and
sad, and severe winter; and thereby were the earth-fruits
greatly injured ; and there was the greatest murrain of cattle
that any man could remember.

An. MC.XII. All this year king Henry abode in Normandy,
in consequence of the hostility that he had against France,
and against the count of Anjou, who held Le Maine against
him. And while he was there he deprived of their lands the
count of Evreux and William Crespin, and drove them out of
Normandy; and to Philip de Braiose, he restored his land, who
had before been deprived of it; and Robert de Belesme he
caused to be taken and put into prison. This was a very good
year, and very abundant in wood and in field ; but it was very
sad and sorrowful one, through a most destructive pestilence.

An. MC.XIII. In this year king Henry was at the Nativity,   370.
and at Easter, and at Pentecost, in Normandy; and afterwards,
in the summer, he sent hither to this country Robert de Be-

---

¹ If the reading of 'Angeow,' for
the senseless 'on cweow' of the text,
be well founded, it shows that Hélie

held of both princes, of Henry, as
count of Normandy, and of the
count of Anjou.

o 2

lesme to the castle at Wareham ; and himself soon after came hither to this land.

An. MC.XIV. In this year king Henry held his court at the Nativity in Windsor; and afterwards this year he held no court oftener. And at Midsummer he went with a force into Wales; and the Welsh came and made peace with the king ; and he caused castles to be built therein ; and afterwards, in September, he went over sea to Normandy. In this year, in the latter end of May, was seen an uncommon star, with a long train, shining many nights. Also in this same year was so great an ebb everywhere in one day as no man before remembered, and so that men went riding and walking over the Thames to the east of the bridge at London. In this year were very great winds in the month of October; but it was excessively great in the night of the octave of St. Martin (Nov. 18th), and that was everywhere manifest, in woods and in towns. Also in this year the king gave the archbishopric of Canterbury to Ralph, who had previously been bishop of Rochester. And Thomas, the archbishop of York, died ; and Thurstân succeeded him, who had previously been the king's chaplain. At this same time the king went towards the sea, and would cross, but the weather hindered him. In the meanwhile he sent his writ after the abbot Ernulf of Peterborough, and commanded him that he should come to him with the utmost speed, because he would speak with him in private speech. When he came to him, he forced upon him the bishopric of Rochester ; and the archbishops, and bishops, and the nobility that were in England supported the king : and he long withstood, but it availed naught. And the king then commanded the archbishop that he should lead him to Canterbury, and bless him for bishop, whether he would or would not. This was done in the town which is called Bourne (Eastbourne). That was on the day the xviiith of the Kal. of October (Sept. 15th). When the monks of Peterborough heard that said, they were so sorry as they never were before; because he was a very good and meek man, and did much good within and without, while he there abode. May God Almighty ever abide with him! Then soon after, the king gave the abbacy to a monk of Séez, named John, at the desire of the archbishop of Canterbury. And soon after, the king and the archbishop of Canterbury sent him to Rome after the archbishop's pall, and a monk with him, who was called Warner, and the archdeacon John, the archbishop's nephew : and they well sped there. This was done on the day the xɪth of the Kal. of October (Sept. 21st), in the town which is called Rowner. And on the same day the king went on shipboard at Portsmouth.

An. ᴍᴄ.xᴠ. In this year, at the Nativity, king Henry was in Normandy; and while he was there, he did so that all the chief men in Normandy did homage and swore oaths of fealty to his son William, whom he had by his queen; and after that, in the month of July, he came hither to this land. In this year there was so severe a winter, with snow and with frost, that no man that then lived ever before remembered a severer; and through that there was an immense mortality of cattle. In this year pope Paschal sent the pall hither to Ralph, archbishop of Canterbury ; and he received it with great worship at his archiepiscopal see in Canterbury. It was brought by abbot Anselm from Rome, who was the nephew of archbishop Anselm, and the abbot John of Peterborough.

371.

An. ᴍᴄ.xᴠɪ. In this year, at the Nativity, king Henry was at St. Alban's, and there caused the monastery to be hallowed; and at Easter at Odiham. And this year also there was a very gloomy winter, both severe and long, for cattle and for all things. And immediately after Easter the king went over sea to Normandy ; and there were many hostile inroads, and plunderings, and castles taken, between France and Normandy. This hostility was chiefly because king Henry supported his nephew, count Theobald of Blois, who then was at war against his lord, Lewis king of France. This was a very grievous year, and deficient in earth-fruits, through the excessive rains that came immediately before August, and greatly troubled and afflicted [people] until the coming of Candlemas (Feb. 2nd). This year was also so wanting in mast, that in all this land, and also in Wales, none was heard spoken of. This land and this people were this year also oftentimes sorely oppressed through the imposts which the king took, both within town and without. In this same year all the monastery of Peterborough was burnt, and all the houses, except the chapter-house and the dormitory ; and in addition thereto, all the greatest part of the town was burnt. All this happened on a Friday, which was the IInd of the Nones of August (Aug. 4th).

An. MC.XVII. All this year king Henry abode in Normandy, on account of the hostility of the king of France, and his other neighbours. And then in the summer came the king of France, and with him the count of Flanders, with a force into Normandy, and remained therein one night, and in the morning returned without a battle : and Normandy was greatly oppressed, both by the imposts, and by the force which king Henry gathered against them. This nation also, through this same, through manifold imposts, was severely oppressed. In this year also, on the night of the Kal. of December (Dec. 1st), there were most violent storms, with thunder and lightning, and rain and hail. And in the night of the IIIrd of the Ides of December (Dec. 11th), the moon was far in the night as if it were all bloody, and afterwards eclipsed. Also in the night of the XVIIth of the Kal. of January (Dec. 16th), the heaven was seen very red, as if it were a conflagration. And on the octave of St. John the Evangelist (Jan. 3rd), was the great earthquake in Lombardy, through which many monasteries, and towers, and houses fell, and did great harm among men. This was a very deficient year in corn, through the rains that ceased not almost all the year. And the [1] abbot Gilbert of Westminster died on the VIIIth of the Ides of December (Dec. 6th); and *Faritz, abbot of Abingdon, died on the VIIth of the Kal. of March (Feb. 23rd) ; and in this same year

* Faricius.

. . . .

372.

An. MC.XVIII. In all this year king Henry abode in Normandy, on account of the war of the king of France, and the count of Anjou, and the count of Flanders. And the count of Flanders was wounded in Normandy, and so wounded went to Flanders. Through the hostility of these the king was sorely troubled, and lost much both in money and also in land; but his own men vexed him most, who frequently revolted from and betrayed him, and turned to his foes; and, to the king's harm and betraying, gave up their castles to them. All

---

[1] A gravestone on the south side of the cloister of Westminster abbey | is supposed to cover the remains of this abbot.

this England dearly bought through the manifold imposts, which all this year did not cease.   This year, in the week of the Epiphany, there was one evening very great lightning, and a most immoderate thunder-clap afterwards.   And queen Matilda died at Westminster on the day of the Kal. of May (May 1st), and was there buried.   And in this year also died count Robert of Meulan.   Also in this year, on St. Thomas' mass (Dec. 21st), there was so very violent a wind that no man who then lived remembered any greater ; and that was everywhere seen, both in houses and also in trees.   In this year also died pope Paschal, and John of Gaëta succeeded to the popedom, whose other name was Gelasius.

An. MC.XIX. ¹All this year king Henry abode in Normandy, and by the war with the king of France, and also with his own men, who with treachery revolted from him and joined his enemy, was oftentimes greatly embarrassed,' until the two kings with their people came together in Normandy.   There was the king of France put to flight, and all his best men taken ; and afterwards many of king Henry's men submitted to him and accorded with him, who before with their castles were against him ; and some of the castles he took by force. In this year went William, the son of king Henry and queen Matilda, to Normandy to his father, and there was given to him and wedded to wife, the daughter of the count of Anjou. On St. Michael's mass-eve was a great earthquake in some places here in the land, though most in Gloucestershire and in Worcestershire.   In this same year died pope Gelasius on this side of the *mountain, and was buried at Cluny.   And after • the Alps. him the archbishop of Vienne was chosen pope, whose name was Calixtus.   He afterwards, on the mass of St. Luke the Evangelist (Oct. 18th), came to France to Rheims, and there held a council.   And the archbishop Thurstân of York went thither ; and because that he, against right, and against the arch-see of Canterbury, and against the king's will, had

---

¹ The integrity of the text seems here more than doubtful ; the sense, however is, I believe, faithfully rendered, and in accordance with the words of the continuator of Florence of Worcester : " Plures Norman-

" norum quam regi Henrico jura-
" verant fidelitatem postposuerunt,
" et ad regem Franciæ Ludovicum
" principesque ejus, adversarios sci-
" licet, ... se transtule-
" runt."

received his ordination from the pope, the king prohibited him from all return to England. And thus he *forfeited his archbishopric, and went with the pope towards Rome. Also in this year died count Baldwine of Flanders of the wounds which he received in Normandy ; and after him Charles, the son of his paternal aunt, succeeded to the government ; he was the son of Cnut the saint, king of Denmark.

An. MC.XX. In this year the kings of England and France were reconciled, and after their reconciliation, all king Henry's own men in Normandy accorded with him, and the counts of Flanders and of Ponthieu. Then, after this, king Henry settled his castles and his land in Normandy after his will ; and so before Advent came hither to this land. And on the passage were drowned the king's two sons, William and Richard, and Richard carl of Chester, and Ottuel his brother, and very many of the king's court, stewards, and chamberlains, and cup-bearers, and from divers habitations, and a countless number of very excellent folk along with them. This death was a two-fold pain to their friends : one, that they were deprived of this life so suddenly ; the other, that few of their bodies were found anywhere afterwards. In this year came that light to the sepulchre of the Lord in Jerusalem twice ; once at Easter, and a second time on the Assumption of St. Mary (Aug. 15th), as credible persons said who came thence. And the arch-bishop Thurstân of York was, through the pope, reconciled with the king, and came hither to this land, and received his bishopric, though it was very displeasing to the archbishop of Canterbury.

An. MC.XXI. In this year king Henry was at Christmas at Brampton ; and afterwards at Windsor, before Candlemas, was given him to wife Adela, and she was afterwards hallowed queen ; she was the daughter of the ¹duke of Louvain. And the moon was eclipsed on the night of the Nones of April (April 5th), and was fourteen days old. And the king was at Easter in Berkeley ; and afterwards, at Pentecost, he held a great court in Westminster ; and afterwards in the summer went with a force into Wales ; and the Welsh came to meet him, and after the king's will they accorded with him. In this

---

¹ Godfrey VII. count of Louvain, duke of Lower Lorraine, and mar- | quis of Antwerp ; afterwards duke of Brabant.

year came the count of Anjou from Jerusalem to his land, and afterwards sent to this land, and caused his daughter to be fetched, who had previously been given to wife to the king's son, William. And in the night of the vigil Natalis Domini was a very violent wind over all this land ; and that was in many things manifestly seen.

An. MC.XXII. In this year king Henry was at Christmas in Norwich, and at Easter in Northampton. And in the Lent-tide before that, the town of Gloucester was burnt while the monks were singing their mass, and the deacon had begun the gospel 'Præteriens Jesus.' Then came the fire on the upper part of the steeple, and burned all the monastery and all the treasures that were there within, except a few books and three mass-robes. That was on the day the VIIIth of the Ides of March (March 8th). And afterwards, on the Tuesday after Palm Sunday, was a very violent wind on the day the XIth of the Kal. of April (March 22nd); after which came many tokens all over England, and many spectres were seen and heard. And on the night of the VIIIth of the Kal. of August (July 25th) there was a very great earthquake over all Somerset-shire and in Gloucestershire. Afterwards, on the day the VIth of the Ides of September, that was on St. Mary's mass-day (Sept. 8th), there was a very great wind from the *third hour of •9 A.M. the day to the swart night. In this same year died Ralph, the archbishop of Canterbury, that was on the day the XIIIth of the Kal. of November (Oct. 20th). Afterwards there were many shipmen on the sea and on (fresh) water, who said that they saw in the north-east a great and broad fire near the earth, which at once waxed in length up to the sky; and the sky separated into four parts, and fought against it as if it would quench it ; but the fire, nevertheless, waxed up to the heavens. The fire they saw in the dawn, and it lasted so long till it was light over all. That was on the day the VIIth of the Ides of December (Dec. 7th).

An. MC.XXIII. In this year at Christmas-tide king Henry 374. was at Dunstable ; and there came envoys from the count of Anjou to him ; and thence he went to Woodstock, and his bishops and all his court with him. Then it befel on a Wednesday, which was on the IVth of the Ides of January (Jan. 10th), that the king was riding in his deer-fold, and the bishop Roger of Salisbury on one side of him, and the bishop

Robert Bloet of Lincoln on the other side of him ; and they
were there riding and talking. Then the bishop of Lincoln
sank down, and said to the king, "Lord king, I am dying." And
the king alighted down from his horse, and lifted him betwixt
his arms, and caused him to be borne to his inn ; and he was
then forthwith dead ; and he was conveyed to Lincoln with
great worship, and buried before St. Mary's altar. And the
bishop of Chester, named Robert Pecceth, buried him. Then
immediately after this the king sent his writ over all England,
and bade his bishops, and his abbots, and all his thanes, that
they should come to his council on Candlemas day (Feb. 2nd),
at Gloucester, to meet him; and they did so. When they were
there gathered, the king bade them that they should choose
them an archbishop of Canterbury, whomsoever they would;
and he would consent to it. Then spake the bishops among
themselves and said, that they never more would have a man
of monkish order for archbishop over them. And they all
went together to the king, and desired that they might
choose a man of the clerical order, whomsoever they would, for
archbishop. And the king conceded it to them. All this was
done previously through the bishop of Salisbury, and through
* abp. Ralph. the bishop of Lincoln, before *he was dead; because they never
loved the rule of monks, but were ever against monks and
their rule. And the prior and the monks of Canterbury, and
all the other men of monkish order who were there, withstood
it full two days ; but it availed naught ; for the bishop of
Salisbury was strong and ruled all England, and was against
it all that he might and could. Then they chose a clerk, who
was named William of Corbeil, he was canon of a monastery
called Chiche (St. Osyth). And they brought him before the
king, and the king gave him the archbishopric, and all the
bishops received him ; almost all the monks, and earls, and
thanes who were there opposing him. At the same time
* of Anjou.   the envoys of the *count went in enmity from the king,
nor recked they aught of his favour. At the same time came
a legate from Rome, named Henry ; he was abbot of the
monastery of St. Jean d'Angely; and he came after the Rome-
scot. And he said to the king that it was against right that a
clerk should be set over monks ; and therefore they had earlier
chosen an archbishop in their chapter according to right.
But the king would not undo it, for love of the bishop of

Salisbury. Then went the archbishop soon after to Canterbury, and was there received, though it was against their will, and was there immediately blessed as bishop by the bishop of London, and the bishop Ernulf of Rochester, and the bishop William Giffard of Winchester, and the bishop Bernard of *Wales, and the bishop Roger of Salisbury. Then soon in Lent * St. David's. the archbishop went to Rome after his pall, and with him went the bishop Bernard of Wales, and Sigfrid abbot of Glastonbury, and Anselm abbot of St. Edmund's, and John archdeacon of Canterbury, and Giffard, who was the king's domestic chaplain. At the same time went the archbishop Thurstân 375. of York to Rome by the pope's command ; and came thither three days before the archbishop of Canterbury came, and was there received with great worship. Then came the archbishop of Canterbury, and was there full seven nights ere he could come to speech of the pope. That was because the pope had been made to understand that he had received the archbishopric in opposition to the monks of the monastery, and against right. But that overcame Rome which overcomes all the world, that is gold and silver. And the pope was pacified, and gave him his pall ; and the archbishop swore subjection to him in all the things which the pope enjoined him, on the altar of St. Peter and St. Paul, and sent him home with his blessing. While the archbishop was out of the land, the king gave the bishopric of Bath to the queen's chancellor named Godfrey : he was born in Louvain. That was on the day of the Annunciation of St. Mary (March 25th) at Woodstock. Soon afterwards the king went to Winchester, and was there all Eastertide; and while he was there he gave the bishopric of Lincoln to a clerk called Alexander : he was the nephew of the bishop of Salisbury. This he did all for love of the bishop. Then the king went thence to Portsmouth, and lay there all through Pentecost week. Then as soon as he had a wind, he went over to Normandy, and committed all England to the care and rule of bishop Roger of Salisbury. Then was the king all this year in Normandy ; and there grew great hostility betwixt him and his thanes, so that the count Waleram of Meulan, and Amauri, and Hugh of Montfort, and William of Roumare, and many others, turned from him, and held their castles against him. And the king held strongly against them. And in this same year he won of Waleram his castle of Pont-Audemer, and of Hugh, Montfort ; and after that he sped ever the longer the better. In this same year, before the bishop of Lincoln came to his bishopric, almost all the town of Lincoln was consumed, and a countless number of people, males and females, were burnt ; and so great harm was there done, that no man could say it to another. That was on the day the xivth of the Kal. of June (May 19th).

An. MC.XXIV. All this year king Henry was in Normandy ; that was on account of the great hostility that he had with the king Lewis of France, and with the count of Anjou, and with his own men most of all. It then happened on the day of the Annunciation of St. Mary (March 25th), that the count Wale- ram of Meulan went from one of his castles, called Belmont, to another castle of his called Wattevile. With him went Amauri, the king of France's steward, and Hugh Fitz Gervase, and Hugh of Montfort, and many other good knights. Then came against them the king's knights from all the castles that were there about, and fought against them, and put them to flight, and took count Waleram, and Hugh Fitz Gervase, and Hugh of Montfort, and five and twenty other knights, and brought them to the king. And the king caused count Waleram and Hugh Fitz Gervase to be imprisoned in the castle of Rouen ; and Hugh of Montfort he sent to England, and caused him to be put in miserable bonds in the castle of Gloucester. And of the others, as many as to him seemed good, he sent north and south to his castles, in durance. Then afterwards the king went and won all the castles of count Waleram that were in Normandy, and all the others which his adversaries held against him. All this hostility was on account of the son of count Robert of Normandy, named William. The same Wil- liam had taken to wife the younger daughter of Fulk, count of Anjou; and therefore the king of France, and all these counts, and all the powerful men, held with him, and said, that the king with wrong held his brother Robert in durance, and unjustly drove his son William out of Normandy. In this same year were many failures in England, in corn and all fruits, so that between Christmas and Candlemas (Feb. 2nd) the acre-seed of wheat, that is, two seedlips, were sold for six shillings; and that of barley, that is, three seedlips, for six shillings; and the acre-seed of oats, that is, four seedlips, for four shillings. That was because there was little corn, and the penny was so bad,

376.

that the man who had at a market a pound could by no means
buy therewith twelve pennyworths.   In this same year died
the blessed bishop Ernulf of Rochester, who was before abbot
of Peterborough; that was on the Ides of March (March 15th).
And thereafter died king Alexander of Scotland, on the day the
ixth of the Kal. of May (April 23rd) ; and David his brother,
who was earl of Northamptonshire, succeeded to the kingdom,
and had them both together, the kingdom of Scotland and the
earldom in England.   And on the day the xixth of the Kal. of
January (Dec. 14th), died the pope in Rome, who was named
Calixtus, and Honorius succeeded to the popedom.   In the
same year, after St. Andrew's mass (Nov. 30th), before Christmas, Ralph Basset and the king's thanes held a court at Huncot
in Leicestershire, and there hanged so many thieves as never
were before, that was, in that little while, altogether four and
forty men ; and six men were deprived of their eyes and
emasculated.   Many righteous men said, that there were many
unjustly deprived ; but our Lord God Almighty, who sees and
knows every secret, sees that the miserable folk are treated
with all injustice ; first they are bereft of their property, and
then they are slain.   A full heavy year it was : the man who
had any goods was bereft of them by violent exactions and
violent courts ; those who had none died of hunger.

An. MC.XXV.   In this year, before Christmas, king Henry
sent from Normandy to England, and commanded that all the
moneyers that were in England should be deprived of their
members ; that was the right hand of each, and their testicles
beneath.   That was because the man that had a pound could
not buy for a penny at a market.   And the bishop Roger of
Salisbury sent over all England, and commanded them all that
they should come to Winchester at Christmas.   When they
came thither they were taken one by one, and each deprived of the right hand and the testicles beneath.   All this
was done within the twelve nights ; and that was all with
great justice, because they had fordone all the land with
their great quantity of false money which they all bought.
In this same year the pope sent from Rome to this land a
cardinal named John of Crema.   He first came to the king
in Normandy, and the king received him with great worship ; commended him afterwards to the archbishop William of Canterbury, and he conducted him to Canterbury,

and he was there received with great worship, and with
a great procession; and he sang the high mass on Easter
day at Christ's altar.   And afterwards he went over all England to all the bishoprics and abbacies that were in this land,
and everywhere he was received with worship, and all gave
him great and noble gifts.   And afterwards he held his council
in London for full three days, on the Nativity of St. Mary, in
September (8th), with archbishops and with suffragan bishops,
and abbots, and clergy, and laity ; and commanded there the
¹same laws that archbishop Anselm had before commanded,
and many more, though it availed little.   And thence he went

377.

over sea soon after St. Michael's mass, and so to Rome ; and
archbishop William of Canterbury, and archbishop Thurstân
of York, and bishop Alexander of Lincoln, and bishop J. of

* Loÿen.

*Lothian, and the abbot G. of St. Alban's ; and they were
there received by pope Honorius with great worship, and were
there all the winter.   In this same year was so great a flood
on St. Lawrence's mass-day (Aug. 10th) that many towns and
men were drowned, and bridges shattered, and corn and mea-
dows totally destroyed, and famine and disease among men
and cattle ; and for all fruits there was so bad a season as
there had not been for many years before.   And in this year
died the abbot John of Peterborough, on the IInd of the Ides
of October (Oct. 14th).

An. MC.XXVI.   All this year king Henry was in Normandy
until quite after autumn ; then he came to this land betwixt
the Nativity of St. Mary (Sept. 8th) and Michaelmas (Sept.
29th).   With him came the queen, and his daughter, whom

* Henry V.

he had formerly given to wife to the emperor *Henry of
Lorraine.   And he brought with him count Waleram and
Hugh Fitz Gervase ; and the count he sent to Bridgenorth in
durance, and thence afterwards to Wallingford, and Hugh to
Windsor, and caused him to be put in hard bonds.   And then
after Michaelmas came David the Scots' king from Scotland
to this land; and king Henry received him with great worship;
and he then abode all that year in this land.   In this same

¹ See them in Flor. Wigorn. edit.   Johnson, Eccles. Laws and Canons,
E. H. S., p. 81, and a curious anec-   II. p. 34; and Spelman, Conc. II.
dote of this legate John, in Hoveden. p. 33.
See also Wilkins, Conc. I. p. 408 ;

year the king caused his brother Robert to be taken from the bishop Roger of Salisbury, and committed him to his son Robert earl of Gloucester, and had him conducted to Bristol, and there put into the castle. That was all done through his daughter's counsel, and through the Scots' king David, her uncle.

An. MC.XXVII. This year king Henry held his court at Christmas in Windsor, where were the Scots' king David, and all the chief clergy and laity that were in England. And there he caused the archbishops, and bishops, and abbots, and earls, and all the thanes that were there, to swear to his daughter [1]Æthelic, who was before the wife of the emperor of Saxland, possession of England and Normandy, after his day; and afterwards sent her to Normandy, and with her went her brother, Robert earl of Gloucester, and Brian, son of *count Alain Fergant; and caused her to wed the son of the * of Brittany. count of Anjou, Geoffrey, surnamed Martel. · Nevertheless, all the French and English thought ill of it; but the king did it to have peace from the count of Anjou, and to have help against his nephew William. In this same year, in Lent-tide, the count Charles of Flanders was slain by his own men in a church, where he lay and prayed to God before the altar, during the mass. And the king of France brought William, the son of the count of Normandy, and gave him the *county, * of Flanders. and the land-folk accepted him. This same William had before taken the count of Anjou's daughter to wife, but they were afterwards divorced on account of consanguinity. That was all through king Henry of England. After that he took the king of France's wife's sister to wife, and on that account the king gave him the county of Flanders. In this same year he gave the abbacy of Peterborough to an abbot named Henry of Poitou, who had in his hand his abbacy of St. Jean d'Angely: and all the archbishops and bishops said that it was against right, and that he might not have two abbacies in hand. But 378. the same Henry gave the king to understand that he had left his abbacy, on account of the dissension that was in the land, and that he acted by the counsel and leave of the pope of

---

[1] This seems to have been the English name of Henry's daughter Matilda.

Rome, and by the abbot of Cluny's, and because he was legate
for the Rome-scot.   But it nevertherless was not so ; but he
would have both in hand, and had so, as long as it was God's
will.   He had in his clerkhood been bishop of Soissons, afterwards he became a monk of Cluny, and then prior of the same
monastery ; and then he became prior of Savenni (Savenay ?);
afterwards, because he was a relation of the king of England,
and of the count of Poitou, the count gave him the abbacy of
the monastery of St. Jean d'Angely ; afterwards, through his
great intrigues he got the archbishopric of Besançon, and had
it in hand three days ; he then lost it with right, because he
had before obtained it with wrong.   Then he got the bishopric
of Saintes, which was five miles from his abbacy : that he had
almost a week in hand.   Then the abbot of Cluny brought
him thence, as he had before done from Besançon.   Then he
bethought him, that if he could be firmly settled in England,
he might have all his will.   He then sought the king, and said
to him, that he was an old and broken-down man, and that he
could not endure the great injustice and the great dissen-
sions that were in their land, and craved in his own name,
and through all his friends by name, the abbacy of Peterborough ; and the king granted it to him, because he was his
relation, and because he was retained to swear on oath and
bear witness, when the son of the count of Normandy and the
daughter of the count of Anjou were parted, on account of
consanguinity.   Thus miserably was the abbacy given at
London between Christmas and Candlemas.   And so he went
with the king to Winchester, and thence he came to Peterborough, and there he abode just as drones do in a hive ; all
that the bees draw towards them, the drones devour and draw
from them; so did he : all that he could take, within and without, from clerical and from lay, he sent over sea, and did no
good there, nor any good left there.   ¹Let it not to any one
seem incredible, [and] that we say not sooth ; for it was fully
known over all the land, that as soon as he came thither, which
was on the Sunday when they sing 'Exurge quare, o Domine,'
then immediately afterwards many men saw and heard many

---

¹ My version of this passage,
though not satisfactory, is the best I
can offer. Without the insertion of
the negative 'ne' in the text, it
seems void of sense.

hunters hunting. The hunters were black, and large, and
ugly, and all their hounds black, and broad-eyed, and ugly ;
and they rode on black horses and on black bucks. This was
seen in the very deer-fold in the town of Peterborough, and in
all the woods that lead from the same town to Stamford ; and
the monks heard the horns blow that they blew in the night.
Truthful men, who observed them in the night, said from what
it seemed to them, that there might well be about twenty or
thirty horn-blowers. This was seen and heard from the time
that he came thither, all the Lenten-tide on to Easter. This
was his entrance ; of his exit we cannot yet say aught. God
provide.

An. MC.XXVIII. All this year king Henry was in Normandy,
on account of the hostility that was between him and his
nephew the count of Flanders. But the count was wounded in
a battle by a peasant, and so wounded he went to the *monas- * St. Omer's.
tery of St. Bertin, and there immediately became a monk, and
lived five days after, and he was then dead and there buried.
May God have mercy on his soul. That was on the day the
VIth of the Kal. of August (July 27th). In this same year
died bishop Ranulf Passeflambard of Durham, and was there
buried on the Nones of September (Sept. 5th). And in this same   379.
year the aforesaid abbot Henry went home to his own monas-
tery at Poitou, by the king's leave. He had given the king to
understand that he would entirely leave that monastery and
that land, and abide with him ¹there in England, and in the
monastery of Peterborough. But nevertheless it was not so :
he did it because he would, through his great wiles, be ¹there,
were it a twelvemonth or more, and then come again. May
God Almighty have his mercy over that wretched place. In
this same year came from Jerusalem Hugo of the Temple to
the king in Normandy, and the king received him with great
worship, and gave him great treasures in gold and in silver.
And afterwards he sent him to England, and there he was
received by all good men, and all gave him treasure ; and
in Scotland also ; and by him sent to Jerusalem great property,
altogether in gold and in silver. And he summoned folk out to
Jerusalem ; and there went with him and after him so many

---

¹ From the use of the word 'þær' (there), it would seem that the
chronicler wrote from abroad.

people as never did before, since the first expedition was in the day of pope Urban ; though it availed little.   He said that a great conflict was resolved on between the Christians and the heathens : when they came thither, it was naught but leasing.   Thus miserably was all the folk harassed.

An. MC.XXIX.   In this year the king sent to England after count Waleram, and after Hugh Fitz Gervase; and they there gave hostages for them; and Hugh went home to his own land in France ; and Waleram remained with the king, and the king gave him all his land, save only his castle.   Afterwards the king came to England in the autumn, and the count came with him, and they became then as good friends as they had before been foes.   Then soon, by the king's counsel, and by his leave,[1] the archbishop William of Canterbury sent over all England, and bade the bishops, and abbots, and archdeacons, and all the priors, monks, and canons, that were in all the cells in England, and after all who had to preserve and watch over Christianity, that they should all come to London at Michaelmas, and should there speak of all God's rights.   When they came thither, the meeting began on Monday, and held on to the Friday.   When it all came forth, it was all about arch-deacons' wives, and about priests' wives ; that they should leave them by St. Andrew's mass (Nov. 30th); and he who would not do that, should forgo his church, and his house, and his home, and never more have any calling thereto.   This ordained the archbishop William of Canterbury, and all the suffragan bishops who were then in England ; and the king gave them all leave to go home; and so they went home, and all the decrees stood for naught : all held their wives, by the king's leave, as they did before.   In this same year died bishop William Giffard of Winchester, and was there buried, on the VIIIth of the Kal. of February (Jan. 25th) ; and king Henry gave the bishopric, after Michaelmas, to the abbot Henry of Glaston-bury, his nephew; and he was hallowed bishop by the archbishop William of Canterbury on the XVth of the Kal. of December (Nov. 17th).   In this same year died pope Honorius.   Before he was well dead there were chosen two popes ; one was

---

[1] For the particulars of this synod at Westminster, in 1127, see Flor. Wigorn Cont. II. p. 85 ; Johnson   'Eccles. Laws and Canons,' II. p. 37 ; Wilkins, Conc. I. p. 410 ; Spelman, Conc. II. p. 35.

named Peter, he was a monk of Cluny, and was born of the richest men of Rome ; with him held those of Rome and the duke of Sicily. The other was named Gregory, he was a clerk, and was driven out of Rome by the other pope, and by his kinsmen. With him held the emperor of Saxony, and the king of France, and king Henry of England, and all those on this side of the mountains. Now there was so much error in Christendom as never before was : may Christ impart counsel for his wretched folk. In this same year, on St. Nicholas' mass-night, a little before day, there was a great earthquake.

An. MC.XXX. In this year the monastery of Canterbury was hallowed by archbishop William, on the day the ivth of the Nones of May (May 4th). There were the bishops John of Rochester, Gilbert Universal of London, Henry of Winchester, Alexander of Lincoln, Roger of Salisbury, Simon of Worcester, Roger of Coventry, Godfrey of Bath, Everard of Norwich, Sigefrid of Chichester, Bernard of St. David's, Owen of Evreux from Normandy, John of Séez. On the fourth day after that, king Henry was in Rochester, and the town was almost burnt down. And the archbishop William hallowed the monastery of St. Andrew, and the aforesaid bishops with him. And king Henry went over sea to Normandy in the autumn. In the same year came the abbot Henry of Angely, after Easter, to Peterborough, and said that he had quite left that monastery. After him came the abbot of Cluny, named Peter, to England, by the king's leave, and was received everywhere whithersoever he came with much worship. To Peterborough he came, and there abbot Henry promised him that he would get him the monastery of Peterborough, that it might be subject to Cluny. But it is said for a proverb, 'The hedge abides that fields divides.' May God Almighty frustrate evil counsels. Shortly after this the abbot of Cluny went home to his country.

An. MC.XXXI. This year after Christmas, on a Monday night,

<hr />

An. MC.XXX. In this year Anagus was slain by the Scots' army; and there was a great slaughter made with him. There was God's right avenged on him, because he was all forsworn.[a]

at the first sleep, the heaven was, on the north side, all as though
it were burning fire, so that all who saw it were so affrighted
as they never were before.   That was on the 11rd of the Ides
of January (Jan. 11th).   In this same year there was so great a
murrain of the cattle, as never was in the memory of men over
all England.   That was in neat and in swine ; so that in the
town where there were ten or twelve ploughs going, there was
not one left; and the man who had two or three hundred swine
had not one left.   After that died the domestic fowls ; then
flesh meat became scarce, and cheese, and butter.   May God
better it when it shall be his will !   And king Henry came
home to England before the autumn, after the mass of St.
Peter ad Vincula (Aug. 1st).   In the same year the abbot
Henry went before Easter from Peterborough over sea to Normandy, and there spoke with the king, and said to him that
the abbot of Cluny had ordered him that he should come
to him and deliver over to him the abbacy of Angely ; and
after that he would come home by his leave.   And so he
went home to his own monastery, and there abode quite to
Midsummer day.   And the second day after St. John's mass-
day (June 26th), the monks chose an abbot from themselves,
and brought him into the church with procession, sang ' Te
Deum laudamus,' rang the bells, set him in the abbot's seat,
showed him all obedience, as they should do to their abbot; and
the earl, and all the chief men, and the monks of the monastery, drove the other abbot Henry out of the monastery.   They
had need : in five and twenty winters they had never enjoyed
one good day.   Here failed him all his great crafts : now it
behoved him to creep, in his great ¹tribulation, into every
corner, if there were at least one miserable trick, that he might
yet deceive Christ and all Christian folk.   He then went to
Cluny, and there he was held so that he could not go east or
west.   The abbot of Cluny said that they had lost St. John's
monastery through him, and through his great sottishness.
Then he knew of no better compensation to them, but to promise them, and swear oaths on relics, that if he might visit
England, he should get them the monastery of Peterborough;
so that he should set there a prior from Cluny, and a church-
ward, and treasurer, and vestment-keeper; and all the things

391.

---

¹ The original word is ' codde,' which I do not understand.

that were within the monastery and without, he should deliver
to them. Thus he went to France, and there abode all the year.
May Christ provide for the wretched monks of Peterborough,
and for that wretched place : now stand they in need of the
help of Christ and of all Christian folk.

An. MC.XXXII. In this year king Henry came to this land.
Then came abbot Henry, and accused the monks of Peterborough to the king; because he would subject that monastery
to Cluny ; so that the king was well nigh deceived, and sent
after the monks ; and through God's mercy, and through the
bishop of Salisbury, and the bishop of Lincoln, and the other
powerful men who were there, the king knew that he proceeded with guile. When he could do no more, he wished
that his nephew should be abbot of Peterborough; but Christ
willed it not. It was not very long after that, that the king
sent after him, and made him give up the abbacy of Peterborough, and go out of the land : and the king gave the
abbacy to a prior of St. Neot's named Martin : he came on
St. Peter's mass-day with great worship to the monastery.

An. MC.XXXIII., MC.XXXIV.

An. MC.XXXV. In this year king Henry went over sea at
Lammas (Aug. 1st); and the second day, as he lay and slept in
the ship, the day darkened over all lands, and the sun became,
as it were, a three-night-old moon, and the stars about it at
midday. Men were greatly wonder-stricken and affrighted,
and said that a great thing should come hereafter. So it did,
for that same year the king died, on the following day after
St. Andrew's mass-day (Dec. 2nd), in Normandy. Then there
was tribulation soon in the land; for every man that could
forthwith robbed another. Then his [1] son and his friends took
his body and brought it to England, and buried it at Reading.
A good man he was, and there was great awe of him. No
man durst misdo against another in his time. He made peace
for man and beast. Whoso bare his burthen of gold and silver,
no man durst say to him aught but good. In the meanwhile
his nephew Stephen of Blois was come to England, and came
to London, and the London folk received him, and sent after
the archbishop William Corbeil, and hallowed him king on

382.

---

[1] Robert earl of Gloucester, the only one of his numerous progeny
present at his death.

Midwinter day. In this king's time all was strife, and evil,
and rapine ; for against him soon rose the powerful men who
were traitors. The first of all Baldwin de Redvers, who held
Exeter against him ; and the king besieged it, and then Baldwin capitulated. Then the others took and held their castles
against him ; and David, king of Scotland, took to vex him.
Then, notwithstanding that, their messengers passed between
them, and they came together, and were reconciled ; though
it was to little purpose.

An. MC.XXXVI.

An. MC.XXXVII. In this year king Stephen went over sea to
Normandy, and was there received ; because they imagined
that he would be such as his uncle was, and because he had
got his treasure : but he distributed it and scattered it foolishly.
Much had king Henry gathered of gold and silver, and no
good was done for his soul thereof. When king Stephen came
to England (a. 1139), he held an assembly at Oxford, and there
he took the bishop Roger of Salisbury, and Alexander bishop of
Lincoln, and the chancellor Roger, his nephew, and put them
all into prison, till they gave up their castles. When the
traitors perceived that he was a mild man, and soft, and good,
and did no justice, then did they all wonder. They had done
homage to him, and sworn oaths, but had held no faith ; they
were all forsworn, and forfeited their troth ; for every powerful man made his castles, and held them against him ;
and they filled the land full of castles. They cruelly oppressed the wretched men of the land with castle-works.
When the castles were made, they filled them with devils and
evil men. Then took they those men that they imagined had
any property, both by night and by day, peasant men and
women, and put them in prison for their gold and silver, and
tortured them with unutterable torture ; for never were martyrs so tortured as they were. They hanged them up by the
feet, and smoked them with foul smoke ; they hanged them by
the thumbs, or by the head, and hung fires on their feet ; they
put knotted strings about their heads, and writhed them so
that it went to the brain. They put them in dungeons, in
which were adders, and snakes, and toads, and killed them so.
Some they put in a 'crucet hûs,' that is, in a chest that was
short, and narrow, and shallow, and put sharp stones therein,
and pressed the man therein, so that they brake all his limbs.

In many of the castles were [instruments called] a **'láð and** *[loathly and grim.]* grim,' these were neck-bonds, of which two or three men had enough to bear one. It was so made, that is, [it was] fastened to a beam ; and they put a sharp iron about the man's throat and his neck, so that he could not in any direction sit, or lie, or sleep, but must bear all that iron. Many thousands they killed with hunger ; I neither can nor may tell all the wounds or all the tortures which they inflicted on wretched men in this land; and that lasted the nineteen winters while Stephen was king ; and ever it was worse and worse. They laid imposts on the towns continually, and called it '*censerie :*' when the wretched men had no more to give, they robbed and burned all the towns, so that thou mightest well go all a day's journey and thou shouldst never find a man sitting in a town, or the land tilled. Then was corn dear, and flesh, and cheese, and butter; for there was none in the land. Wretched men died of hunger; some went seeking alms who at one while were rich men; some fled out of the land. Never yet had more wretchedness been in the land, nor did heathen men ever do worse than they did; for everywhere at times they forbore neither church nor churchyard, but took all the property that was therein, and then burned the church and altogether. Nor forbore they a bishop's land, nor an abbot's, nor a priest's, but robbed monks and clerks, and every man another who anywhere could. If two or three men came riding to a town, all the township fled before them, imagining them to be robbers. The bishops and clergy constantly cursed them, but nothing came of it; for they were all accursed, and forsworn, and lost. However a man tilled, the earth bare no corn; for the land was all fordone by such deeds : and they said openly that Christ and his saints slept. Such and more than we can say, we endured nineteen winters for our sins. In all this evil time abbot Martin held his abbacy twenty winters and a half year, and eight days, with great trouble ; and found the monks and the guests all that behoved them, and held great charity in the house; and, notwithstanding, wrought on the church, and

383.

---

¹ In the MS. 'tenserie.' Censerie is, no doubt, the same as 'cens,' in Low Latin *censaria*, "rente seig-" neuriale et foncière, dont un héri- "tage est chargé envers le seigneur" "du fief d'où il dépend." Roque-fort, Glossaire Romain.

added thereto lands and rents, and greatly endowed it, and [1] had it provided with vestments, and brought them (the monks) into the new monastery, on St. Peter's mass-day, with great worship. That was in the year from the incarnation of the Lord MC.XL., from the burning of the place XXIII. And he went to Rome, and was there well received by pope [2] Eugenius, and there got privileges: one for all the lands of the abbacy, and another for the lands which are adjacent to the [3] church-dwelling ; and if he might have lived longer, he meant to do so for the treasurer's dwelling. And he got back the lands that powerful men held by force : from William Malduit, who held the castle of Rockingham, he obtained Cotingham and Easton ; and from Hugo of Walteville he obtained Irling-borough and Stanwick ; and from Oldwinkle sixty shillings every year. And he made many monks, and planted a vine-yard, and made many works, and rendered the town better than it ere was ; and was a good monk and a good man, and therefore God and good men loved him. Now we will say a part of what befel in king Stephen's time. In his time the Jews of Norwich bought a Christian child before Easter, and tortured him with all the same torture with which our Lord was tortured ; and on [4] Longfriday hanged him on a rood, in [5] hatred to our Lord, and afterwards buried him. They ima-gined that it would be concealed, but our Lord showed that he was a holy martyr. And the monks took him and buried him honourably in the monastery; and through our Lord he makes wonderful and manifold miracles, and he is called St. William.

An. MC.XXXVIII. In this year came David, king of Scotland, with an immense force to this land : he would win this land. And against him came William, count of Albemarle, to whom the king had intrusted York, and [6] two other chief men, with

---

[1] Or perhaps *had the walls adorned with hangings.* The meaning is very doubtful.

[2] Eugenius II. did not reign till 1145.

[3] Probably the inhabited part of the abbey, as distinguished from the abbey-church.

[4] The Scandinavian nations still say Langfredag for Good Friday.

[5] For 'luue' of the text I suspect we should read laðe, *hate.* At p. 382 of the text there is appa-rently a similar error of 'lof' for lað.

[6] Perhaps Roger of Monbrai and Walter Espec.

few men, and fought against them, and put the king to flight
at the Standard, and slew very many of his followers.

An. MC.XXXIX. .

An. ¹MC.XL. In this year king Stephen would take Robert
earl of Gloucester, the son of king Henry; but he could not, for
he was aware of it. Afterwards in Lent, the sun and the day
darkened about the noontide of day, when men were eating,
and they lighted candles to eat by ; and that was on the XIIIth
of the Kal. of April (Mar. 20th). Men were greatly wonder-
stricken. After that died William, archbishop of Canterbury ;
and the king made Theobald archbishop, who was abbot of
Bec. After this waxed a very great war betwixt the king
and Randolf earl of Chester ; not because that he gave him
not all that he could ask from him, as he did to all others ; but
ever the more he gave them, the worse they were to him.
The earl held Lincoln against the king, and took from him all
that he ought to have. And the king went thither and besieged him and his brother William de Roumare in the castle.
And the earl stole out, and went after Robert earl of Gloucester, and brought him thither with a great force; and they
fought obstinately on Candlemas day (Feb. 2nd) against their
lord, and took him; for his men deserted him and fled. And
they led him to Bristol, and there put him into prison, and
. . . . .   Then was all England stirred more that it ere was,
and all evil was in the land. After that came king Henry's
daughter, who had been empress of Almaine, and was now
countess of Anjou, and came to London; and the London folk
would take her, and she fled and ²lost thus much.' Afterwards the bishop of Winchester, Henry, the brother of king
Stephen, spoke with⁻ earl Robert and with the empress, and
swore oaths to them that he never more would hold with the
king his brother, and cursed all the men who held with him ;
and said to them, that he would give Winchester up to them,
and made them come thither. When they were therein, then
came the king's queen ˈwith all her strength and besieged

384.

---

¹ Under this date are included
events belonging to following years.
    ²ˈ MS. 'þas mycel,' which I do
not understand ; but supposing that
' þas ' may be an error for ' þus,' I

have translated accordingly. Florence of Worcester has : " omni sua
" suorumque supellectile post ter-
" gum relicta."

them, so that there was great hunger therein. When they could no longer hold out, they stole out and fled. And they without were aware, and followed them, and took Robert earl of Gloucester, and led him to Rochester, and there put him in prison; and the empress fled to a monastery. Then went wise men betwixt the king's friends and the earl's friends, and so agreed : that the king should be let out of prison for the earl, and the earl for the king, and they so did. After that, the king and earl Randolf agreed at Stamford, and swore oaths, and plighted troth, that neither of them should prove traitor to the other ; but it stood for naught ; for the king afterwards took him at Northampton, through wicked counsel, and put him in prison, and eftsoons, through worse counsel, he let him out, on the condition that he should swear on a relic, and find hostages, that he would give up all his castles. Some he gave up, and some he gave up not ; and then did worse here than he should. Then was England much divided ; some held with the king and some with the empress ; for when the king was in prison, the earls and the great men imagined that he never more would come out; and agreed with the empress, and brought her to Oxford, and gave her the burgh. When the king was out, he heard that say, and took his force, and besieged her in the tower; and she was let down by night from the tower with ropes, and she stole out, and fled, and went on foot to Wallingford. After that she went over sea, and they of Normandy all turned from the king to the count of Anjou, some voluntarily, some by compulsion, for he besieged them till they gave up their castles ; and they had no help from the king. Then went Eustace, the king's son, to France, and took the king of France's *sister to wife, imagining to get Normandy thereby ; but he sped little, and by good right, for he was an evil man, for wheresoever he was, he did more evil than good. He robbed the lands, and laid great imposts on them. He brought his wife to England, and put her in the castle of . . . . . A good woman she was, but she had little bliss with him; and Christ would not that he should long rule ; and he died, and his mother also ; and the count of Anjou died, and his son Henry succeeded to the county. And the queen of France parted from the king, and she came to the young count Henry, and he took her to wife, and all Poitou with her. He then went with a great force to England, and

* Constance.

won castles; and the king went against him with a much larger
force; and yet they fought not; but the archbishop and the wise
men went betwixt them and made this agreement : That the
king should be lord and king while he lived; and after his day
Henry should be king ; and he should hold him as a father, and
he him as a son, and peace and concord should be betwixt them
and in all England.   This and the other compacts which they
made, the king, and the count, and the bishops, and all the
powerful men, swore to observe.   The count was then received
at Winchester and at London with great worship ; and all
did him homage, and swore to hold the pacification.   And it
was soon a very good pacification, such as never had been
before.   Then was the king stronger than he ever was before;
and the count went over sea ; and all folk loved him ; for he
did good justice and made peace.

An. MC.LIV. In this year king Stephen died, and was buried
where his wife and his son were buried, at Faversham, the
monastery which they had founded.   When the king was dead
the count was beyond sea ; but no man durst do other than
good, for the great awe of him.   When he came to England he
was received with great worship, and blessed for king in London on the Sunday before Midwinter day; and there he held
a great court.   That same day that Martin, abbot of Peterborough, should have gone thither, he sickened and died, on
the ivth of the Nones of January (Jan. 2nd) ; and the monks
within a day chose another for themselves, William de Walte-
vile, a good clerk and good man, and well loved of the king
and of all good men.   And all the monks buried the abbot
honourably; and soon the abbot elect went, and the monks
with him, to the king at Oxford ; and the king gave him the
abbacy; and soon went to Peterborough . . . . and
he was also at Ramsey . . . .

385.

CHRONOLOGICAL INDEX.

CHRONOLOGICAL INDEX,

A.D.	—	Pages of	
		A.S. text.	Transl.

A.D.	—	Pages of	
		A.S. text	Transl.
1012	Ælfhûn, bishop of London, receives and buries the body of abp. Ælfheah	268, 269	118
1013	accompanies Æthelred's sons to Normandy {	271, 272, 273	} 119
792	Ælfled, wife of Æthelred, king of Northumbria .	99	48
1011	Ælfmær, abbot of St. Augustine's, betrays Canterbury to the Danes	266, 267	117
1056	Ælfnoth, shire-reeve, slain	326	158
853 }	Ælfred, son of Æthelwulf—his genealogy—sent to		
854 }	Rome	2,122,123	4, 57
853 }			
854 }	consecrated king by pope Leo	123, 127	57, 58
868	marches to Nottingham, in aid of Burhred, king of Mercia	132, 133	59
871	succeeds to the kingdom of Wessex . .	140 141	62
871	defeated by the Danes at Wilton . . .	140, 141	62
871	fights nine battles with the Danes in one year . .	140, 141	62
875	defeats the Danes at sea	144, 145	63
876	makes peace with them	144, 145	63
877	pursues them to Exeter	146, 147	64
877	takes refuge in Athelney	146, 147	64
878	defeats the Danes and becomes sponsor for Guthorm	148, 149	65
882	fights with the Danes at sea	150, 151	66
883	sends alms to Rome and India . . .	152, 153	66
885	raises the siege of Rochester	152, 153	66
885	sends a naval force to the mouth of the Stour .	152, 153	66
885	conflicts with the vikings at sea . . .	152, 153	66
885	obtains the freedom of the English school at Rome	154, 155	67
886	restores London and commits it to the aldorman Æthelred	156, 157	67
887 }			
888 }	sends alms to Rome	158, 159	68
890 }			
891 }			
892 }	receives three Scottish (Irish) pilgrims . .	160, 161	69
894	defeats of the Danes at Farnham . . .	166, 167	70
896	blockades the river Lea	172, 173	73
897	orders the construction of long ships . .	174, 175	74
897	his conflict with Danish ships at the Isle of Wight	176, 177	74
901	dies	178, 179	75
906	Ælfred, reeve of Bath, dies	182, 183	77
1013	Ælfred, son of king Æthelred and Emma, sent abroad	271, 272	119
1036	comes to England, and is cruelly murdered .	292	129
634	Ælfric, father of Osric, king of Northumbria . .	45	22
983	Ælfric, aldorman of Mercia	236, 237	103
985	banished	236, 237	105
992 }		238, 239	104
1003 }	his treachery . . . . . {	252, 253	112

| A.D. | — | Pages of | |
| | | A.S. text. | Transl. |

C.

J.

A.D.	—	Pages of	
		A.S. text.	Transl.
924	Scotland, acknowledges the supremacy of Eadward the Elder	196, 197	84
933 934	invaded by king Æthelstân	200, 201	85
946	submits to king Eadred	212, 213	90
1031	„ to Cnut	290, 291	128
1073	„ to William I.	340	179
1073 1072	Scotland (Scolland), abbot of St. Augustine's, Canterbury	386	—
	Scots, of Ireland	3	5
430	Palladius sent to the	18, 19	11
684	of Ireland, attacked by king Ecgferth . .	63	34
891	three pilgrims from Ireland visit king Ælfred .	160, 161	69
	Scrocmail, Scromail. See Brocmail.		
	Scurfa jarl. See Skurfa.		
	Seaxburh. See Sexburh.		
654 655	Seaxulf (Saxulf), abbot of Medeshamstede . .	51, 52	25
675	attests charter to Medeshamstede . . .	59	33
675	bishop of the Mercians (Lichfield) . . .	53	29
705	dies	68	38
656	Sebbi, king of Essex, attests charter to Medeshamstede	53	28
	Sefred. See Sigfrid.		
746	Selred, king of Essex, slain	80, 81	41
852	Sempringham, land at, leased for life to Wulfred .	122	56
774	Serpents, extraordinary, in Sussex	90, 93	45
188 189	Severus, invades Britain—makes the wall from sea to sea	14, 15	9
639 640	Sexburh, wife of Erkenberht, king of Kent . .	47	23
672	Sexburh, queen of Wessex	1, 56, 57	3, 30
832	Shepey, ravaged by the pagans (Danes) . .	114, 115	54
855	pagans winter in	124, 125	57
1052	plundered by earl Godwine	319	151
897	Ships, built by king Ælfred	174, 175	74
1008	„ king Æthelred	258, 259	114
894	Shoebury, Danes raise a fort at	168, 169	71
1124	Sibylla, daughter of the count of Anjou, married to William, son of count Robert of Normandy .	375	220
1127	divorced	377	223
789	Sicga, slays king Alfwold of Northumbria . .	99	48
793	dies	101	48
977	Sideman, bishop of Devon (Crediton), dies suddenly	230	99
871	Sidroc jarl, the elder, slain	138, 139	61
871	Sidroc jarl, the younger, slain	138, 139	62
	Sigbald. See Hygbald.		
754	Sigebryht, king of Wessex	1, 80, 81	3, 42 ✓
755	deposed and slain	82, 83	42
905	Sigebryht, son of Sigulf, slain	182, 183	76
962	Sigeferth, king, kills himself	218	92
1015	Sigeferth, thane, murdered by Eadric aldorman .	274, 275	120

321

A GLOSSARY

OF

A FEW ANGLO-SAXON TERMS NECESSARILY RETAINED IN THE
TRANSLATION, FOR WHICH THERE IS NO EXACT EQUIVALENT
IN ENGLISH.

Aldorman (Ealdorman), *dux;* for
so the Saxon appellation is usually
rendered in Latin; though we
also find, as its equivalent, *prin-
ceps, comes.* Although originally
signifying *prince,* it appears in
later times, rather to designate a
title of office, than as *eorl,* a dis-
tinction of caste. The aldorman
was the governor, civil and military, of a shire. In the Kentish
laws the title of aldorman does
not occur, its place being supplied
by that of eorl; a difference
arising probably from its being
unknown to the Jutish followers
of Hengest, to whom the dignity
of eorl, or jarl was, no doubt,
native and familiar.

Æscman. See p. 83, *note.*

Bonde-land; p. 46. This species
of land, as far as I am aware,
occurs only in this place: it is
probably part of the bôcland
rented to a 'bonda' or husband-
man.

Butse-carl. *See* p. 147, *note.*

Censerie. *See* p. 231, *note.*

Cild, *child.* A title nearly synonymous with æðeling; though un-
VOL. II.

like it in being given not only to
the younger branches of royalty,
but to those of the highest fami-
lies : as Wulfnoth cild, Eadric
cild : even Eadgar ætheling is
sometimes called Eadgar cild.
So in France, under the old
regime, we have *enfants de
France;* also in Spain.

Cotlif, a vill, or small holding, the
precise nature of which is not
known.

Eorl, *Dan.* Jarl, *earl, comes.* A
title of honour which, though in
early use amongst us, particularly
among the Jutes of Kent, may, as
designating an office, be regarded
as a Danish innovation, and to
have been substituted by Cnut for
the Saxon title of ealdorman, as
governor of a shire or province.
Unlike ealdorman, it denoted, at
least originally, a caste or order,
in contradistinction to 'ceorl';
the antithesis of 'eorl and ceorl'
signifying the highest and lowest
orders of freemen; hence an
'corlcund man' signified one of
the noblest birth; the wēr (capi-
tis æstimatio) of the former being
sixfold that of the latter; whence

x

the expressions 'twelfhind man' and 'twihind man.'

Gerefa, *reeve*. A fiscal officer appointed by the king, but subordinate to the aldorman of the shire. This definition, however, applies strictly only to the highest class of gerefan, to the scîr-gerefan, or sheriffs, the *vicecomites* of the Latin chroniclers, a title introduced probably when that of aldorman was supplanted by that of eorl, *comes*. In the Sax. Chron. (a. 897), mention occurs of a 'Wealh-gerefa,' with whose functions we are unacquainted. We have also a wîc-gerefa, a *village* or *town-reeve*, a denomination probably equivalent to port-gerefa, the title anciently borne by the official of later times styled *mayor* and *lord mayor*. Besides the king we find other dignitaries having their reeves, as aldormen, bishops, and others.

Hold. *See* p. 76, *note*.

Hors-þegn. *See* þegn.

Hûs-carl. *See* p. 130.

Infangenþef. The privilege of executing summary justice on a thief, if captured on the land with the stolen property in his possession.

Kenepas. *See* p. 158, *note*.

Lidwiccan. *See* p. 67, *note*.

Mitta, *modius*, a corn measure of uncertain capacity.

Niðing, a *vile person, outlaw*, from niðerian, *to lower, humiliate*. To declare a man a niðing, was to proclaim him infamous and outlaw.

Saca and Sôcn (from sacan, *to con-*

tend, litigate, and secan (secean), *to seek*). Saca is the privilege enjoyed by a lord of hearing and deciding causes in his court. The two terms are usually conjoined, and seem nearly synonymous, one standing occasionally for both. Sôc sometimes signifies the court itself.

Scegð. *See* p. 114, *note*.

Sædleap (from sǽd, *seed*, and leap, *basket*). *A measure of seed-corn*.

Sester, *Sextarius: one horse-load*, according to Hen. Huntend., who, speaking of the famine in 1044, says, " Circa hoc tempus tanta " fames Angliam invasit, quod " sextarius frumenti, qui equo " uni solet esse oneri, venunda- " retur quinque solidis, et etiam " plus." A sester of honey was thirty-two ounces, Cod. Diplom., No. 950.

Sôcn. *See* Saca and Sôcn.

Stallere, *the comes stabuli*, or *constable :* from steall, *stall, stable*, and here, *lord, master*. The steallere was an official of the highest rank. The title does not appear till the later times of the Saxon monarchy. In what his functions differed from those of the king's hors-þegn, is uncertain; the latter may probably have been subordinate to the former, if not an earlier denomination of ' steallere.'

Tenseri. *See* Censerie.

Þegn (þegen), *thane* (from þegnian, *servire, ministrare*). Though signifying originally a domestic servant, a king's thane (like a king's minister now) was a high dignitary, and a noble by service. Of thanes there were many degrees and kinds, as *the king's horsethane,* perhaps the subordinate of, or identical with, the steallere ; the hrægl-þegn, or wardrobe keeper ; the bûr-þegn, *bowerthane,* or *chamberlain.* The idea of service seems at length to have become obsolete, as a ' ceorl,' or simple freeman might, by owning a certain quantity of land, attain to thane-right, or the rank of thane. In fact, the thanes were the gentry of the kingdom.

Team. The privilege possessed by a lord of taking cognizance in cases of tracing, from one to another, property that had been stolen, or, as it is termed, *vouching to warranty.* It is thus defined by Spelman : " Jurisdictio " cognoscendi in curia sua de " advocationibus ; hoc est, ut ju- " risconsulti loquuntur, de voca- " tis ad warrantiam."

Toll. The right of the lord of levying toll on all sales and purchases on his land.

Viking (Ut-viking). *See* p. 65, *note.*

Witan (plur. of wita, gen. plur. witena), the councillors, or member of the great national assembly (môt, gemôt), or witena gemôt.

CORRIGENDUM.

Page 143, *after* AD. M.XLVIII. *add* (M.L.), *and* p. 146, *at foot, for* E., *read* E.F.

LONDON:

Printed by GEORGE E. EYRE and WILLIAM SPOTTISWOODE.
Printers to the Queen's most Excellent Majesty.
For Her Majesty's Stationery Office.

LIST OF WORKS

PUBLISHED

By the late Record and State Paper Commissioners,
or under the Direction of the Right Hon. the
Master of the Rolls, which may be had of
Messrs. Longman and Co.

PUBLIC RECORDS AND STATE PAPERS.

ROTULORUM ORIGINALIUM IN CURIA SCACCARII ABBREVIATIO. Henry
III.—Edward III. *Edited by* HENRY PLAYFORD, Esq. 2 vols.
folio (1805—1810). *Price,* boards, 12s. 6d. each, or 25s.

CALENDARIUM INQUISITIONUM POST MORTEM SIVE ESCAETARUM.
Henry III.—Richard III. *Edited by* JOHN CALEY AND J.
BAYLEY, Esqrs. 4 vols. folio (1806—1808 ; 1821—1828), boards:
vols. 2 and 3, separately, *price,* boards, each 21s.; vol. 4, boards,
24s.

LIBRORUM MANUSCRIPTORUM BIBLIOTHECÆ HARLEIANÆ CATALOGUS.
Vol. 4. *Edited by* The Rev. T. H. HORNE, (1812) folio, boards.
Price 18s.

ABBREVIATIO PLACITORUM, Richard I.—Edward II. *Edited by* The
Right Hon. GEORGE ROSE, AND W. ILLINGWORTH, Esq. 1 vol.
folio (1811), boards. *Price* 18s.

LIBRI CENSUALIS vocati DOMESDAY-BOOK, INDICES. *Edited by* Sir
HENRY ELLIS. Small folio (1816), boards (Domesday-Book,
vol. 3). *Price* 21s.

LIBRI CENSUALIS vocati DOMESDAY, ADDITAMENTA EX CODIC. ANTI-
QUISS. *Edited by* Sir HENRY ELLIS. Small folio (1816), boards
(Domesday-Book, vol. 4). *Price* 21s.

STATUTES OF THE REALM, in very large folio. Vols. 1 to 11 (except vols. 5 and 6.) including 2 vols. of Indices (1810—1828). *Edited by* Sir T. E. TOMLINS, JOHN RAITHBY, JOHN CALEY, and WM. ELLIOTT, Esqrs. *Price* 31s. 6d. each.

₊ The Alphabetical and Chronological Indices may be had separately, *price* 30s. each.

VALOR ECCLESIASTICUS, temp. Henry VIII., Auctoritate Regia institutus. *Edited by* JOHN CALEY, Esq., and the Rev. JOSEPH HUNTER. Vols. 4 to 6, folio (1810, &c.), boards. *Price* 25s. each.

₊ The Introduction is also published in 8vo., cloth. *Price* 2s. 6d.

ROTULI SCOTIÆ IN TURRI LONDINENSI ET IN DOMO CAPITULARI WESTMONASTERIENSI ASSERVATI. 19 Edward I.—Henry VIII. *Edited by* DAVID MACPHERSON, JOHN CALEY, AND W. ILLINGWORTH, Esqrs., and the Rev. T. H. HORNE. 2 vols. folio (1814—1819), boards. *Price* 42s.

" FŒDERA, CONVENTIONES, LITTERÆ," &c. ; or, Rymer's Fœdera, A.D. 1066—1391. New Edition, Vol. 2, Part 2, and Vol. 3, Parts 1 and 2, folio (1821—1830). *Edited by* JOHN CALEY and FRED. HOLBROOKE, Esqrs. *Price* 21s. each Part.

DUCATUS LANCASTRIÆ CALENDARIUM INQUISITIONUM POST MORTEM, &c. Part 3, Ducatus Lancastriæ. Calendar to the Pleadings, &c. Henry VII.—Ph. and M. ; and Calendar to Pleadings, 1—13 Elizabeth. Part 4, Calendar to Pleadings to end of Elizabeth. *Edited by* R. J. HARPER, JOHN CALEY, and WM. MINCHIN, Esqrs. Part 3 (or Vol. 2) (1827—1834), *price* 31s. 6d. ; and Part 4 (or Vol. 3), boards, folio, *price* 21s.

CALENDARS OF THE PROCEEDINGS IN CHANCERY IN THE REIGN OF QUEEN ELIZABETH, to which are prefixed examples of earlier proceedings in that Court from Richard II. to Elizabeth, from the originals in the Tower. *Edited by* JOHN BAYLEY, Esq. Vols. 2 and 3 (1830—1832), boards, each, folio, *price* 21s.

PARLIAMENTARY WRITS AND WRITS OF MILITARY SUMMONS, together with the Records and Muniments relating to the Suit and Service due and performed to the King's High Court of Parliament and the Councils of the Realm. Edward I., II. *Edited by* Sir FRANCIS PALGRAVE. (1830—1834). Vol. 2, Division 1, Edward II., 21s. ; Vol. 2, Division 2, 21s.; Vol. 2, Division 3, folio, boards, *price* 42s.

ROTULI LITTERARUM CLAUSARUM IN TURRI LONDINENSI ASSERVATI. 2 vols. folio (1833—1844). The first volume commences A.D. 1204 to 1224. The second volume 1224—1227. *Edited by* THOMAS DUFFUS HARDY, Esq. Together, *price* 81s. cloth ; or the volumes may be had separately. Vol. 1, *price* 63s. cloth ; Vol. 2, cloth, *price* 18s.

THE GREAT ROLLS OF THE PIPE FOR THE SECOND, THIRD, AND FOURTH YEARS OF THE REIGN OF KING HENRY THE SECOND, 1155—1158. *Edited by* the Rev. JOSEPH HUNTER. 1 vol. royal 8vo. (1844), cloth. *Price 4s. 6d.*

THE GREAT ROLL OF THE PIPE FOR THE FIRST YEAR OF THE REIGN OF KING RICHARD THE FIRST, 1189—1190. *Edited by* the Rev. JOSEPH HUNTER. 1 vol. royal 8vo. (1844), cloth. *Price 6s.*

PROCEEDINGS AND ORDINANCES OF THE PRIVY COUNCIL OF ENGLAND, commencing 10 Richard II.—33 Henry VIII. *Edited by* Sir N. HARRIS NICOLAS. 7 vols. royal 8vo. (1834—1837), cloth 98s.; or any of the volumes may be had separately, cloth. *Price 14s.* each.

ROTULI LITTERARUM PATENTIUM IN TURRI LONDINENSI ASSERVATI, A.D. 1201 to 1216. *Edited by* THOMAS DUFFUS HARDY, Esq. 1 vol. folio (1835), cloth. *Price 31s. 6d.*

*** The Introduction is also published in 8vo., cloth. *Price 9s.*

ROTULI CURIÆ REGIS. Rolls and Records of the Court held before the King's Justiciars or Justices. 6 Richard I.—1 John. *Edited by* Sir FRANCIS PALGRAVE. 2 vols. royal 8vo. (1835), cloth. *Price 28s.*

ROTULI NORMANNIÆ IN TURRI LONDINENSI ASSERVATI, A.D. 1200—1205. Also from 1417 to 1418. *Edited by* THOMAS DUFFUS HARDY, Esq. 1 vol. royal 8vo. (1835), cloth. *Price 12s. 6d.*

ROTULI DE OBLATIS ET FINIBUS IN TURRI LONDINENSI ASSERVATI, tempore Regis Johannis. *Edited by* THOMAS DUFFUS HARDY, Esq. 1 vol. royal 8vo. (1835), cloth. *Price 18s.*

EXCERPTA E ROTULIS FINIUM IN TURRI LONDINENSI ASSERVATIS. Henry III., 1216—1272. *Edited by* CHARLES ROBERTS, Esq. 2 vols. royal 8vo. (1835, 1836), cloth, *price 32s.*; or the volumes may be had separately, Vol. 1, *price 14s.*; Vol. 2, cloth, *price 18s.*

FINES SIVE PEDES FINIUM SIVE FINALES CONCORDIÆ IN CURIA DOMINI REGIS. 7 Richard I.—16 John (1195—1214). *Edited by* the Rev. JOSEPH HUNTER. In Counties. 2 vols. royal 8vo. (1835—1844), together, cloth, *price 11s.*; or the volumes may be had separately, Vol. 1, *price 8s. 6d.*; Vol. 2, cloth, *price 2s. 6d.*

ANCIENT KALENDARS AND INVENTORIES (THE) OF THE TREASURY OF HIS MAJESTY'S EXCHEQUER; together with Documents illustrating the History of that Repository. *Edited by* Sir FRANCIS PALGRAVE. 3 vols. royal 8vo. (1836), cloth. *Price 42s.*

DOCUMENTS AND RECORDS illustrating the History of Scotland, and the Transactions between the Crowns of Scotland and England; preserved in the Treasury of Her Majesty's Exchequer. *Edited by* Sir FRANCIS PALGRAVE. 1 vol. royal 8vo. (1837), cloth, *Price 18s.*

ROTULI CHARTARUM IN TURRI LONDINENSI ASSERVATI, A.D. 1199—
1216. *Edited by* THOMAS DUFFUS HARDY, Esq. 1 vol. folio
(1837), cloth. *Price* 30s.

REGISTRUM vulgariter nuncupatum "The Record of Caernarvon," e
codice MS. Harleiano, 696, descriptum. *Edited by* Sir HENRY
ELLIS. 1 vol. folio (1838), cloth. *Price* 31s. 6d.

ANCIENT LAWS AND INSTITUTES OF ENGLAND ; comprising Laws
enacted under the Anglo-Saxon Kings, from Æthelbirht to Cnut,
with an English Translation of the Saxon ; the Laws called
Edward the Confessor's ; the Laws of William the Conqueror, and
those ascribed to Henry the First ; also, Monumenta Ecclesiastica
Anglicana, from the 7th to the 10th century ; and the Ancient
Latin Version of the Anglo-Saxon Laws ; with a compendious
Glossary, &c. *Edited by* BENJAMIN THORPE, Esq. 1 vol. folio
(1840), cloth. *Price* 40s.

—— 2 vols. royal 8vo. cloth. *Price* 30s.

ANCIENT LAWS AND INSTITUTES OF WALES; comprising Laws supposed
to be enacted by Howel the Good ; modified by subsequent Regu-
lations under the Native Princes, prior to the Conquest by Edward
the First ; and anomalous Laws, consisting principally of Insti-
tutions which, by the Statute of Ruddlan, were admitted to continue
in force. With an English Translation of the Welsh Text. To
which are added a few Latin Transcripts, containing Digests of
the Welsh Laws, principally of the Dimetian Code. With
Indices and Glossary. *Edited by* ANEURIN OWEN, Esq. 1 vol.
folio (1841), cloth. *Price* 44s.

—— 2 vols. royal 8vo. cloth. *Price* 36s.

ROTULI DE LIBERATE AC DE MISIS ET PRÆSTITIS, Regnante Johanne.
Edited by THOMAS DUFFUS HARDY, Esq. 1 vol. royal 8vo.
(1844), cloth. *Price* 6s.

DOCUMENTS ILLUSTRATIVE OF ENGLISH HISTORY in the 13th and 14th
centuries, selected from the Records in the Exchequer. *Edited
by* HENRY COLE, Esq. 1 vol. fcp. folio (1844), cloth. *Price*
45s. 6d.

MODUS TENENDI PARLIAMENTUM. An Ancient Treatise on the Mode
of holding the Parliament in England. *Edited by* THOMAS
DUFFUS HARDY, Esq. 1 vol. 8vo. (1846), cloth. *Price* 2s. 6d.

REPORTS OF THE PROCEEDINGS OF THE RECORD COMMISSIONERS, 1800
to 1819, 2 vols., folio, boards. *Price* 5l. 5s. From 1819 to 1831
their proceedings have not been printed. A third volume of
Reports of their Proceedings, 1831 to 1837, folio, boards, 8s.
3 vols. together, boards. *Price* 5l. 13s.

THE ACTS OF THE PARLIAMENTS OF SCOTLAND. 11 vols. folio (1814–1844). Vol. I. *Edited by* THOMAS THOMSON and COSMO INNES, Esqrs. *Price* 42s.

₊ Also, Vols. 4, 7, 8, 9, 10, 11, 10s. 6d. each Vol.

THE ACTS OF THE LORDS OF COUNCIL IN CIVIL CAUSES. A.D. 1478–1495. *Edited by* THOMAS THOMSON, Esq. Folio (1839). *Price* 10s. 6d.

THE ACTS OF THE LORDS AUDITORS OF CAUSES AND COMPLAINTS. A.D. 1466–1494. *Edited by* THOMAS THOMSON, Esq. Folio (1839). *Price* 10s. 6d.

REGISTRUM MAGNI SIGILLI REGUM SCOTORUM in Archivis Publicis asservatum. A.D. 1306–1424. *Edited by* THOMAS THOMSON, Esq. Folio (1814). *Price* 15s.

ISSUE ROLL OF THOMAS DE BRANTINGHAM, Bishop of Exeter, Lord High Treasurer of England, containing Payments out of His Majesty's Revenue, 44 Edward III., 1370. *Edited by* FREDERICK DEVON, Esq. 1 vol. 4to. (1835), cloth. *Price* 35s.

—— Royal 8vo. cloth. *Price* 25s.

ISSUES OF THE EXCHEQUER, containing similar matter to the above, temp. Jac. I., extracted from the Pell Records. *Edited by* FREDERICK DEVON, Esq. 1 vol. 4to. (1836), cloth. *Price* 30s.

—— Royal 8vo. cloth. *Price* 21s.

ISSUES OF THE EXCHEQUER, containing like matter to the above, extracted from the Pell Records ; Henry III. to Henry VI. inclusive. *Edited by* FREDERICK DEVON, Esq. 1 vol. 4to. (1837), cloth. *Price* 40s.

—— Royal 8vo. cloth. *Price* 30s.

LIBER MUNERUM PUBLICORUM HIBERNIÆ, ab an. 1152 usque ad 1827 ; or, The Establishments of Ireland from the 19th of King Stephen to the 7th of George IV., during a period of 675 years ; being the Report of Rowley Lascelles, of the Middle Temple, Barrister-at-Law. Extracted from the Records and other authorities, by Special Command, pursuant to an Address, an. 1810, of the Commons of the United Kingdom. With Introductory Observations by F. S. THOMAS, Esq. (1852.) 2 vols. folio. *Price* 42s.

NOTES OF MATERIALS FOR THE HISTORY OF PUBLIC DEPARTMENTS. By F. S. THOMAS, Esq. Demy folio (1846). *Price* 10s.

HANDBOOK TO THE PUBLIC RECORDS. By F. S. THOMAS, Esq. Royal 8vo. (1853.) *Price* 12s.

STATE PAPERS DURING THE REIGN OF HENRY THE EIGHTH. 11 vols. 4to. (1830—1852) completing the work in its present form, with Indices of Persons and Places to the whole. *Price 5l. 15s. 6d.*
Vol. I. contains Domestic Correspondence.
Vols. II. & III.—Correspondence relating to Ireland.
Vols. IV. & V.—Correspondence relating to Scotland.
Vols. VI. to XI.—Correspondence between England and Foreign Courts.

* Any Volume may be purchased separately, *price 10s. 6d.*

MONUMENTA HISTORICA BRITANNICA, or, Materials for the History of Britain from the earliest period. Vol. 1, extending to the Norman Conquest. Prepared, and illustrated with Notes, by the late HENRY PETRIE, Esq., F.S.A., Keeper of the Records in the Tower of London, assisted by the Rev. JOHN SHARPE, Rector of Castle Eaton, Wilts. Finally completed for publication, and with an Introduction, by THOMAS DUFFUS HARDY, Esq., Assistant Keeper of Records. (Printed by command of Her Majesty.) Folio (1848). *Price 42s.*

HISTORICAL NOTES RELATIVE TO THE HISTORY OF ENGLAND; embracing the Period from the Accession of King Henry VIII. to the Death of Queen Anne inclusive (1509 to 1714). Designed as a Book of instant Reference for the purpose of ascertaining the Dates of Events mentioned in History and in Manuscripts. The Name of every Person and Event mentioned in History within the above period is placed in Alphabetical and Chronological Order, and the Authority from whence taken is given in each case, whether from Printed History or from Manuscripts. By F. S. THOMAS, Esq., Secretary of the Public Record Office. 3 vols. 8vo. (1856.) *Price 40s.*

CALENDARS OF STATE PAPERS.

[IMPERIAL 8vo. *Price* 15s. each Volume.]

CALENDAR OF STATE PAPERS, DOMESTIC SERIES, OF THE REIGNS OF EDWARD VI., MARY, ELIZABETH, 1547–1580, preserved in the State Paper Department of Her Majesty's Public Record Office. *Edited by* ROBERT LEMON, Esq., F.S.A. 1856.

CALENDAR OF STATE PAPERS, DOMESTIC SERIES, OF THE REIGN OF JAMES I., preserved in the State Paper Department of Her Majesty's Public Record Office. *Edited by* MARY ANNE EVERETT GREEN. 1857–1859.

Vol. I.—1603–1610.
Vol. II.—1611–1618.
Vol. III.—1619–1623.
Vol. IV.—1623–1625, with Addenda.

CALENDAR OF STATE PAPERS, DOMESTIC SERIES, OF THE REIGN OF CHARLES I., preserved in the State Paper Department of Her Majesty's Public Record Office. *Edited by* JOHN BRUCE, Esq., V.P.S.A. 1858–1859.

Vol. I.—1625–1626.
Vol. II.—1627–1628.
Vol. III.—1628–1629.
Vol. IV.—1629–1631.

CALENDAR OF STATE PAPERS, DOMESTIC SERIES, OF THE REIGN OF CHARLES II., preserved in the State Paper Department of Her Majesty's Public Record Office. *Edited by* MARY ANNE EVERETT GREEN. 1860.

Vol. I.—1660–1661.

CALENDAR OF STATE PAPERS relating to SCOTLAND, preserved in the State Paper Department of Her Majesty's Public Record Office. *Edited by* MARKHAM JOHN THORPE, Esq., of St. Edmund Hall, Oxford. 1858.

Vol. I., the Scottish Series, of the Reigns of Henry VIII., Edward VI., Mary, Elizabeth, 1509–1589.

Vol. II., the Scottish Series, of the Reign of Queen Elizabeth, 1589–1603; an Appendix to the Scottish Series, 1543–1592; and the State Papers relating to Mary Queen of Scots during her Detention in England, 1568–1587.

CALENDAR OF STATE PAPERS relating to IRELAND, 1509–1573, preserved in the State Paper Department of Her Majesty's Public Record Office. *Edited by* H. C. HAMILTON, Esq. 1860.
Vol. I.

CALENDAR OF STATE PAPERS, COLONIAL SERIES, preserved in the
State Paper Department of Her Majesty's Public Record Office.
Edited by W. NOËL SAINSBURY, Esq. 1860.
Vol. I.—1574-1660.

CALENDAR OF STATE PAPERS, FOREIGN SERIES, OF THE REIGN OF
EDWARD VI. *Edited by* W. B. TURNBULL, Esq., of Lincoln's Inn,
Barrister-at-Law, and Correspondant du Comité Impérial des
Travaux Historiques et des Sociétés Savants de France. 1861.

In the Press.

CALENDAR OF STATE PAPERS RELATING TO IRELAND, preserved in the
State Paper Department of Her Majesty's Public Record Office.
Edited by H. C. HAMILTON, Esq.
Vol. II.

CALENDAR OF STATE PAPERS, DOMESTIC SERIES, OF THE REIGN OF
CHARLES II., preserved in the State Paper Department of Her
Majesty's Public Record Office. *Edited by* MARY ANNE EVERETT
GREEN.
Vol. II.

CALENDAR OF STATE PAPERS OF THE REIGN OF HENRY VIII.
Edited by the Rev. J. S. BREWER, M.A., Professor of English
Literature, King's College, London, and Reader at the Rolls.

CALENDAR OF STATE PAPERS, COLONIAL SERIES, preserved in the
State Paper Department of Her Majesty's Public Record Office.
Edited by W. NOËL SAINSBURY, Esq.
Vol. II.

CALENDAR OF STATE PAPERS, FOREIGN SERIES, OF THE REIGN OF
MARY. *Edited by* W. B. TURNBULL, Esq., of Lincoln's Inn,
Barrister-at-Law, and Correspondant du Comité Impérial des
Travaux Historiques et des Sociétés Savants de France.

CALENDAR OF STATE PAPERS, DOMESTIC SERIES, OF THE REIGN OF
CHARLES I., preserved in the State Paper Department of Her
Majesty's Public Record Office. *Edited by* JOHN BRUCE, Esq.,
V.P.S.A.
Vol. V.

THE CHRONICLES AND MEMORIALS OF GREAT BRITAIN AND IRELAND DURING THE MIDDLE AGES.

[ROYAL 8vo. *Price 8s. 6d.* each Volume.]

1. THE CHRONICLE OF ENGLAND, by JOHN CAPGRAVE. *Edited by* the Rev. F. C. HINGESTON, M.A., of Exeter College, Oxford.

2. CHRONICON MONASTERII DE ABINGDON. Vols. I. and II. *Edited by* the Rev. J. STEVENSON, M.A., of University College, Durham, and Vicar of Leighton Buzzard.

3. LIVES OF EDWARD THE CONFESSOR. I.—La Estoire de Seint Aedward le Rei. II.—Vita Beati Edvardi Regis et Confessoris. III.—Vita Æduuardi Regis qui apud Westmonasterium requiescit. *Edited by* H. R. LUARD, M.A., Fellow and Assistant Tutor of Trinity College, Cambridge.

4. MONUMENTA FRANCISCANA ; scilicet, I.—Thomas de Eccleston de Adventu Fratrum Minorum in Angliam. II.—Adæ de Marisco Epistolæ. III.—Registrum Fratrum Minorum Londoniæ. *Edited by* the Rev. J. S. BREWER, M.A., Professor of English Literature, King's College, London, and Reader at the Rolls.

5. FASCICULI ZIZANIORUM MAGISTRI JOHANNIS WYCLIF CUM TRITICO. Ascribed to THOMAS NETTER, of WALDEN, Provincial of the Carmelite Order in England, and Confessor to King Henry the Fifth. *Edited by* the Rev. W. W. SHIRLEY, M.A., Tutor and late Fellow of Wadham College, Oxford.

6. THE BUIK OF THE CRONICLIS OF SCOTLAND ; or, A Metrical Version of the History of Hector Boece ; by WILLIAM STEWART. Vols. I., II., and III. *Edited by* W. B. TURNBULL, Esq., of Lincoln's Inn, Barrister-at-Law.

7. JOHANNIS CAPGRAVE LIBER DE ILLUSTRIBUS HENRICIS. *Edited by* the Rev. F. C. HINGESTON, M.A., of Exeter College, Oxford.

8. HISTORIA MONASTERII S. AUGUSTINI CANTUARIENSIS, by THOMAS OF ELMHAM, formerly Monk and Treasurer of that Foundation. *Edited by* C. HARDWICK, M.A., Fellow of St. Catharine's Hall, and Christian Advocate in the University of Cambridge.

9. EULOGIUM (HISTORIARUM SIVE TEMPORIS), Chronicon ab Orbe condito usque ad Annum Domini 1366 ; a Monacho quodam Malmesbiriensi exaratum. Vols. I. and II. *Edited by* F. S. HAYDON, Esq., B.A.

10. MEMORIALS OF KING HENRY THE SEVENTH : Bernardi Andreæ Tholosatis de Vita Regis Henrici Septimi Historia ; necnon alia quædam ad eundem Regem spectantia. *Edited by* J. GAIRDNER, Esq.

11. MEMORIALS OF HENRY THE FIFTH. I.—Vita Henrici Quinti, Roberto Redmanno auctore. II.—Versus Rhythmici in laudem Regis Henrici Quinti. III.—Elmhami Liber Metricus de Henrico V. *Edited by* C. A. COLE, Esq.

12. MUNIMENTA GILDHALLÆ LONDONIENSIS ; Liber Albus, Liber Custumarum, et Liber Horn, in archivis Gildhallæ asservati. Vol. I., Liber Albus. Vol. II. (in Two Parts), Liber Custumarum. *Edited by* H. T. RILEY, Esq., M.A., Barrister-at-Law.

13. CHRONICA JOHANNIS DE OXENEDES. *Edited by* Sir H. ELLIS, K.H.

14. A COLLECTION OF POLITICAL POEMS FROM THE ACCESSION OF EDWARD III. TO THE REIGN OF HENRY VIII. Vol. I. *Edited by* T. WRIGHT, Esq., M.A.

15. The "OPUS TERTIUM" and "OPUS MINUS" of ROGER BACON. *Edited by* the Rev. J. S. BREWER, M.A., Professor of English Literature, King's College, London, and Reader at the Rolls.

16. BARTHOLOMÆI DE COTTON, MONACHI NORWICENSIS, HISTORIA ANGLICANA (A.D. 449—1298). *Edited by* H. R. LUARD, M.A., Fellow and Assistant Tutor of Trinity College, Cambridge.

17. The BRUT Y TYWYSOGION, or, The Chronicle of the Princes of Wales. *Edited by* the Rev. J. WILLIAMS AB ITHEL.

18. A COLLECTION OF ROYAL AND HISTORICAL LETTERS DURING THE REIGN OF HENRY IV. Vol. I. *Edited by* the Rev. F. C. HINGESTON, M.A., of Exeter College, Oxford.

19. THE REPRESSOR OF OVER MUCH BLAMING OF THE CLERGY. By REGINALD PECOCK, sometime Bishop of Chichester. Vols. I. and II. *Edited by* C. BABINGTON, B.D., Fellow of St. John's College, Cambridge.

20. THE ANNALES CAMBRIÆ. *Edited by* the Rev. J. WILLIAMS AB ITHEL.

21. THE WORKS OF GIRALDUS CAMBRENSIS. Vol. I. *Edited by* the Rev. J. S. BREWER, M.A., Professor of English Literature, King's College, London, and Reader at the Rolls.

22. LETTERS AND PAPERS ILLUSTRATIVE OF THE WARS OF THE ENGLISH IN FRANCE DURING THE REIGN OF HENRY THE SIXTH, KING OF ENGLAND. Vol. I. *Edited by* the Rev. J. STEVENSON, M.A., of University College, Durham, and Vicar of Leighton Buzzard.

23. THE ANGLO-SAXON CHRONICLE, ACCORDING TO THE SEVERAL ORIGINAL AUTHORITIES. Vol. I., Original Texts. Vol. II., Translation. *Edited by* B. THORPE, Esq., Member of the Royal Academy of Science at Munich, and of the Society of Netherlandish Literature at Leyden.

In the Press.

RICARDI DE CIRENCESTRIA SPECULUM HISTORIALE DE GESTIS REGUM ANGLIÆ. (A.D. 447—1066.) *Edited by* J. E. B. MAYOR, M.A., Fellow and Assistant Tutor of St. John's College, Cambridge.

LE LIVERE DE REIS DE BRITTANIE. *Edited by* J. GLOVER, M.A., Chaplain of Trinity College, Cambridge.

RECUEIL DES CRONIQUES ET ANCHIENNES ISTORIES DE LA GRANT BRETAIGNE A PRESENT NOMME ENGLETERRE, par JEHAN DE WAURIN. *Edited by* W. HARDY, Esq.

THE WARS OF THE DANES IN IRELAND : written in the Irish language. *Edited by* the Rev. Dr. TODD, Librarian of the University of Dublin.

A COLLECTION OF POLITICAL POEMS FROM THE ACCESSION OF EDWARD III. TO THE REIGN OF HENRY VIII. Vol. II. *Edited by* T. WRIGHT, Esq., M.A.

A COLLECTION OF SAGAS AND OTHER HISTORICAL DOCUMENTS relating to the Settlements and Descents of the Northmen on the British Isles. *Edited by* GEORGE W. DASENT, Esq., D.C.L. Oxon.

A COLLECTION OF ROYAL AND HISTORICAL LETTERS DURING THE REIGN OF HENRY IV. Vol. II. *Edited by* the Rev. F. C. HINGESTON, M.A., of Exeter College, Oxford.

LETTERS AND PAPERS OF THE REIGNS OF RICHARD III. AND HENRY VII. *Edited by* JAMES GAIRDNER, Esq.

MUNIMENTA GILDHALLÆ LONDONIENSIS ; Liber Albus, Liber Custumarum, et Liber Horn, in archivis Gildhallæ asservati. Vol. III. Translations from the Anglo-Norman portions of the Liber Albus ; Appendix ; Glossaries ; and Index. *Edited by* H. T. RILEY, Esq., M.A., Barrister-at-Law.

EULOGIUM (HISTORIARUM SIVE TEMPORIS), Chronicon ab Orbe condito usque ad Annum Domini 1366 ; a Monacho quodam Malmesbiriensi exaratum. Vol. III. *Edited by* F. S. HAYDON, Esq., B.A.

LETTERS AND TREATISES OF BISHOP GROSSETETE, illustrative of the Social Condition of his Time. *Edited by* the Rev. H. R. LUARD, M.A., Fellow and Assistant Tutor of Trinity College, Cambridge.

THE WORKS OF GIRALDUS CAMBRENSIS. Vol. II. *Edited by* the Rev. J. S. BREWER, M.A., Professor of English Literature, King's College, London, and Reader at the Rolls.

LETTERS AND PAPERS ILLUSTRATIVE OF THE WARS OF THE ENGLISH IN FRANCE DURING THE REIGN OF HENRY THE SIXTH, KING OF ENGLAND. Vol. II. *Edited by* the Rev. J. STEVENSON, M.A., of University College, Durham, and Vicar of Leighton Buzzard.

DESCRIPTIVE CATALOGUE OF MANUSCRIPTS RELATING TO THE EARLY HISTORY OF GREAT BRITAIN. *Edited by* T. DUFFUS HARDY, Esq.

In Progress.

HISTORIA MINOR MATTHÆI PARIS. *Edited by* Sir F. MADDEN, K.H., Chief of the MS. Department of the British Museum.

CHRONICON ABBATIÆ EVESHAMENSIS, AUCTORIBUS DOMINICO PRIORE EVESHAMIÆ ET THOMA DE MARLEBERGE ABBATE, A FUNDATIONE AD ANNUM 1213, UNA CUM CONTINUATIONE AD ANNUM 1418. *Edited by* the Rev. W. D. MACRAY, M.A., Bodleian Library, Oxford.

A ROLL OF THE IRISH PRIVY COUNCIL OF THE 16TH YEAR OF THE REIGN OF RICHARD II. *Edited by* the Rev. JAMES GRAVES.

POLYCHRONICON RANULPHI HIGDENI, with Trevisa's Translation. *Edited by* C. BABINGTON, B.D., Fellow of St. John's College, Cambridge.

February 1861.